A Brief & Lively, No-Nonsense Guide to Writing

A Brief & Lively, No-Nonsense Guide to Writing

Sandra Kurtinitis

Prince George's Community College

Scott, Foresman and Company
Glenview, Illinois

Dallas, Tex. Oakland, N.J. Palo Alto, Cal. Tucker, Ga. London

To my family: my children, who gave up a lot, and Jerry, who never lost faith.

Acknowledgments

From Camero Advertisement, *Car and Driver,* January 1980. Reprinted by permission of General Motors Advertising Division.

"War Is Cancer of Mankind" by Sydney J. Harris from *The Best of Sydney J. Harris* published by Houghton Mifflin Company. Copyright © 1975 by Sydney J. Harris. Reprinted by permission of the publisher.

Library of Congress Cataloging in Publication Data

Kurtinitis, Sandra, 1943-
A brief and lively, no-nonsense guide to writing.
Includes index.
1. English language—Rhetoric. 2. English language—Style. 3. English language—Grammar—1950- I. Title.
PE1421.K8 808'.042 80-16002
ISBN 0-673-15240

Printed in the United States of America.

1 2 3 4 5 6-VHJ-86 85 84 83 82 81 80

Preface

In his book *The Unembarrassed Muse,* Russel Nye surveys the development of the popular arts in America—comic books, films, popular fiction, and so on. In this book, Nye cites a nineteenth-century pulp magazine editor as saying:

> The game is to give the ordinary guy what he wants, that is, the transitive verb—action, excitement, blood, love, a little humor, a taste of sex, a pepper of passion, a lot of escape.

A Brief & Lively, No-Nonsense Guide to Writing is built upon the spirit, if not the letter, of that advice. That transitive verb—coupled with its potent relatives the concrete noun and the deftly used modifier—holds a secret for anyone who has the task of writing or teaching writing. We can all be verbal and concrete when we talk about a "great car" or take a political stand, describing in detail what we mean. However, confronted with a blank piece of paper, we often have trouble lifting our language from the vague, flat prose too many writers use once they stop talking and start writing. As a teacher of writing, I have made a pledge to myself: I want my students to produce not only well-structured essays, but *interesting* ones as well. Thus, concrete language—that transitive verb and its relatives—is not only the beginning but the very heart of this book.

Since one can never be sure just exactly what skills students possess as they begin a composition course, this book starts with the most basic building block, the word, and works upward. *A Brief & Lively, No-Nonsense Guide to Writing* develops the idea of the individual and collective power of words, and how words can be plugged into workable paragraph and essay patterns. It gives students a one-semester survival kit for dealing with their writing needs.

The text is based on four separate but interlocking steps:

1. Developing students' sensitivity to the power of concrete language tailored to audience and purpose.

2. Encouraging students to use words concretely in effective sentences.
3. Helping them knit those sentences into tightly written paragraphs from which basic errors can be edited.
4. Guiding them to build those paragraphs into the larger structure of an essay, which becomes a conscious blend of words, sentences, and paragraphs.

The bonus for the instructor in this steady progression is that much of the mechanical grading of grammatical and syntactical errors occurs at the beginning of the course, when it is far easier to deal with such problems.

Other features of this book should also help your students write better. Each chapter, for example, ends with a "Chapter Checklist" that briefly summarizes the main points of the chapter; these checklists are both reminders of chapter content and lists of what the student should have learned.

Numerous examples, many written by students, illustrate the concepts and show what students can realistically expect to accomplish. Aimed at a typical college audience—adults and teenagers of many different backgrounds—the examples range from mundane images of a used-car dealer to a critique of two contemporary photographers.

Ample exercises following most chapter subsections provide practice in the concepts presented and encourage participation in the prewriting as well as the writing processes. These exercises range from identification of errors to writing phrases to combining sentences to writing and revising paragraphs and essays.

In addition to the general movement of the text from simple to complex, three of the chapters give additional advice about specific writing tasks. Chapter 8, on logic, illustrates that clear thinking is an antecedent to clear writing, and logical writing is necessary to all modes of essays. A thorough yet readable chapter on research begins with a sample paper; students seem better able to deal with a research paper if they see the whole *before* its parts are dissected. Then, a brief handbook provides easy access to quick review of standard topics.

Overall, I hope this book makes traditional rhetorical principles easily understandable through a nonthreatening exposure to the standards of good writing. But as every writing instructor knows, you go where your students need to go, and you do what your own philosophy and style dictate. You may follow a book step by step, or you may vary the order to suit other preferences. And so it can be with this book.

Whether you start with Chapter 1 or Chapter 5, *A Brief & Lively,*

No-Nonsense Guide to Writing will help the beginning writer organize and transfer his or her thoughts to paper. It offers some hints, guidelines, and tricks for writing a clear, readable essay for a composition class, or for a political science final exam, a complaint to the Better Business Bureau, or an office memo. It tries to set up a writing program that combines some good sense, some humor, and some humanism to produce a system that builds both confidence and skill.

Many people helped this book emerge from thought to object. I wish gratefully to thank:

The reviewers who carefully examined the several layers of manuscript from which this book grew: Joan N. Murray, Cosumnes River College; James M. Williams, Johnson County Community College; Alan Meyers, Harry S Truman College; Mary Northcutt, Richland Community College; Aspasia Anastos, Mt. Wachusett Community College; Richard L. Harp, University of Nevada, Las Vegas; Donald W. Sieker, Purdue University, Calumet Campus; and Julia A. Alexander.

My colleagues at Prince George's Community College who have watched and commented, encouraged and advised, especially John Bodnar, a valued mentor; Bill Fry and Pat Tatspaugh, dear friends and gentle taskmasters; Diana Hacker, Marianne Strong, and Vera Wentworth, believers way back when.

My students who contributed not only writing samples but challenges and inspiration as well: Juanita Abelmann, Mary Jo Alderman, Lynn Alexander, Eileen Baca, Kate Baird, Diane Baker, Robert Bean, James Behun, Richard Brown, Rosemarie Bryant, Kathy Buckner, Russ Burgess, Beverly Burns, Craig Castellana, Terry Clark, Steve Crane, Louise Dayney, Margaret DeCampo, Dave Eddleman, Kathleen Fern, William Finch, Kathy France, Donna Fritts, Dave Gallaghan, Robin Garrett, Delia Gerace, Kay Hillebrand, Elizabeth Griffin, Manuel Hernandez, Robert Hohensee, John Irvin, Joyce Jarrell, Kathy Lanata, John Lineberger, Joseph Luszcz, Linda Mills, Melissa Mooney, Jan Motyczynski, Rebecca Norman, Tom O'Donnell, Stanley Ostazeski, William Overman, Georgette Parker, Jennifer Rochlin, Gayle Stearns, Judith Stigelman, Karen Sullivan, Larry Sweeney, Ron Taylor, Paul Vass, Kathy Walker, John Ware, Claude Waters, Maralyn Weihe, Felicia Wilkerson, Patti Williams, Lynn Winbigler, Carol Workinger, Luis Zuniga, and many others such as Jude, Barbara, and Agnes who keep on proving that education can be exciting for both teacher and student.

SK

Contents

Some Initial Advice

For years, students have been shivering or slouching through that academic monstrosity known as freshman composition. This course has long rivaled the Loch Ness Monster, the Bermuda Triangle, and the Abominable Snowman in legendary fame. Not surprisingly, then, many students, fearing pain or boredom, dread their freshman composition class before they even step into it. They could be far happier escaping it completely by nestling in front of an afternoon soap opera or playing frisbee out on a lawn far away from that mausoleum where nouns and topic sentences are entombed. As you glance through this book, the course may seem just as menacing or just as boring as the legend suggests. And in reality it is indeed a lot of hard work. But these chapters try to make the labor, if not very much lighter, at least a little sweeter.

Good writing is hard work no matter who does it. Professional writers are rarely Basil Rathbones who don a velvet smoking jacket, pour a flask of martinis, pick up a quill pen, and summon a muse to guide a bejeweled hand across the page. Emily Dickinson wrote her poems on backs of envelopes and paper bags which she then stitched into packets. James Thurber claims to have spent nearly two thousand hours doing fifteen revisions of a story that was only twenty thousand words long. Flannery O'Connor frequently adopted the unglamorous posture of sitting with her feet soaking in a pan of water to keep her working in one place. And it is said that Tennessee Williams, when fired with an idea, would sit down at a typewriter and type spontaneously, tossing unnumbered pages over his shoulder onto the floor.

In a very real way you are probably already aware of the vagaries of the writing process from your own experience. Wearing anything from blue jeans to bathrobe, you no doubt have tackled an essay while you sat at your kitchen table or in front of your television set. Sipping cups of cold coffee or munching on potato chips, you have scrawled or typed sheets of crossed-out pages, very much aware that muses rarely visit Sioux City or Poway or Brooklyn.

Good writing is by no means beyond a student's achievement. Writing is not good just because the author is well known. Leo Tolstoy, Gertrude Stein, and William Shakespeare have all had their leaner moments. Nor is writing good just because the publisher is prestigious. Articles in *Road and Track* or *Time* are often as well written as those in *Harper's* or *Atlantic Monthly*. Writing is good when it has something to say and says it well. Although you may not have the polish of a professional, your writing can speak to a reader clearly and concisely whether you are giving directions for changing the oil in a car, presenting an argument for outlawing handguns, or preparing a research essay on the ideological backgrounds of the American Revolution. Good writing has the power to make the thoughts of the writer visible to the reader, no matter how humble the author or the idea.

Producing clear, readable writing, then, will be the challenge. When you speak, you can shout, whisper, grind your teeth, or grin. You can shrug a shoulder or wave a hand. Or you can say "You know what I mean," and your listener will usually nod sympathetically. But writing is a series of ink marks on a bare page. Your ideas are frozen there. You usually do not get a chance to explain or to edit by saying, "Oh, right here I meant . . ." or "You know what I meant. . . ." Every one of those little black marks on the page must count; they are the only tools a writer has. Your opinions may be radical or conservative, but unless a reader—your history teacher, your insurance agent, your sister—can understand what you mean, a gap exists. If your readers misunderstand what you are trying to tell them, you have not succeeded in communicating.

As you begin this course, your problems are likely to be similar to those of many other freshman writers. On one level, you may have trouble with grammar, punctuation, and spelling. On another you may struggle with organization and content. Most beginning writers share these problems to some degree, and yet some simple guidelines can help overcome them.

Poor grammar and punctuation block communication. As a reader, you are startled and often confused by missing periods or an overdose of commas. As a writer, therefore, you should not expect others to tolerate such errors. At this point in your writing career, after close to a dozen years of telling noun from pronoun or subject from verb, you probably have some natural control over grammar. If you were driving along a turnpike and saw a tollbooth sign which said "Tollway repairs begins April 24," you would quickly sense that something was wrong with that sentence even if you could not label it a subject/verb agreement problem. If you turned to the sports page and saw the headline "Oilers and Steelers meet again in combat. Win easily," you would be just as confused about who won whether or not you recognized the fragment. And you would certainly be amused if you read this line in a short story: "Hastening down the street with high heels clicking, the bus left without her." While common sense will tell you it is a rare bus that can wear high heels, you may not know how to label the dangling participle.

Most of us can sense the problems in the above sentences, but if asked in class to identify them, we might well put our heads down, stare at the floor, or remember something urgent tucked away in a notebook. However, remembering that "shall have run" is the future perfect tense of "run" or that "to have" is an infinitive is not nearly as important as knowing how to use those parts of speech naturally or knowing how to look them up if you do not. The handbook guide at the back of this book will give you a ready frame of reference to clear up such problems.

Poor spelling plagues a writer as much as poor grammar does. While good spelling is a silent asset to any piece of writing, poor spelling can be a major detractor. When a road sign reads "14′ Clea*ren*ce" or a ticket window says "Adm*isi*on 50¢," you get the point, but you still lift an eyebrow. Someone taking a stand against the use of "fowl" language by women's rights groups, a Vietnam veteran explaining how he fought against "gorilla" warfare, a newspaper headline citing awards to six "atheletes" will all make their reader flinch. Writers who spell like Huckleberry Finn raise some questions about their credibility. The problem is rarely serious enough to cause a communication breakdown, but flagrant misspelling does suggest something about the writer. To avoid embarrassment, an architect should not speak of "multi*pained*" windows; a poet would sound silly writing lyrically, "This is love at its *peek*"; and a psychiatrist should not write in a report, "The client's mind, *torchered* by emotional stress . . . ." Poor spelling requires attention. Do not be embarrassed to use a dictionary to help you spell correctly. And if your problem is really serious, memorize the spelling rules, take a quick review spelling course, or buy a special dictionary for poor spellers which lists thousands of words by their common misspellings.

But grammar and spelling aside, by far the main problems you may have in this course will stem from organization and content. Putting all of the pieces together logically and clearly is the hardest part of writing. Presenting your thoughts so that they will make sense to your reader . . . and even interest him or her . . . is not always easy. However, even though you are just beginning your freshman composition course, as a reader you can probably see the difference between the following two short passages written in a freshman composition class.

> Training to become an athlete. You need physical features as well as the ability to perform as an athlete. I am in the process of training for the coming fall football season. Where I attend school. The athlete has to be a person with good coordination, stamina, disire, and deadication to the sport he or she is pertisipating in. I need to run every day to build up my indurence and to have a weight training program to become physicly strong. The athlete must be physicaly strong and mentaly strong. To perform well and maintain. Like myself. The athlete should at his best at all times.

> Our small, though sturdy, sailboat was being tossed around by strong waves, resembling some child's toy boat in his bathtub. We were buffeted by rising winds which howled through the rigging, making the mainsail slap irritatingly against the boom.
>
> Warm stinging rain fell heavily, plastering our hair and clothes to our bodies. Our gym shoes squelched as we moved around the boat. I was no longer able to see clearly due to rainwater on my glasses so I removed them and peered shortsightedly through the curtain of rainwater.
>
> The thunder now cracked overhead followed by lightning so bright that there was no need for our riding lights as our boat was illuminated every thirty seconds. But with every crack of lightning, we instinctively cringed lower into the cockpit all but praying lightning would not hit our exposed mast.
>
> As I moved forward to attempt to drop the anchor, I slipped on the water covered foredeck and as the boat tilted with the wind, I fell overboard into the river.

Even without a composition course, you can see the difference between the two. The first flounders and stumbles about; poor organization, careless spelling, and sloppy grammar make it hard to read. The second is clear and direct. Its content, its organization, its presentation make it a well-written account which speaks easily to the reader and is thus effective.

Overall, the main purpose of the book is to help you to speak easily to a reader, to express your ideas on a piece of paper so that someone else can read them and understand them. The chapters that follow should gradually help you refine the skill you already possess in meshing words and sentences into paragraphs and essays. They will also give you some idea of the many different strategies you can use to shape your thought to your purpose and reader. Such information can be useful whether you are preparing a report on electronic typewriters for your office, documenting the discovery of the Cro-Magnon race for a history paper, or tracing the origins of the Nantucket Basket for a museum display. These chapters try to show you how language, structure, and thought work together to produce clear, readable writing. Each chapter contains some passages by professional writers as well as many examples of the writing of other students to show you that good writing is not only the province of famous authors; it lies very much in the grasp of the student as well.

This book makes no demands on you to imitate Norman Mailer or Jane Austen. It makes no claim to be the only right way to learn to write. Its aim is to be a practical rhetoric offering some basic guidelines for clear, concise prose. While there are few absolute laws in writing, there are some reliable standards as well as some hints about when to obey the rules and when to defy them. These pages offer a survival kit containing those standards to help you organize and transfer your thoughts to paper.

Writing well is not just an antiquated academic exercise, nor is it a convenient method for legitimizing B.S. It is as valuable a skill for the X-ray technician who must file a medical report as it is for the architectural engineer preparing a justification for a new building. It is as vital for the reporter doing a story on a flood in North Dakota as it is for the scholar documenting research on the animal imagery in *King Lear.* Writing is a way of communicating on paper with somebody else—auditor, client, critic, layman, or teacher. And the sole aim of this book is to give you the wherewithal to do just that.

1

Starting with Words

Most of us use words well. Without any special training, we fill our everyday speech with fascinating word patterns. The CB'er warns that a "Smokie is taking pictures"; the trucker carries a "load of doughnut holes"; the surveyor "shoots a line." All three are being eloquent in their own way. Religious revelations shouted from soapboxes, recipes swapped in kitchens, four-letter words scrawled on restroom walls with lipstick or bobby pins or pocketknives all bear living testimony to our natural skill with our own language. If we allow them, words can be powerful. A few strong, well-chosen words will convey a message far more forcefully than several hundred weak ones. That lesson may be one of the most valuable ones we can learn about writing.

Everyday language flows smoothly and easily. With it we buy shoes, complain about parking tickets, and order hamburgers. Every word, every phrase from "right on" to "logical positivism" has a place, a meaning. Some of this language is mere convention which fills in a blank or acts out a formula. When we go through the "Hello, how are you" ritual with others, for instance, we may not really want to hear how they are. We are making pleasant noises to signal our goodwill or to begin a conversation. At other times language works in a more calculated way—using words designed to conceal thoughts or modify real meanings. Television ads speak of "underarm wetness" rather than "sweat." Executives are often not "fired"; they are "dehired" or "selected out." Funeral arrangements sometimes shade the reality of death with a "slumber room" instead of a "funeral parlor," "professional car" instead of "hearse," and "memorial park" in place of "cemetery."

Choosing Words

Words, then, in speech or in print, perform many functions. They inform, they persuade, they command, they apologize, they plead, they laugh, they cry. But in the final analysis, words, just like McDonald's golden arches, are *symbols;* the sounds themselves have no real meaning. We—nations, towns, groups, individuals—give them meanings from common experience. The British cruise in trams and lorries, while Americans ride on buses and trucks. They wear Wellies and Macs, and we clomp about in boots and raincoats. We have one all-purpose word for snow; Eskimos carefully distinguish between "ganit," snow that is falling, and "aput," snow that is lying on the ground. And although Tibetans may not have the vocabulary to distinguish split-level from ranch-style houses, they have far more words than we for describing the ailments of yaks.

The ability to link these symbols into effective communication with a reader separates the good writer from the poor. A vital step in learning to write well, then, is to steep yourself in words, to see them as fundamental building blocks. To give an exact picture or an exact impression, you need words that are strong in their own right before they can be strong together. As Mark Twain once said, the difference between the right word and the wrong word is like the difference between lightning and a lightning bug.

The careful selection of these right words over wrong words is a matter of *diction*. Simply put, diction is word choice. You choose one word over another according to your audience, the nature of your subject, and your own attitude or opinion. When you meet a friend at school or in a shopping center, you chat in an easy, casual way; if you were introduced to the state governor at a ribbon-cutting ceremony for a new hospital, your speech would be much more formal. In writing, you would speak differently in a report on the problems of educating autistic children than you would in a note to ask your mother to send money or in a memo to alert employees to a new fire-alarm system. Your audience is different; your intent is different; your language will be different.

Audience and purpose determine what we can say and how we can say it. Looking at almost any magazine will teach us this lesson of tailoring message to audience. Editors work hard to combine articles, graphics, and advertisements into a consistent pose. For instance, *Better Homes and Gardens* besieges its homemaker audience with advice on flu viruses, drapery care, and potato soufflés. It illustrates with photographs of living rooms and crescent rolls and advertises for Sears Superplush towels, Land O'Lakes butter, Litter Green kitty litter, and

Maytag washers. On the other hand, to lure its supposedly sophisticated reader, the *New Yorker* follows a different format. It might review an off-Broadway play or a Woody Allen film or invite Arthur Schlesinger to talk about the White House. It often illustrates with Charles Saxon cartoons and contains ads for Mercedes Benz, Strega liqueur, and Charles of the Ritz cosmetics. In quite another style, *Sports Illustrated,* the sports fan's bible, packs photographs of baseball players and race cars into accounts of the World Series and the Daytona 500, while advertising for Marlboro, Adidas tennis shoes, Old Spice, and Fruit of the Loom. An essay on Hemingway's *The Sun Also Rises* would no more find a place in *Better Homes and Gardens* than an ad for Rossignol skis. An article on canning tomatoes would not fit in *Sports Illustrated* any better than a photograph of Albert Camus. Editors consider audience and purpose very carefully. So, too, should you as you write.

Exercises

1. Bring to class a few advertisements from different types of magazines. Consider their appeal according to their intended reader and purpose and the way they use words or pictures. Consider how effective those same ads would be if they appeared in different magazines. Try to design a new ad for one of the products for a different magazine.
2. Bring to class a magazine or newspaper that you have examined carefully. Be prepared to discuss its audience and purpose from internal evidence. Who is its intended reader? How does it tailor language and graphics to that reader? What types of articles does it publish? What types of ads does it rely on?
3. Select a well-known product—Lipton tea, Clairol Herbal Essence shampoo, Black and Decker drills, for example—and try to devise an ad with a particular magazine in mind. Then, rewrite the ad to suit a different type of magazine. You might try one first for *Ms. Magazine* and then *Cosmopolitan* or for *National Geographic* and *Humpty Dumpty's Magazine.*
4. Write a short piece (one or two paragraphs) geared to a particular audience—hunters, football fans, chemists. Choose a simple subject relevant to the group you select—a comment on a film or newspaper item or a short autobiographical sketch. Then, rewrite the piece aiming it at a different audience. You might, for instance, pretend you are a critic

reviewing the Grammy Award presentation for the *New York Times* television section and then do the same for *Rolling Stone.*

Levels of Usage

Depending on audience and purpose, then, the choice of which word to use is vast. It ranges over several levels of standard and nonstandard English. Standard English, dialect of most educated people, is the dialect we most often see in print. Nonstandard English—"Ain't youse goin'" or "I couldn't hardly do it"—is the label for many regional or social dialects. It is usually a spoken language that appears in print largely as dialogue, like this speech by one of William Faulkner's characters:

> "It's a public street," the man says. "I reckon we can stop to buy something same as airy other man. We got the money to pay for hit, and hit ain't airy law that says a man can't spend his money where he want."
>
> *As I Lay Dying*

Words, pronunciations, and grammatical differences separate standard English from nonstandard. Nonstandard English has as many variations as groups of speakers; standard English, while also having some regional or other variations, is more uniform, although it can vary among formal, informal, or general language. Formal occasions (speeches, dedications, serious articles) demand formal language; informal occasions (picnics, letters to friends, some newspaper articles) call for informal language. If language is to match audience and intent, then we cannot always be formal and we cannot always be informal. More likely, when we write or speak as students or as professionals, we strike a balance between the two by using *general English.* This is the language most of us speak and write, the language of many magazines, the language of this textbook. Your task as a writer is to pick the right words to suit your audience and your intent and to tailor those words to meet the occasion.

Formal English

Formal writing avoids the colorful quirks of daily speech. Its language is elevated, dotted frequently with Latinate words (*celebration* or *reticent,* for example); its sentences are often long and complex. The writer, acknowledging the dignity of both subject and reader, speaks on the page in ways that differ from normal conversation. We are all familiar with some of the more well-known examples of formal writing. Some are time-honored documents such as the Declaration of Independence or the Constitution. The first sentence of the Constitution, for instance, reads:

> We, the people of the United States, in order to form a more perfect union, establish justice, insure domestic tranquility, provide for the common defense, promote the general welfare, and secure the blessings of liberty to ourselves and our posterity do ordain and establish this Constitution for the United States of America.

Other familiar examples, such as the one below, come from the King James Bible:

> Blessed is the man that walketh not in the counsel of the ungodly, nor standeth in the way of sinners, nor sitteth in the seat of the scornful.
>
> Psalm 1

These passages have a rhythm, a body of language, and a balance of parts that distinguish them from other less formal types of writing. The Gettysburg Address, the speeches of Winston Churchill or John Kennedy, the literary masterpieces of the eighteenth and nineteenth centuries such as *Gulliver's Travels* and *The Rubaiyat* show that formal writing can be intellectual and objective, inspiring and exciting, or even witty and personal.

Although the casualness of the sixties has generally decreased the amount of formal writing done in America, formality still fits in many places besides graduation speeches. Anyone wishing to grant dignity to the subject and distance to the reader needs a formal style. Textbook writers for subjects such as philosophy or chemistry adopt a formal pose. Most of us tend to be formal in business correspondence: applying for a job, accepting an award, complaining about an excessively high electric bill. Writers addressing a community of scholars, thinkers, or intellectuals of any kind—be they political analysts, scientific researchers, or university professors—often formalize language and construction. A typical critic, Richard David, writes about *Macbeth* in the journal *Shakespeare Survey* in this fashion:

> . . . During the season 1954–5 the Shakespeare theatres of both London and Stratford confined themselves to a single—and the same—tragedy: *Macbeth.* The two productions were diametrically opposed in in-

> tention and method. A comparison between the two is therefore interesting in itself. I hope it may also demonstrate the nature of the tragic curve, how it runs in *Macbeth,* and in what ways actors and producers may sustain or suppress it.

David tailors his language to his audience. Writing for other literary critics, for readers who know *Macbeth* well, he has to address them in language appropriate to his thought, his subject, and his audience's expectations. Not to do so might reflect poorly on his critical abilities.

While a high formal style may be more commonly the language of scholars and critics, occasionally students must be formal, too. Many teachers expect it; many future employers demand it. Certain purposes or audiences demand a more controlled tone and more formal language: A chatty style would be disastrous in a letter accepting a scholarship offer or a position at the National Institutes of Health and equally out of place in a research paper about nuclear waste or an account of child abuse or Indian land rights.

Problems with formality. Phony formality surrounds us. Despite the movement begun by some government officials to translate bureaucratic jargon into common English, all types of people—housing inspectors, police officers, bank presidents, insurance agents—frequently hide behind pretentious language (phony formality) as part of their jobs. The building inspector finds a leak and leaves you a note solemnly stating:

> Please be advised to procure the services of a plumber.

A police officer gives you a speeding ticket which does not say, "This person was speeding." It says instead:

> As prescribed by the Motor Vehicle Administration pursuant to Article 66-½, Section 16–117, the defendant named above did unlawfully violate Article 11001.

The passbook for your savings account might well say:

> The objects of this Association shall be the encouraging of the saving of money; the accumulation of a capital in money to be derived from the savings and accumulations by its members thereof to be paid into the Association in such sums and at such times as herein designated. . . .

And if you ever have to read your insurance policy to discover if the company will pay for your broken window, you must wade through passages such as this:

> In consideration of the provisions and stipulations herein or added hereto and of the premium above specified (or specified in endorsements made a part hereof), this company, for the term shown above from inception date shown above at noon (Standard Time) to expiration date shown above at noon (Standard Time) at location of property involved, to an amount not exceeding the limit of liability above specified, does insure the insured named in the declarations above and legal representatives, to the extent of the actual cash value of the property at the time of loss. . . .

The audience for each of these documents is the average person—the home owner, the worker who wants to save money. The language is so pretentious, though, that it hinders rather than furthers communication.

Students who think that college writing should be formal often end up sounding pretentious themselves. Trying hard to be formal, they instead become ponderous, wordy, or even bombastic; they create colossal sentences and fill them with fancy words—like *ponderous, bombastic,* and *colossal.* A student is not writing good formal prose when he or she states:

> I hope to recuperate in some manner of fashion from the toil of the previous week and drench myself in liquid sunshine.

And it would certainly be pretentious for a student to describe hitting a baseball with:

> I have made contact with the oncoming projectile and deflected it from its course leaving me free to advance to Station One.

Likewise, inappropriate formality deadens this comment on a mother's birthday party:

> Mother walked around in bewilderment and continued passing out expressions of her gratitude for their presence in her celebration.

The circumstance, the audience, and the attitude of these three subjects—a tired worker, a baseball player, a grateful mother—would call for more straightforward, down-to-earth prose. The students, however, seem to be striving for a formal respectability they associate with college writing. They may be sincere, but their expression does not ring true. You may recall feeling the same way about the language of former Vice-President Spiro Agnew in the early Nixon administration. In complicated sentences, he railed against "pusillanimous pussy-footing," "hopeless, hysterical hypochondriacs of history," and the "effete corps of impudent snobs who characterize themselves as intellectuals."

Pretentious language blocks communication. We expect Kojak to say to his villains, "If you don't tell me the truth, sweetheart, I'll beat your guts out." He would sound phony if he said instead, "If you continue to prevaricate or distort the truth, sir, I will be forced to deal roughly with you." The language would fit neither the man nor the circumstance. And think of your reaction if a friend mentioned while you were walking to class together, "A skunk sprayed my car today with an odoriferous aroma" or "I met the love of my life while masticating a McDonald's hamburger." *Odoriferous* and *masticate* are fine words, but they do not fit into the friendly chatter of friends. The sign in the Greyhound bus station which reads "Please Do Not Expectorate" creates the same kind of problem. *Expectorate* may not be the best word to use to people who spit on the floor.

A problem similar to that of using inappropriate words occurs when a writer, again trying hard to be formal, uses *malapropisms,* words which actually mean something else. Mrs. Malaprop is not just a character from Richard Sheridan's eighteenth-century play *The Rivals;* she is alive and well today. Straining for a note of formal sophistication, we sometimes use words that mean something other than what we think they do. The effect can be confusing or comical. Think of Archie Bunker solemnly announcing to Edith after his one flirtation, "The sexual act was never constipated." Imagine the effect of the letter to the insurance agent which says, "Unless I get my husband's money soon, I will be forced to lead an immortal life." *Constipated* and *immortal* sound a little bit like *consummated* and *immoral,* but their meanings could not be more different.

Be careful not to tie yourself into tortuous verbal knots for the sake of formality. An undeniable touch of charm lies in the sign in the parking lot of a very staid British hotel:

> Vehicles and their accessories and contents are left here at the owner's risk and whilst every endeavor is taken to ensure the safety thereof, the proprietors will not be responsible for loss or damage thereof and thereto however caused.

But what works for the British does not necessarily work for us. A similar sign in an American parking lot makes the same point more quickly and forcefully:

> Park at your own risk.

The sign on the gate of the Old Charing Cross Hospital in London announces:

> You are kindly requested to make as little noise as possible in the interests of the patients of this hospital.

Its American counterpart might read:

> QUIET
> HOSPITAL

If you can use a large vocabulary naturally, do so. But do not strain. The words must fit the context and match the audience, or they will betray you. Some occasions demand that you refer to a janitor as a maintenance engineer or a library as a learning resource center. But even with formal language, the title of Jack Teagarden's verse "Say It Simple" is often very good advice. Sometimes you need to call a spade a spade instead of an agricultural implement.

Exercises

1. Tape a short conversation with a friend. Transcribe the tape. Then, write up the transcription so that you summarize the topics of conversation. What is the difference between spoken and written English?
2. Bring to class a passage of formal writing which you find in some outside source. Be ready to describe its context, its purpose, and its intended audience.
3. Try to find some samples of pretentious language that show formality gone bad. Revise at least one of them into good formal prose.
4. Write a short passage of your own in which you are consciously as pretentious as possible. Exaggerate as much as you like. Then rewrite the piece so that it is still formal but not pretentious. Comment on the changes you consciously made to improve it.

Informal English

Informal English is the language of coffee klatches, barrooms, and PTA meetings. It is the language spoken around most supper tables, swimming pools, and television sets. Informal writing, unlike formal writing, maintains the rhythm and sounds of everyday speech. It is the language of the familiar—of letters, of diaries, or of almost any other instance in which a writer speaks personally to a reader. An informal thank-you note to a grandmother might say:

> Dear Gram,
> Thanks for the neat sweater you made for me. I thought it was going to be a little baggy until I put it on. But wow! It fits great!
>
> Love ya,
> Gwen

With possibly a few exceptions, the language of lawyers' briefs or of policy debates is not the idiom for the sincere outpouring of feeling and affection from grandchild to grandparent. Attempts at formality may lead to ill-suited, strained prose if what you need instead is the ease and flexibility of informality.

A passage from an article in *Sports Illustrated,* in which a young wrestler talks about an overnight trip for a high-school meet, illustrates the informal style:

> I spent the night with the Carpenter family. . . . Rance Prokoff from Lewis and Clark shared the Carpenter basement with me. We shot a game of eight ball to see who got the davenport, and Rance won. I slept under the pool table. Actually, it was pretty cozy. I managed to hook up a little desk lamp and read *The Autobiography of Malcolm X* till pretty late.
>
> "As I Did It," *Sports Illustrated,*
> November 6, 1978

When audience and purpose permit, informal English is as functional in its way as formal English, yet its rules are more flexible. It uses shortcuts that would be out of place in formal diction; short sentences, fragments, and contractions are common. The agility of informal language springs from devices such as colloquialism, regionalism, slang, and jargon.

Devices of informality. *Colloquial* language refers to our everyday speech, words that are more often spoken than written. No matter what your degree of education, you usually speak to your friends in language that is less formal than your written language. You might refer to your younger brother as a "little kid," you might go to a "movie" instead of a "film," or you might "get mad" instead of "angry." Colloquial language contributes shortcuts to informality: contractions such as *can't* or *shouldn't* or abbreviations such as *TV* or *phone.* A colloquial style fits writing occasions when you want to seem to be chatting informally.

Certain colloquial words or phrases native to particular parts of the country are *regionalisms.* While most Americans will "turn out the light," some will "shut out the light," and the Pennsylvania Dutch might "outen the light." Southerners say "you-all" or "y'all"; some mountain people say "you-uns"; some Northeasterners say "youse." The standard form, though, remains *you.* The shopper in Southern Illinois puts groceries in a "sack," the shopper in Baltimore or even Chicago puts them in a "bag," and shoppers in West Virginia stuff their boxes of spaghetti and cans of beans into a "poke."

Another type of nonstandard diction more often spoken than written is *slang.* Frequently colorful initially, slang quickly becomes dated, thereby losing its effectiveness. Often, too, it is peculiar to a certain group. At some high schools, for instance, different groups of students might be called "jocks and jockettes," "greasers," and "freaks." Other high-school students may not recognize these labels at all. Likewise, some motorcyclists refer to their bikes as "hogs," while for some "street dude," a "hog" is a big pink Cadillac. Many variations of slang slip into our daily language. We might refer to a pair of sunglasses as "shades," to money as "dough" or "bread," or to a silly friend as a "turkey."

An even more limited kind of slang is *jargon,* the technical or specialized language of a trade, profession, sport, or other special-interest group. In a way, jargon is shoptalk. Like slang, it is effective only when its audience understands it. Teachers can discuss "correlative objectives" and "competency based curricula." Computer programmers understand a colleague who must "debug" a "program" because it "bombed" on the first "run." Monday night football fans have no trouble understanding Frank Gifford when he pinpoints a "red dog" or a "blitz."

Problems with informality. While an informal style can be appropriate to casual writing situations, it is ill-suited when the reader/writer contact is impersonal. Colloquialisms, regionalisms, slang, and jargon, which breathe life into informal English, can also create problems when mixed with a more formal diction or when aimed at the wrong audience.

In a serious essay discussing Arab/Israeli relations, you should not say "The Palestinian Liberationists are a bunch of jerks." A paper on investment options should not make a statement such as "People who mess with the stock market are ill-informed." You might say these things to friend in conversation, but the informality of the phrases "bunch of jerks" and "mess with" do not belong in writing that has a more dignified tone. Although an occasional informal expression sometimes adds an interesting touch to a more formal posture, unless the writer is skillful, its placement can be jarring.

Just as with formal English, informality can backfire if aimed at the wrong audience. Readers who do not understand the special meaning of the slang or the jargon or the regionalism will be confused. Some regionalisms transcend boundaries of states or sections of the country and some slang and jargon have grown common enough to have broader meanings. Still, these devices work best with a special audience and a special context. In *Midnight Cowboy,* for instance, Joe can say to Rico, "Keep your meathooks off my radio," or John in Kurt Vonnegut's *Cat's Cradle* can say, "Papa was rolled away in the airport's big red meat wagon." The language matches the speakers and the situations, so the slang is acceptable. If you ever want to talk on a CB radio, you cannot timidly say, "Uh, excuse me." You must use the jargon and say "Breaker, breaker" loud and clear or no one will pay any attention to you. On the other hand, these informal expressions are out of place when the audience is more general. This ad proclaiming the superior design of a Chevrolet Camaro fits well into *Car and Driver* magazine:

> It's engineered, from the ground up, with the most sophisticated suspension in the Camaro line, with special shocks, anti-sway bars and springs to help stabilize the ride. It's equipped with steel-belted radials. Bold new cast-aluminum wheels are available in three colors. There's a four-speed gearbox that delivers the power from the smooth 5.7 Liter V8 engine. A new solenoid-operated air induction scoop helps the engine breathe. The exhaust sings through dual resonators. The Z28 bristles with a good-looking front air dam, fender flares, and a rear spoiler.

But imagine its effect on the readers of *Woman's Day* magazine or even of *Newsweek.* Audience is important in dictating informality of word choice.

A last problem of informality comes from the use of cliché. A *cliché* is a word or phrase used too many times by too many people. It is informality at its worst. A cliché is worn out. It has lost most of the effect it might once have had. In the sixties, someone announced that she would "tell it like it is," and someone else decided to "do his own thing." These were clever phrases—then. But after they were seen in every newspaper and heard in every conversation, they lost most of their original punch. The same problem arises if you say your niece is "pretty as a picture" or "cute as a button." The phrase "bold as brass," which many of us still use, is so old that James Joyce used it in *Ulysses,* a book written more than seventy years ago.

You may easily slip into clichés when you are talking. They are, as the cliché goes, "on the tip of your tongue," and they do, after all, generally make a point. But people react to clichés much as they process the ring of a door bell or a telephone—with an automatic response. Clichés therefore blunt rather than sharpen a writer's meaning and defeat the purpose of writing. With a little care you can usually edit out the cliché and rephrase your ideas more freshly and cleverly.

Exercises

1. Write two examples of each of the following: colloquialism, regionalism, slang, jargon, cliché.
2. Make a list of five clichés. Try to express the thought of each one in a different, more original way.

   Example: They were as different as day and night.
   Sugar and lemon juice could not have been more different.

3. Sit in a lounge, cafeteria, bus, restaurant, or the like and listen to the conversation around you. Try to write down what you hear without the speakers' knowledge. See if you can make some observations about the nature of informal language.
4. Try rewriting a formal piece of writing (possibly one from the exercises on formality) to make it very informal. Define your new audience and purpose and comment on the changes you make. Do you think the piece has improved?

Balancing Formal and Informal Language

Unless the situation demands otherwise, you do not want your writing to be too formal and rigid, but you also may want to avoid the casualness of colloquialism and slang. General English lets you strike a balance between the two. It is the language of most newspapers and magazines as well as of most educated people, whether they are journalists, personnel officers, or students. While it usually follows standard grammatical practices, such as subject/verb agreement, general English pays less heed to formal distinctions, such as between *shall* and *will.* Words are usually Anglo-Saxon rather than Latinate. Sentences are usually shorter and less complicated than in a formal style, but they are not as simple or unstructured as they may be in informal English.

The following passage shows the kind of consistency of language and shape which characterizes general English:

> In many countries, such as Iran, Northern Africa, and Scotland, laws exist specifically against wife abuse. However, in America, only three states, California, Texas, and Hawaii, consider spouse abuse a felony. In most other states, such laws get scant support when they are introduced in male-dominated legislatures. Therefore, the United States government must institute a nationwide law that protects the battered wife, a law which judges, lawyers, and policemen can not ignore and will be required to enforce.

The sentences in this paragraph are fairly short and only occasionally complicated; grammar and punctuation are used correctly; diction is consistent. The language reflects the seriousness of content and purpose by choosing words considered more formal than informal: *abuse* instead of *beating, battered* instead of *punched out, male-dominated legislatures* instead of *the chauvinist pigs in Congress, institute* instead of *pass.* At the same time, however, some terms that could have been very formal have been stated more informally: *laws* instead of *legal entities, scant* instead of *minimal, required* instead of *compelled.* In other words, the passage is looser than the level of formal English, yet tighter than the level of informal.

There are times when you will write a paragraph with a certain audience and purpose in mind and then find you have to alter it for a more general audience, using general English. For example, this passage was written very informally:

> Four months after Carter was released, he and Artis were picked up and charged again. The state had found a grand jury who could swallow its story. Solomon also points out the fact that one time in this same city Carter was arrested on a trumped-up charge and was able to bribe the arresting officer when the cop approached Carter and informed him of the opportunity to beat the rap.

The language in this research paper should have been general rather than informal. Colloquial and slang expressions such as "picked up," "swallow their story," "trumped-up charge," "cop," and "beat the rap" distort the tone, making it much too informal. Given the purpose and audience of the paper, such phrases are inappropriate. Recast into general English, the passage reads like this:

> Four months after Carter was released, he and Artis were arrested and charged again. The state had found a grand jury now willing to indict the pair. Solomon also states that at one time in this same city, Carter was arrested on a false charge. He was able to avoid prosecution when the arresting officer, willing to accept a bribe, gave him an opportunity to escape.

A slightly different problem with language appears in this passage taken from a research paper about Buckminster Fuller's many talents:

> Fuller's education started at the Milton Academy, an exclusive New England school for which his mother sacrificed dearly to send him. He was very athletic and quarterbacked for the school football team. He later described athletics as "an enthusiastically broad experience in the historically differentiated family of controlled physical principles, which greatly heightened . . . the intuitive dynamic sense, a fundamental . . . of competent anticipatory design formation." Howard Cosell, eat your beans.

Although Fuller's language is little short of incredible, the allusion to Cosell's verbal gymnastics, while very clever, is definitely out of place. It changes the tone of the writing from serious to cute, hurting the writer more than helping.

One final example comes from a paper discussing witchcraft. This student quoted a long passage from Herbert Malloy Manson's *Secrets of the Supernatural* outlining the tortures endured by one poor woman accused of being a witch in medieval Germany:

> "Her hands were bound, her hair shorn and alcohol was doused on her and set alight. Sulphur strips were placed under her arms and around her neck and set on fire. She was suspended by a rope from the ceiling with her hands bound behind her back and left dangling for hours. Alcohol was poured on her back and lighted. Her thumbs were put in vices and crushed. She was lashed with a rawhide whip. A heavy plank studded with nails was pressed against her body and left there. She was, of course, fainting repeatedly but was revived by sluicing with cold water and having vinegar pumped in her nose. The next day was the same but without pushing things quite so far." Witches back then really had it rough.

After reading through the horrors described by Manson, bumping into the student's colloquial analysis is quite a shock. "Witches back then really had it rough" destroys the tension built up through the list of tortures so crucial to Manson's point. The student's comment trivializes the woman's ordeal and puts it on the level of a teenager bemoaning the fate of a friend who cannot borrow his father's car for a date. The torture of human beings merits more sympathetic language.

Chapter Exercises

1. Compare samples of formal, general, and informal writing (you should be able to use material from previous exercises). Decide what makes each passage effective or ineffective by considering its use of language, the intended reader, and the purpose of the passage.
2. Find an old business letter you or someone in your family wrote—an application for a job or a complaint about a product. Then, remember how you told your family and friends about the job application or the complaint. What is the difference between formal, informal, or general English? Can you see any further differences between formal written English, general written English, and informal spoken English?
3. Watch Walter Cronkite read his nightly script. Listen to Dick Enberg announce a basketball game. Are there differences in their diction? Compare their language (which is basically standard American English) with the colloquial American English we more normally speak.
4. Find one or more word usage problems in each of the following passages from student papers. Try to correct them by revising, deleting, or rewording.

   a. Buckminster Fuller was sent to the Connecticut Canada Textile Company in Sherbrooke, Canada, as an apprentice mechanic for his punishment. After getting back into the good graces of his family, he returned to Harvard in 1914 only to be dismissed for "lack of sustained interest in the process of the University." Well, he was never accused of being a conformist.

   b. The only diversion these handicapped children had was throwing a ball upside the shed.

c. Chris Hanburger, the Redskins' right linebacker, broke up several passes and dumped Herb Lusk behind the line of scrimmage on a crucial third-down play.
d. Although they do not grow as humongous as a Great Dane or greyhound, dalmatians are nowhere near the size of a Yorki or a tea-cup poodle.
e. As he walked away as if he were stepping to "Mister Magic" by Grover Washington, Jr., he was so cool I nearly fell out of my seat.
f. The midnight blue horizon quickly blanketed the foreboding sky with huge bellowing black clouds.

5. Here are the introductory paragraphs from two student papers. Considering the intended reader, the writer, and the purpose, discuss the effectiveness of their diction.
a. This is the age of modern medicine, miracle drugs, and advanced technology. Doctors can repair unbelievably broken bodies and burned skin. In some hospitals, they can even transplant human organs. But the wonders of modern medicine are limited. Working in Respiratory Therapy in Doctors' Hospital, I have seen cases in which patients were kept alive through artificial means for weeks or months. This not only prolongs the patient's suffering but places terrible hardships, both emotional and financial, on the family. In some cases, modern medicine, while trying to save lives, denies death with dignity to its patients.
b. Alcoholism among young people has been a problem for years. Drunk teenagers are a common sight on Saturday night. They spend a lot of time partying and sometimes destroy property until the police show up to bust a few heads. Drinking affects young people both physically and mentally. It changes their personalities as well as physical beings.

Chapter Checklist

1. When you write, think carefully about your words. A few well-chosen words can say more than a hundred weak ones.
2. Since you rarely write the way you speak, try to strike a good balance between formality and informality. Be consistent. Audience and purpose determine what you can say and how you can say it.

3. When your style is formal, watch out for wordiness and pretentiousness.
4. When your style is informal, use colloquialisms, slang, jargon, or regionalisms when they fit your reader and your writing task. Otherwise avoid these very informal kinds of speech in your writing.

Being Specific

Often we sit down to prepare an essay and start the first sentence with a phrase like "In the modern world of today . . . ." Or we write on a postcard "Having a nice time. Wish you were here." In a letter to a friend working at the seashore for the summer, we might send such important information as "I met a good-looking girl at Joe's party last week."

Whether our language is formal, informal, or general, we often have trouble lifting it from the vague, flat prose that too many of us use once we stop talking and start writing. We get tongue-tied on paper. We grab at timeworn phrases. We slip into traditional patterns. We puff up our writing with long words. We generalize, we temporize, we stumble and fumble. In this way we perpetuate vagueness and flatness. While we can't all be witty and we can't all be clever, with some effort we *can* break the habit of vague, nonthinking language. We can all produce clear, readable writing that is concrete and specific.

If words are the only real tools we have to fashion our thoughts, then we must make them work for us and not against us. The words must *show* the laughter, the complexity, the love, the sweetness, the joy, the agony, the seriousness, or the pain . . . not simply *tell* it. As the solid common denominator of most good writing, concrete language is complementary to the freshness and vigor of your thoughts. To communicate those thoughts to someone else, there is no alternative. You must learn to be specific.

Abstract and Concrete Words

Loveliness, truth, beauty, hatred, envy—these words indicate concepts. They cannot be held in a hand like an egg or a baseball; they cannot be seen by an eye like a painting or a television screen. Such words are *abstractions:* concepts, emotions, relationships that you cannot perceive through your senses. On the other hand, something that is *concrete* is an object, a shape, a person, a sound, a sensation—any of the clear, sharp images which can be felt or seen or heard or smelled or tasted. Pyramids of oranges in a Safeway store, the rough touch of an army blanket, the wail of a hungry baby—unlike infatuation or greed or laziness, these are images our senses perceive. While writers need both abstract and concrete words, concrete images let your reader respond to your writing by translating message into shape.

Abstractions are not undesirable; they are just more difficult to use because they offer neither reader nor writer a ready image or picture. In discussing the theory of relativity, the philosophy of existentialism, or some other intellectual concept, you need abstractions. For example, in her book *Against Interpretation,* Susan Sontag can make a powerful abstract statement such as, "Writing criticism has proved to be an act of intellectual disburdenment as much as of intellectual expression." Abstractions fit in other places as well—a report on inflation, for instance, or a study of the energy needs of the United States. A typical newspaper article predicting a recession might contain a statement such as this one:

> The nonpartisan Congressional Budget Office has privately warned Congress to expect a full-fledged recession this year and through most of 1980, with inflation continuing at a double-digit pace and the jobless rate rising to well above normal.
>
> *Washington Post,* June 10, 1979

Abstractions can be precise and meaningful, but if not used with care they can dominate writing, making it vague and flat, as in this paragraph taken from a student essay:

> Today's youth are brighter, more assertive, more articulate, and they possess a far deeper commitment to social justice than their parents, because today's youth are today. Today's youth are brighter because of their youth. There is more life before them than behind them. Their parents have had as much life behind them as well as before them. Their parents see what is now as well as what has been now. Today's youth see only now. Today's youth are more assertive because

> they maintain today. Their parents have maintained yesterday to today, but today's youth maintain today to tomorrow. Today's youth are their parents' only link to tomorrow.

While there are problems other than an over-reliance upon abstract ideas in this paragraph, you become almost dizzy trying to follow the student's thought. You continually bump into the abstract notions of youth, commitment, social justice, life, now, today, yesterday, tomorrow, and so on. Naturally, you become confused. Abstractions need concrete images or words to limit, define, and illustrate them. Otherwise they begin to bore and frustrate us.

Writers often cope with abstract concepts, by linking the filmy notions of beauty, truth, and love to concrete images. Shakespeare writes of the "hollow bubble of pride" or the "tree of life." James Joyce describes death with the image, "She lies laid out in stark stiffness in the secondbest bed. . . ." This brief passage beginning an essay about America's food habits is very concrete:

> Supermarket shelves, the great barometer of what America eats, all seem to be colored brown now. Instant cereals, white flours, refined sugars appear solemnly packaged in their tan sacks to persuade us that there has been hardly any intervention between the manure that nourished them and the recycled paper that wraps them.
>
> Ruth Gay, "Fear of Food"

Supermarket shelves, instant cereals, white flour, refined sugar, tan sacks, manure, and recycled paper—Ruth Gay uses many concrete images to make her point about the recent marketing techniques that take advantage of the shift in America from processed to natural foods. Her choice of images suggests her own slight intolerance of what may be yet another American fad. In this way, she translates an abstract idea into a concrete statement, quickly understood by the reader. Her message would not be quite as effective if she had written instead:

> The products in grocery stores suggest that America's dietary habits have changed. Lately there has been a move back to natural foods, and manufacturers have taken advantage of the trend in the way they package their products.

Paul Simon spoke for prose writers as well as singers and songwriters when he pleaded, "Don't take my Kodachrome away." Sharp, technicolor pictures show the reader what is in our minds more clearly than do unfocused abstract concepts.

Exercises

1. Make a list of the five senses. Following each, add five concrete words that show a sensory image.

   Examples: touch: icy
   taste: peppery

2. Make a list of ten unrelated concrete images. Each should be something you can hear, see, smell, taste, or touch. You might stand or sit in a fixed place and record what you see, or you might use your imagination to devise this list. There is no need to use complete sentences.

   Examples: troops at picket-fence attention
   bags crackling

3. Make a list of five abstractions. Then, write a concrete sentence to clarify each one.

   Example: love: Two teenagers dig their toes in wet sand as they amble hand in hand on a beach.

4. Analyze the use of abstract and concrete language in the following passages taken from student essays. If appropriate, suggest ways to make the abstractions more concrete.
   a. The imperfections of every society have been dramatized in numerous ways, and although various cultures within a society are quite distinct from one another, the problems themselves remain consistent. This can be attributed to the individuals who form the community and whose social interaction is motivated by each person's attitudes or needs.
   b. The forlorn figure of the duck lies amidst the debris on the beach, its oil soaked feathers plastered to its lifeless form. With its head craned outward, feet partially covered by sand, and battered wings folded by its side as if pleading for mercy, the duck symbolizes the victims of mankind's carelessness.
   c. Running away from home can be dangerous. When you run out of money, you will turn to crime. You may become

involved with the wrong person or people. You may get involved with gangs or with criminals. It is very dangerous to run away from home since many problems arise.

Being More Concrete

The management of a college cafeteria, annoyed at the daily lunch mess, taped the following note onto each table:

PLEASE
Give the next person who uses this table a break.
Clean your own table!

At one table a student had handwritten underneath the typed lines:

Why?
The food is cold and lousy!

Another student came along and added:

. . . and my pickle had a hair on it!

The vague phrase "cold and lousy" suggests that the first student isn't too pleased with the cafeteria food. But the second student's pickle with the hair on it so strongly suggests the cafeteria's poor service that you can almost feel a gag welling up in your throat as you read it. The hair on the pickle is a good example of being specific.

The words *cold* and *lousy* are not really abstractions; instead they vaguely express an attitude. We often use such general phrases to express a point of view: "That was a neat party; I had a blast"; "Her dress is a putrid color"; "The meal was great." But such general phrases don't mean much by themselves. You know what specifics made you conclude "neat," "blast," "putrid," and "great," but unless you supply those specifics, the vague language lets the reader insert his or her own meaning. If you danced until 4:00 A.M. or drank sixteen bottles of Michelob, say so. If her dress is chartreuse or mauve or tangerine, say so. If the meal was chili dogs and sauerkraut, beefburgers and baked beans, or pâté and caviar, say so. Only you can tell exactly what you mean. If you choose not to, then your comments pale as written communication. They are too dependent upon your presence for explanation.

You have to show that the "well-dressed woman" is wearing a

gray pin-striped suit and crisp white blouse; the "nice house" is a brown-shingled ranch or a green clapboard Victorian; your yard is "a mess" because a thousand dandelions poke through the unmowed lawn. Joseph Conrad once wrote, "My task is, by the power of the written word, to make you hear, to make you feel—it is, above all, to make you see." Concrete writing, then, means showing, not telling. Concrete detail changes the vague and general into the specific.

Omitting specifics produces this type of writing:

> Not long ago, I went fishing. I had a swell time. It was an awfully hot day. The fish didn't bite for a long time. Suddenly, I caught a really big fish. Boy did he put up a fight. It was tough going, but I finally landed him all right.

This short paragraph is very similar to much that you hear, read, and perhaps write. What kind of response can you have to this piece of writing, however? Does it excite you, move you, insult you, scandalize you, or even interest you? Unless you wrote it—or unless you are the doting parent or tolerant friend of the writer—probably not. The writer is proud of landing the fish, but the real tale is still locked up. We know that the writer went fishing and caught a big fish, but we get only a series of vague, general statements about what happened, few specific, concrete images. A concrete picture of that same event would be filled with specific images which would catch the vigor and excitement of the violent struggle of man *vs.* beast:

> My palms were sweaty. I was driving myself insane waiting. Waves snapped in front of me. The sun seared my bare body. The 95 degree heat seemed to curdle my fiberglass boat while the engine's constant hum made me drowsy. Finally, the violent struggle began. I had hooked a lunker, the granddaddy of all bluefish. He had no intention of letting some young sprout like me reel him in. The guts of my Penn 60 were practically stripped; the super stiffness of my Tru Temper rod had no effect on him. I wrenched the drag as tight as I could, almost twisting it off. I reeled and reeled, finally reaching my leader to start the last lap. The veins in my arms were enormous. Between the sweat and the flies and the bees, I thought I would never outlast this almighty beast. But finally, there he was, a tired old fool, who had eaten my artificial bait, floating aimlessly alongside by boat.

Whether or not you are an angler, you can probably see the difference between this paragraph and the original. The second is concrete. The battle with the fish is vigorous. The lull of waiting, the labored struggle, the tired finish are all there. Strong, concrete phrases set the scene: waves snapping, the sun searing the bare body, the reel stripping. Unlike the general references in the previous paragraph to "swell time" and "awfully hot," the specific images help draw a sharp picture of the fishing trip so it not only becomes clearer but grows into something in which you can participate on the writer's terms.

A simple reminiscence of childhood offers another example of the value of the concrete. You could not express warm memories of your own mother's concern in this general way:

> Mothers can really be corny sometimes. My mother used to worry about the silliest things. But every now and then, her fears would turn out to be justified.

This general comment about motherly wisdom says very little to a reader. The subject is almost any mother and undoubtedly the reader will think of his or her own experiences, not yours: the time he played hooky, or the swimming pool she was not allowed in, or the dog that bit him after his mother warned him not to pull its tail. More concrete details could make your remembrance vivid and alive:

> My mother always used to scold me about jumping across the stream in the woods next to our house. She warned me that one day I would fall in and get soaked. Sure enough, on my eighth birthday, clad in a new yellow taffeta dress and black patent leather shoes, I jumped across the stream for a group of admiring cousins. My foot slipped; I fell with a splat. I sat in the mud, yellow ribbon dangling in my eyes, while seven cousins gleefully ran to tell my mother what I had done.

Such a specific statement of the experience would leave little room for readers to guess at your meaning or to superimpose their own memories on yours.

To make your meaning absolutely clear, then, you—the writer, the picture drawer—use specific, concrete images to depict abstractions and generalities. To describe a scene as "romantic" is not enough. When you mention satin sheets on a water bed or a ski lodge in Vermont or sitting together in a library studying for a physics exam, you define "romantic" as *you* see it at a given moment. If happiness is a dozen warm Toll House cookies or a *B* on a political science final, you should say so. If a "slick" car for you is a Jaguar XJ12L, you must say so to keep your reader from dreaming about a shiny, dechromed 1956 Ford Fairlane.

Exercises

1. Illustrate the following general sentences with at least one specific sentence.
   a. It was a lovely day.
   b. We had a nice time.
   c. He is a handsome boy.
   d. I was in an ugly mood.
   e. She wore a beautiful outfit to the theater party.
2. Take some of the abstractions and general phrases given in the list below and offer three specific details to make them more concrete. You need not make complete sentences.

   Example: *noise in the cafeteria*
   straws gurgling through ice
   money jangling in coin changers
   the blare of Kiss

   a. an evening of television
   b. writing all over the blackboard
   c. a delicious aroma
   d. an interesting person
   e. hair that is a real mess
   f. a Friday-night date
   g. elegant clothing
   h. children playing
   i. frightening
   j. many kinds of football fans
3. In the manner of the fishing example or the motherly concern passages, try writing two paragraphs about the same thought or experience. First discuss the experience in the general terms you might use initially to describe it; then, consciously rewrite the paragraph to make it more specific.
4. Try to write several short, specific items that highlight some human folly. To make the exercise more interesting, try to achieve a humorous or tongue-in-cheek twist.

   Example: Listening to my "devout Buddhist" roommate go on about his pure, natural diet and finding him eating a packaged macaroni and cheese dinner.

Using Nouns, Verbs, and Modifiers

You may easily imagine Emily Dickinson delicately placing specific images of shadows and bells and birds into her poems. You may more easily think of Edgar Allan Poe using the concrete details of coffins and black cats and madmen to build up the tension in one of his chilling short stories. But what a trouble when you try to do it yourself.

Being concrete is not easy. It takes thought and practice. But you need not be a professional writer; there are tricks any of us can use. If you remember that language must suit situation, you can usually be concrete without being phony and specific without being overdressed. Concrete writing does not come from just tacking on another modifier. It comes from using precise, specific words. And more precise words may well mean lean, tough Hemingway prose as well as the rounder, fuller style of a Thomas Wolfe. Well-chosen nouns, verbs, and modifiers can help you achieve either.

Nouns

Nouns are the people, places, and things we write about. The butterflies, Christmas trees, and solar energy collectors that we need to fill out our ideas are all nouns. There are several different types of nouns. We spoke earlier of the abstract nouns such as "ugliness" or "transcendentalism." Then there are the more common, concrete nouns which can be either general or particular: *occupation* is general, *plumber* is particular; *pen* is general, *Bic Banana* is particular; *dog* is general, *Dachshund* particular.

Fix your writing on the most workable and believable concrete level. Most nouns fit somewhere in a chain that lets them move from the more general to the more specific. The word *performer,* for instance, can break down this way:

General → Specific → More Specific

Performer → Singer → Rock Star → Elton John

That same general word *performer* could evolve quite differently by altering the specifics:

Performer → Dancer → Ballerina → Margot Fonteyn

Let specifics work for you as much as they can. Saying "I bought an antique car" lets you pass on a certain amount of information by using the general noun *car.* Saying "I bought a 1943 Cadillac" would let you say even more the first time around. Saying "The book was written by Eldridge Cleaver" is ambiguous until you specify the book as *Soul on Ice.* You can only go so far with general nouns; it would be pointless to say, "In love with small cars, she bought a small car." Whenever possible, consider using *Coke* instead of *drink, Ben* instead of *boy, Rembrandt* instead of *artist.* Whenever, in other words, you can use a particular noun, do so, for it gives your reader a clearer picture of your meaning.

As always, though, use caution. Sometimes a more general noun is more appropriate. At times you will want to say, "I put the knife on the table" rather than "I put the meat cleaver on the Duncan Phyfe." Or you might prefer to say "I strapped my tennis racquet to the handlebars of my bicycle" instead of "I strapped my Wilson T-3000 to the handlebars of my Sears Free Spirit bicycle." And it would sound awkward to say, "The woman lifted her glass of 1961 San Martin Mountain Chablis in a toast to her husband." In instances such as these, there would be little reason to be so specific as to use a brand name. The more general noun sounds better, makes good sense, and conveys the right degree of specificity.

Exercises

1. Below are three sets of related nouns. In each set, the first noun is abstract, the second general, and the third specific. Use each noun separately in a sentence to show circumstances requiring different degrees of specificity.
   a. driving/automobile/Chevy Monza
   b. reading/book/*Gone with the Wind*
   c. communication/telephone/Princess phone
2. For each of the following words, develop a chain of nouns going from general to specific to more specific. Start with the given word as the general and work down to the more specific.

   Example: circus performer→trapeze artists→Harvey Wallenda

   a. chair
   b. recording
   c. truck
   d. guitar
   e. ballet
3. Look at each of the nouns below and suggest one that is more general and one that is more specific.

   Example: *millionaire*
   rich man
   Howard Hughes

a. Marine
b. fern
c. sofa
d. automobile
e. thoroughbred

4. Bring to class two or three paragraphs from a textbook, newspaper, or magazine. Be prepared to comment on the use of nouns in the passage. If it can be more specific, rewrite it, substituting more specific nouns.

Verbs

Verbs usually provide the action in a sentence. Using strong, active verbs helps make your writing concrete. Such verbs not only speak for themselves, but they carry the image of the sentence.

> Sandals **slapped** the pavement.
> The chalk **screeched** and **tapped** its way across the blackboard.
> The trees **lurked** in the night.

All three of these sentences generate a power and tension through their verbs. You hear the slap of the sandals of someone walking behind you. You cringe as the chalk screeches on the blackboard. And you shudder at the eerie image of the dark, lurking trees. Unlike the linking verbs *be, is, are* or *has, have, had,* verbs with strong action built into them do not need to depend on other words in the sentence. If someone frantically entered a crowded room and shouted "Run," the people in the room would respond more immediately than if that same person entered the same room and frantically shouted "Be." With *run,* the comprehension is immediate. Linking verbs have many functions, but to accent the concrete, use active verbs if you can.

As with nouns, some verbs are closer than others to the precise meaning you intend, letting you draw a sharper picture with them. When you say, "Tarzan *dashed* through the trees," you say more with one verb than you do with, "Tarzan *swung quickly* through the trees." In this situation, "dashed" has a strength which "swung quickly" lacks. In another, such as "The monkey *swung* nimbly to the ground," "swung" is better. If you say, "The baby *snuggled* against her father," rather than, "The baby *sat next to* her father," you take advantage of the contented, cozy image built into the word *snuggled.* You also gain some economy from using one word instead of three. In another sentence, though, "sat" would be more exact: "Too scared to move, the boy *sat* next to his mother in the dentist's office."

Verbs can be either active or passive. Active verbs help their subjects act:

The sailor **knotted** the rope.
The man **cooked** the fish.
The frog **ate** the fly.

Passive verbs emphasize the objects rather than the subjects. The subject in a sentence with the passive voice is acted upon by someone or something:

The rope **was knotted by** the sailor.
The fish **was cooked by** the man.
The fly **was eaten by** the frog.

When the verb is active, the sailor does the knotting, the man does the cooking, and the frog does the eating. But the passive voice robs the sentences of some of their thrust. Passive voice requires more words than the active voice to convey the same information. Like heavily abstract writing, verbs in the passive voice frequently generate vague, flat writing, especially if you use too many of them. Passive voice often becomes a way of evading an issue. Phrasing such as "The paper *was turned* in late" or "The tapes *were erased*" offers too ready a means by which someone can sidestep taking direct responsibility for an action.

At times, however, the passive voice helps emphasize or deemphasize an idea. Sometimes, as in "The car was smashed on the parking lot," you do not know who has performed the action and a vague "somebody" would serve poorly as the subject of the sentence. Sometimes, also, you want to remain neutral or disinteresed as in "The test *must be taken* by all applicants simultaneously" or "*Romeo and Juliet was danced* beautifully by the Royal Ballet."

In most cases, though, you will find that the active voice is more useful or forceful. There are few occasions when "The coat was bought by me" would be better than "I bought the coat." And it is certainly awkward to say, "The house was walked into by the boy." As a rule, avoid the passive voice. Use it occasionally to gain some formality or to add variety; otherwise, even though you carefully use concrete nouns and verbs, the lazy passive will rob your writing of vigor. Active verbs give you a built-in concrete image.

Exercises

1. While any of the following verbs can be effective, suggest three other verbs of roughly the same meaning that would make the sentence more specific:

   Example: *The boy* ran *down the street.*
   sped, scampered, scurried

   a. The dinosaur *walked* in the jungle.
   b. The men *ate* the pumpkin pie.
   c. The bell *rang.*
   d. The housekeeper *washed* the dirty pots.
   e. She *read* the newspaper.
   f. Dick Cavett *talked* with his guests.
   g. She *laughed* at the joke.
   h. Angry at his brother, the boy *went* into the house.
   i. Quickly changing her clothes, the girl *went* to meet her date.
   j. The child *asked* for a set of *Star Wars* figures.
2. The following verbs function well in certain writing situations, but the thoughts are often better expressed by common synonyms. List as many as you can.
   a. calculate
   b. annihilate
   c. postulate
   d. theorize
   e. redound
3. Use each of the following verbs in an appropriate sentence.
   a. rinse
   b. juggle
   c. shoot
   d. massage
   e. pinch
4. Write five sentences using strong, active verbs that carry the meaning of the sentence.
5. Find a piece of professional prose and analyze its use of verbs. Try to make suggestions for any that might be improved. Bring the original to class.

Modifiers

People often think that the way to be concrete is to add modifiers—words such as adjectives, adverbs, and participles that help explain the meaning further. True enough . . . sometimes! Modifiers do let you enrich the stark noun/verb combination. While the simple noun *lollipop* is concrete, you can create a more specific lollipop with modifiers: "a child's fuzzy lollipop," one that has been stuffed into a pocket or clutched by mittens. The noun *boat* speaks of many different kinds of boats, but modifiers can shape it into "an oyster boat in the shabby gray morning." The word *hat* suggests all kinds of hats, but modifiers transform it into a "furry, black hat nestling against an accounting book." Any of those nouns, *lollipop, boat, hat,* can function quite nicely on its own. The modifiers, however, carefully placed, sharpen the picture.

The most common modifiers, adjectives and adverbs, are by nature weaker than the nouns and verbs they modify. Adjectives particularize nouns and pronouns by qualifying them: *gold* watch, *mushroom* soup, *greedy* fish. Adverbs, on the other hand, explain the other words in a sentence—verbs, adjectives, other adverbs—by showing degree (*really* sorry), manner (walked *rapidly*), place (lived *there*), or time (cried *then*). Inserted carefully, these modifiers add a discriminating touch to nouns and verbs by pinpointing the distinctions that make them unique.

Trouble with modifiers comes more from their overuse or misuse than from lack of use. Some of us automatically tack adjectives onto most nouns and slip adverbs behind every verb. With a single sentence, this tactic raises few problems. In paragraphs full of such sentences, though, especially when many of the modifiers are vague or general, such as "*interesting* story," "*very* nice," "*fantastic* dress," so many modifiers pale. Strengthening the nouns and verbs themselves can sometimes lessen a preponderance of adjectives and adverbs. A stronger noun and verb can change a sentence such as "The *immediate superior* of the men *walked angrily* out of the factory" to "The foreman of the men stomped out of the factory." *Hurried* can replace *walked quickly; wardrobe* is more direct than *big clothes cupboard;* and *mural* is more precise than *wall painting*. Sometimes, too, one strong adjective can clinch an image faster than several weaker ones, as in "scrawny child" rather than "very small and thin child."

Yet another misuse of modifiers occurs when we dip into the common stock of predictable or canned phrases which we haul out for certain occasions. Thus we sing of "raging fires," "babbling brooks," "fighting valiantly," and "growing old gracefully." These packaged phrases are clichés, code words for particular situations or emotions.

For best effect, then, choose modifiers carefully to complement nouns and verbs rather than to smother or dilute them. Too many modifiers will insult your reader's imagination; too few may allow too much leeway. You do not always need modifiers, but when you do, the right kind and the right number make the difference between concrete writing and purple prose. Without modifiers, the nouns and verbs must be very specific so that your writing will not sound flat.

With too many, though, the prose may sound silly, as, for instance, if the lollipop becomes

> a scrawny, dirty little child's sticky, fuzzy, lemon lollipop with a bite taken out of it.

And it would be laughable if the boat became

> an ancient, fading yellow fossil of a wooden oyster boat loaded to the gills with booty, floating noisily, clumsily, and slowly in the shabby, gray, misty morning.

Modifiers, carefully added, create a striking effect. Ernest Hemingway's spare style won him praise. The more fanciful prose of writers like John Updike and William Faulkner gained critical approval for them. No one way is right; no one way is wrong. What works is what is best. This passage illustrates how effective a controlled application of modifiers can be.

> He looked about twenty-two years old. His skin was pale; his body was stiff. His scarred right arm seemed made of plastic. His short, curly black hair shone with sweat. His heart had stopped; he did not breathe. The carbon monoxide flowing through a hose from his truck's tailpipe had drained every ounce of life from Robert Bowman.

Exercises

1. To help you determine the value of modifiers used with control, describe something or someone in a brief paragraph without using any modifiers. Then, write a second description using an overabundance of modifiers. Examine the two and write a final paragraph which would be an appropriate blend of the two.
2. While adjectives sometimes overburden an image, frequently they strengthen a description. Add to each of the following nouns one or several modifiers to make the noun more concrete.

   Example: chair
   a tattered armchair with cotton stuffing dripping from the arm.

Avoid something like

tree
beautiful tree

a. elephant
b. glass
c. swing
d. wristwatch
e. house
f. boy
g. knife
h. woman
i. tree
j. fish

3. Find a short piece of professional writing and analyze its use of modifiers. Try to make suggestions for any that might be improved. Bring the original to class.

Some cautions about nouns, verbs, and modifiers

Concrete writing does not just happen. The Duchess in *Alice in Wonderland* is wrong when she tells Alice "Take care of the sense, and the sounds will take care of themselves." The sounds will not take care of themselves; you have to labor to produce concrete writing. You will not achieve it by pasting long lists of modifiers onto a sentence or by pushing alien verbs into doubtful service or by making every noun particular to the *n*th degree. Excessive detail confuses rather than clarifies. Ill-fitting verbs can be awkward or create comical, mismatched images. And overly picky nouns at times encumber ideas. Too much concreteness is like the overdressed courtesan, caked with too much make-up and jingling with bangles and beads. You must balance concreteness with grace. Keeping that limitation in mind, you should be able to enrich your writing without cluttering it, to free your style from a dominance of abstractions or generalities, and to enhance your ideas with clear, concrete prose. Then, not only will your writing be vivid, it will be taut and firm, without flab.

Exercise

Write a concrete sentence for each of the following subjects and verbs. Try to create some interesting and imaginative, yet controlled sentences. Change the nouns and verbs to be more specific if you wish.

a. monster ate
b. boy skipped
c. woman sang
d. fish swam
e. bracelet fell

Using Similes, Metaphors, and Allusions:

Other devices also prod language toward the specific. Similes, metaphors, and allusions are all figures of speech which explain through comparison. If concrete language works to clarify abstract or vague ideas by being specific, the metaphor, the simile, and the allusion define abstract concepts by comparing them to concrete images or experiences. These devices are not just ornaments. They work hard to vitalize ideas by suggesting relationships your reader may not have thought of before.

Similes

Similes compare by saying that X is *like* Y; they compare by using the words *like* or *as*. In describing a muddy football game between the Eagles and the Rams, you might say:

> The muddy football field was **like** a giant suction cup pulling the players to the ground.

To describe a fall bonfire, you might muse:

> The burning paper was shriveling **like** a black butterfly folding its wings.

Maya Angelou, in "A Lesson for in Living," wrote:

> For nearly a year, I sopped around the house, the store, the school, and the church, **like** an old biscuit, dirty and inedible.

A simile lends clarity to a thought by relating one idea or experience to a more familiar one. Someone you know may have "twig*like* fingers," a garter may strangle a thigh *like* a boa constrictor, and stinging rain may bounce off the hard pavement *like* tiny golf balls. All of these images are similes, describing one thing by showing its similarity to something else.

Metaphors

Metaphors do not use *like* or *as*. They are more dramatic than similes; they say directly that X *is* Y. Instead of saying that the muddy football field is like a giant suction cup, the metaphor says:

> The muddy football field **was** a giant suction cup pulling the players to the ground.

The burning paper shriveling like a black butterfly folding its wings becomes

> The shriveling, burning paper **was** a black butterfly folding its wings.

Poet/novelist Josephine Johnson uses several metaphors to describe a rain-soaked morning in a short piece entitled "April":

> An intermittent rain this morning, now ceasing. The quail are very shrill. Soggy but nervous. The woods are still bare except for **the thousand limp umbrellas of the buckeyes.** . . . This **delicate, shaking carpet of wild flowers!** Ferns, violets, squirrel corn, bluebells, spring beauties, bloodroot leaves, wild poppies.

The range of such comparisons is endless. You can make vivid the hard life of the tenant farmer by referring to the farm wife's "rough, sandpaper hands." With a minimum of description, the familiar properties of sandpaper say much about the larger aspects of poverty exhibited by rough, chapped hands. The figurative image of footsteps "exploding down an empty hall" draws the familiar image of the bursts of noise as someone walks down an empty hall.

Allusions

Allusions are special kinds of metaphors. They explain much about an object, person, or event by comparing it to some object, person, or event drawn from history, literature, contemporary politics, or pop culture. We use allusions every day, almost unconsciously. If a friend of yours always has his arm slipped around someone's waist, you might call him a Don Juan or a Casanova. You might describe your father-in-law's real or imagined tyranny by referring to him as a "little Hitler" or "Attila the Hun." Or you might put your "John Hancock" on a permission slip, automobile title, or life insurance policy. These familiar allusions are clichés, but their metaphoric base works by explaining one thing or person by relating it to another. Other allusions are more spontaneous, called up by the occasion. Watching people as they pass in front of your car at a red light, you might contrast the bobbing, two-hundred pound woman struggling to manage her packages with the gorgeous Lola Falana type sashaying behind her. After a tennis match, you might congratulate your opponent by telling her she plays like Chris Evert. Then, too, many other allusions are more studied and academic. We hear left-wing liberals refer to the political tenor of the seventies as "the New McCarthyism" while almost any new political scandal gets dubbed "a new Watergate."

Some cautions about similes, metaphors, and allusions

Similes, metaphors, and allusions are all interesting ways of making abstract statements concrete. Used in moderation, they vitalize your writing through their quick, vivid images. When you speak of a sandwich as being "paved" with peanut butter rather than spread with it, or refer to a cucumber as "nude" instead of "peeled," you are using language in a vigorous, metaphoric way. Figurative language clarifies; the image speaks clearly enough to lessen the need for other explanation.

Unless you are careful, though, figurative language can backfire. Stuffing sentences with metaphors and similes can bloat them. Excess can hurt just as much as absence. You must also beware of worn-out metaphors that become clichés, limply drawing comparisons for the nine hundredth time. Writing "your cheeks are like roses" or "your eyes are like the stars" will not send romantic shivers up your reader's spine. Such clichés are more apt to bring a grimace. Furthermore, you may puzzle or amuse your reader if you use exaggerated metaphors that confuse instead of convince. Do not, as one student did, describe a police officer blowing a whistle like this: "The policeman blew his bird-sounding mechanism." Don't say, "I used a neighbor's speaking box" when you mean "I used a neighbor's telephone." Too great a metaphoric urge can grow ridiculous.

Another problem for even the best writers is the mixed metaphor. It combines two metaphors that do not fit together. The statement, "Her gnarled hands were samurai swords flailing wildly," compares the hands at once to gnarled branches and to samurai swords. But the swords are not gnarled; they are clean, sharp weapons of destruction. The old and twisted image of the gnarled branch contradicts the smoothness and sharpness of the sword. The image doesn't clarify; it confuses.

An unfamiliar or obscure allusion also reduces the impact of the metaphor. If your sixty-nine-year-old uncle, Chester Hawkins from Queen Creek, Arizona, looks like Harry Truman, you might write a delightful sketch of your uncle by referring to his Harry Truman features. But if you were writing an essay about Harry Truman, you would not say that Harry Truman had Chester Hawkins features. No one outside your family and the small population of Queen Creek would know what you mean. If you write a paper about Frank Lloyd Wright and you also happen to be an ancient history buff, you still should not describe Wright as the Imhotep of modern architecture. You might be very pleased with your learned allusion, but few people would be aware that Imhotep was an important architect of the Old

Kingdom of Egypt. Your allusion would obstruct communication instead of furthering it.

Combined with strong nouns, verbs, and modifiers, metaphoric language lends strength to a writer's style, vitalizing and coloring it, offering options otherwise unavailable. A passage from a typical tongue-in-cheek Tom Wolfe essay, "The Frisbee Ion," illustrates how all of these devices can come together in a collage of images. Wolfe speculates on a doomsday prophecy that "due to the rape of the atmosphere by aerosol spray users, by 2000 a certain ion would no longer be coming our way from the sun." Then he fantasizes the horror to descend upon us:

> Suddenly I could see Lexington Avenue, near where I live in Manhattan. The presence of the storm troopers was the least of it. It was the look of ordinary citizens that was so horrible. Their bones were going. They were dissolving. Women who had once been clicking and clogging down the Avenue up on five-inch platform soles, with their pants seams smartly cleaving their declivities, were now mere denim & patent-leather blobs . . . oozing and inching and suppurating along the sidewalk like amoebas or ticks. . . . A cabdriver puts his arm out the window . . . and it just dribbles down the yellow door like hot Mazola. A blind news dealer tries to give change to a notions buyer for Bloomingdale's, and their fingers run together like fettucine over a stack of *New York Posts*. . . . It's horrible . . . it's obscene . . . it's the end—

The startling images with which Wolfe depicts a de-spined human race are what make this piece come alive. His mastery of specific language forges the images in visible form. Noun/modifier combinations such as "five-inch platform soles" (not shoes), "denim and patent-leather blobs," "blind news dealer/notions buyer" mix with similes such as "oozing and inching and suppurating along the sidewalk like amoebas or ticks," "dribbles down the yellow door like hot Mazola," and "fingers run together like fettucine over a stack of *New York Posts*." Central to all of these pictures are strong and unusual verbs and verb forms: "dissolving," "clicking," "clogging," "cleaving," "oozing," "inching," "suppurating," and "dribbles." In miniature, the Wolfe passage capsules the desired qualities of sharpness and clarity at which we aim.

Exercises

1. Listed below are several simple nouns. From each one, create a metaphor, simile, or allusion. You need not write complete sentences.

Example: *tea kettle*
a tea kettle whistling for
help from the burning fire

a. mirror
b. shoestring
c. finger
d. coat
e. bicycle
f. lilac
g. pencil
h. button
i. sandal
j. typewriter

2. Write three sentences of your own, the first using a simile, the second a metaphor, and the third an allusion.
3. Think of three stale metaphors and similes and try to revive them.

Example: *Her eyes are like the stars.*
Her eyes flashed like the sequins on her black lace dress.

4. Find the metaphors, similes, and allusions in the passage given below. Explain why they are effective or ineffective.

The night was dark. Lightning flashed in the distance. Charles Lindbergh personified, I hopped into the plane. "Why can't I do these things in the daytime?" I asked myself. I looked back at my passenger. He was a quiet, peaceful type. I pulled back on the yoke and took off.

Looking back at the quiet of the airport, I wanted desperately to reach my destination. The clouds closed in like madmen; the air wrestled the little plane. Never once did my companion complain. I kept staring back. What the hell was he doing back there? My hand was sweating; I pulled back on the throttle, knowing my speed unreasonable. Why do I do these things . . . money? The fear built up in me. I wanted to turn back. I felt his hand touch my back, and I turned with horrid anticipation. It wasn't his hand, just my shoulder strap which had fallen off after the plane hit an air pocket. Feeling uncomfortable, I looked down to see that I had wet my pants.

Pale lights shimmered in the distance. Soon the friendly chatter of the controller filled the cockpit. As my tires blackened the runway, I hurried my taxi and stopped dead on the ramp. I was out of my plane like a flicker of light from a candle. Two men walked over, opened the back door of the plane, and grabbed the handles on the coffin. I walked to the hangar, thanking God I would be alone on the next flight.

5. Bring to class a few lines of fiction or nonfiction in which you find some figurative language. Analyze the use of metaphor, simile, or allusion.

Denotation and Connotation

The denotations and connotations of words offer still another way for a writer to be concrete. To the writer who is trying to be exact, trying to draw upon each word for economy and concreteness, connotations and denotations are crucial. The denotation of a word is its literal meaning, its dictionary meaning. "Father," for example, is "a male parent." A connotation, on the other hand, "packs" a word; it suggests other meanings that are emotionally charged or meanings that have special significance to us based on our personal or general experiences. "Father," then, would connote a different figure for each of us: that warm and loving creature to whom we can turn when we feel battered by the world or the stern face of discipline behind "Mow the lawn." Connotations of words set off chain reactions of meanings. The color red denotatively means a primary color in the spectrum. Connotatively, however, red can suggest blood, urgency, emergency, danger, prostitution, anger, Communism, heat, sexual attractiveness, stop signals, and so on.

Connotations of words are important to a writer for the shade, the color, the force, or the meaning they add to language. One word or one phrase can generate a lot of meaning. The word "mother-in-law" suggests to many people such notions as loud, tyrannical, pushy, controlling, gossipy, meddling, ugly, money monger, and so on. *My Fair Lady*'s Henry Higgins sums up all of these emotional responses when he describes the mother of his potential wife like this:

> She'll have a large Wagnerian mother with a voice that shatters glass!

In reality, though, many mothers-in-law are sweet, kind, and generous women who do not fit that stereotype.

Sometimes a word will possess several distinct, even conflicting connotations. When some little boy clutches a skirted leg and mumbles shyly, "This is my mother," he is saying something quite different from the dude who mutters through clenched teeth, "I'm a mean mother." Think of the connotations of "freak." According to the *American Heritage Dictionary,* a freak is:

1. a thing or an occurrence that is very unusual or irregular.
2. an abnormally formed organism; especially a person or animal regarded as a curiosity or a monstrosity.

Once, the connotations as well as the denotations of "freak" were negative. Now all sorts of people describe themselves as "freaks" to indicate their deep and sincere involvement in something. A health-food addict may label himself an "Adele Davis freak"; someone else may describe herself as a "country-and-western freak."

At times not knowing or not heeding the connotations of words can get you in trouble. You should not say, "The woman waddled" if you mean "The woman strolled" or "The girl is skinny" if you mean "The girl is slender." *Waddled* and *strolled* and *skinny* and *slender* mean roughly the same thing, but *waddled* and *skinny* connote less complimentary concepts than *strolled* and *slender*. Sometimes a thesaurus—a book that lists synonyms—can be a source of this problem. The thesaurus lists words with similar denotations but often very different connotations. In the thesaurus, words such as *intemperate, self-indulgent, dissipated, debauched,* and *drunk* are approximate synonyms for *intoxicated.* But *intemperate* and *self-indulgent* have far more delicate connotations than *dissipated* or *debauched.* Depending on who is describing the state of inebriation, one might say "intemperate"; another might just say "drunk."

Connotations play an important role in shaping our daily speech and thought. Examples are almost endless. Think of the middle-aged man who was born "colored," turned into a "Negro" as a teenager, and was transformed into a "black" as an adult. Think of the connotations attached to such place names as Auschwitz or My Lai or Bay of Pigs and of our reactions to the people connected with them. Or consider why entertainers so often feel a compulsion to adopt stage names. What impelled Archibald A. Leach in the early 1930s to change his name to Cary Grant? Why did Arnold G. Dorsey in the 1960s decide to become Englebert Humperdink? And why are there no more rock groups called The Marvellettes or The Ponytails?

Exercises

1. Following are several sentences containing a choice of words. Explain how each word changes the meaning of the sentence.
   a. The sergeant (barked, shouted, gave) orders to his men.
   b. The local Democratic Committee (pleaded, begged, asked) for money.
   c. Alice Cooper (gyrated, walked, strutted) across the stage.
   d. The woman wore a (kaftan, robe, housedress) to the embassy ball.

e. Each evening he drank mulled wine from a (goblet, jelly glass, mug).

2. For each word in the following list, think of several synonyms with different connotations; use each in an appropriate setting in a sentence.

   Example: *fat*
   chubby, plump, roly-poly

   a. thin
   b. fancy
   c. elegant
   d. stingy
   e. fastidious

3. Make a list of five words or terms. Write down both their denotative and connotative meanings.

   Example: *middle class*
   denotation: The members of society occupying an intermediate social and economic position between the laboring classes and those who are in land or money.
   connotation: often a derogatory adjective to make a negative comment about someone's style, taste, etc. Also suggests, positively, solid values, family life, getting ahead.

Chapter Exercises

In the following exercises, use this list of attributes of language to help you make some judgments about the quality of the prose:

level of diction
use of colloquialism, jargon, slang, cliché
degree of abstraction or concreteness
degree of vagueness or specificity
strength of nouns, verbs, modifiers
use of simile, metaphor, allusion
denotation and connotation

1. Select a paragraph of nonfiction from a newspaper or magazine. Bring it to class and be prepared to consider its many aspects of language usage. Repeat the same exercise with a short piece of fiction.
2. Take a few sentences from a well-known fiction writer: Faulkner, Oates, Bellow, etc. Try to find some synonyms for most of the main words. If the original remains the most effective, tell why.

3. Look at the following pieces of writing. Be ready to discuss their language.
   a. This country is the best in the world. No place else in the world has people who have so much. Except for the small minority of troublemakers (who should, by the way, either shape up or ship out), the people of this country are good, hard-working citizens. They love their flag and would fight to the death for it. The Bicentennial proved this.

      Some people say this country is going to the dogs. But that isn't true. This country is as strong as ever. It makes me proud to be an American.
   b. In the miniature cubicle of an office, surrounded by staring frogs and mutilated worms, I made up my mind to do it. My hand moved in quick jerks toward the gray drawer. Grasping the cold, silver handle made chills go through my tight body. This was it! Magnified in my pounding ears, the squeaks of the drawer seemed to turn into cries for help. Now the steel mouth finally opened; my wet hand reached inside. Clammy fingers felt the smooth paper and pulled it from its resting place. The exam, the coveted biology exam, was in my hands. As the thought of a fat, red *A* flashed across my mind, the sweat on my face turned cold. The white sheet containing questions to which I did not know the answers slid back to its resting place and resumed its yearly nap. The drawer stopped its pleas for help and quietly rolled shut. I hated myself for having so damn many morals.
   c. Riding down the mountainside with blown-out glass packs booming backfires, our pickup headed for Blue-Bend Creek. Crossing an erector set bridge, we made a quick right and nearly pitched into the swollen creek. The heaving, bumping ride over, we made our way to the water's edge.

      The creek bottom was covered with mossy velvet boulders, the water chilly and swift. I had not brought my cutoffs, so I took off my shirt and waded in with my jeans. Joe and Bill were right behind me. Everyone was quickly shocked into wetness by the slippery rocks and the tugging current. We stood chest high in the middle of the creek.

      It was easy swimming with the current; Joe and I went about a hundred yards downstream in no time. We now veered to the edge where a young couple was fishing.

They saw us coming and left. I wish they had stayed.

"Kind of scary when you can't touch bottom, ain't it?" It sure was. I was pretty pooped from fighting the fast water in the pool and suddenly realized that I had over fifteen more yards to get to the branch Joe was standing on. I went under, pushed off the sandy bottom toward air, got a gulp and went under again. In a hoarse, frantic gurgle, I got out, "Joe, help me, man!" While I thrashed at that menacing creek, I clutched quickly for a saving shoulder and went blank. Someone upstream on a raft had seen me bobbing and beating at the water and came to help. I was a pale, gagging mass of thankfulness when I came to on that branch.

d. Not once in four days had the rain ceased to hammer down upon us from the gray sheet that had once been bright blue sky. The rice paddies that give this country its life had long since filled and overflowed. Only an occasional thatched hut and the jungle remained above the surface of the lake that the surrounding area had become. Beneath the surface of the water a quagmire of slimy, black mud pulled at our boots. Walking was difficult, tiring. Submerged VC handiwork, punji sticks—sharpened bamboo—mines, and booby traps made walking actually hazardous. Death comes suddenly in this water-soaked land; hopefully, we will not meet ours on this fifth day of rain.

e. Strings and strings of automobiles loiter impatiently while choking on one another's stale exhausts. Cars pant for water as red-faced owners mutter and grumble at their unworthy automobiles. Blaring radios screech the top forty records and the ear-piercing horns trumpet repeated calls for help. Summertime motorists skim frisbees from the roofs of their autos. The Bay Bridge silently moans with anguish as it pleads with traffic controllers to move the awesome weight from its back.

4. Write a short description of a place or person you know, some joy or pain you have had, something you see at this very moment, some experience you have had. Make the chief aim of this exercise to translate your thoughts into concrete images. Try to achieve sharp, specific details by concentrating on your use of language. Try to heighten the reader's perception of what you see or of what happened to you by presenting it in exciting, living, graphic words.
5. Try writing a paragraph of what you consider to be terrible

prose. Mix up the diction; abuse colloquialism, slang, jargon, regionalism, and clichés; make the piece as abstract as possible; fill it with vague and flabby or excessively flashy nouns, verbs, and modifiers. Fill it with as much inaccurate, imprecise, or purple prose as you can. Then label the errors you have consciously created. Discuss these with another student in the class.

Chapter Checklist

1. Make abstract and general concepts as concrete as context will allow.
2. Use strong, vivid language, but be careful not to become too flashy. Use concrete nouns, active verbs, and colorful modifiers, but use them appropriately.
3. Use metaphors, similes, and allusions to strengthen and clarify your writing. Do not let them become confusing or ridiculous or trite.
4. Take advantage of both the denotative and connotative meanings of words.

Generating Sentences

Just as you have been a master of words from childhood, you have also been a clever shaper of those words into sentences. You speak naturally in whole sentences that boldly state your meaning or in pieces of sentences that hint at it. Even grunts and stammers have a place. By changing tone, pausing, speeding up, slowing down, your voice lets you punctuate in many ways. You can say rather ordinary things:

> I'm hungry.
>
> Beat it!
>
> I'll finish the laundry after I watch the soccer game.

Or you can say more complicated things:

> John Donne's poetry exhibits a brilliant display of wit through a tight structure of thought and argument.

You can speak all of these sentences of varied length and shape without thinking about whether they are simple, compound, or complex. Our speech has an unlearned eloquence which lets us state our thoughts in groups of words naturally formed into a sentence.

But when we write, when we are dealing only with print and not with gestures and voice, sentences have to be more precise. Good sentences frequently do not just happen. Sometimes, despite all efforts, people who can speak very well put together clumsy bundles of written words that may sound like one of these:

> The first approach of fulfilling my dream of becoming an expert rock climber started with a thirty-foot tower in which we will eventually be cast off the side of it.
>
> The next day I woke up, as I tried to think it was a dream, however, it wouldn't leave my mind as fantasy, for it was a reality.

These sentences are hard to read. As listeners, we might be able to pick up some or most of the meaning—or we could ask questions if we could not. But readers cannot help stumbling as they read them. The writers no doubt knew what they wanted to say, but without the crutches of gesture, vocal inflection, pauses, or instant rephrasing, their words became a tangle. Because writing lacks these speech tools, written words must be more precise in meaning and in position.

Sentence Types

To use words well, you must consider the sound and meaning of each one individually. To use sentences well, you must consider the sound and meaning of several words as you bring them together. The words should be welded into a firm unit designed to do one thing—express your thought clearly and concretely. Thus, you could, in good confidence, make statements such as these:

> My date was elegantly dressed in faded Levis and a navy-blue silk shirt with French cuffs.
>
> The blazing yellow Avanti roared around the corner, coughing up gravel and shattering the stillness of the sultry afternoon.
>
> Sounds of cracking bones echoed through the cave; the monster sat stuffing himself like a fat Buddha before a feast.

While the earlier sentences made difficult reading, these flow smoothly and their meaning is clear. They vary in length, but each one links at least one subject and one verb together to express a thought:

date	was dressed
Avanti	roared
sounds	echoed
monster	sat

The other words are spare parts as far as the essence of the sentence goes. Adjectives, adverbs, nouns, pronouns, interjections, participles, gerunds, or infinitives expand and complete the central subject/verb thought. Each pair of subject and verb above makes an *independent,* or *main, clause,* which can express a thought by itself. Other subjects and verbs unable to stand by themselves are *dependent,* or *subordinate, clauses.* Clauses such as "When I grow up" or "before he took out the trash" must lean on the main clause for meaning since they cannot stand alone. Designing a sentence is choosing a strategy. Depending on what you are trying to say, you bring these independent and dependent parts together in different ways, thus forming the *four* traditional types of sentences: simple, compound, complex, and compound-complex:

A *simple sentence* contains one independent clause stating or emphasizing one thought:

independent clause

S V

The old woman sat nibbling on a potato chip.

A *compound sentence* contains two or more independent clauses connecting closely related ideas:

independent clause

S V

The old woman sat nibbling on a potato chip,

+

and

independent clause

S V

her aged dog lay sleeping on the ground beside her wheelchair.

A *complex sentence* contains one independent clause plus one or more dependent clauses. It shows how one main idea relates to one or more lesser ones:

dependent clause

S V

While the old woman sat nibbling on a potato chip,

+

independent clause

S V

her aged dog lay sleeping on the floor beside her wheelchair.

A *compound-complex* sentence has two or more independent clauses plus one or more dependent clauses. This combination adds variety to the possible relationships between independent and dependent ideas:

dependent clause

S V

While the old woman sat nibbling on a potato chip,

+

independent clause

S V

her aged dog lay sleeping on the floor beside her wheelchair,

+

and

independent clause

S V

her grandchildren built puzzles on a nearby table.

There is no single or right way to show the scene surrounding this old woman as she sits nibbling on a potato chip. Tone, meaning, and context all play a part in deciding just how elaborate or simple the sentence needs to be. Your purpose in writing a sentence is communication. Having four options to construct what you mean gives you considerable flexibility since each one lets you confront an idea from a different direction.

Exercises

1. Label each of the following sentences as simple, compound, complex, or compound-complex.
   a. My first car was a 1965 Austin Healey Sprite.
   b. The handsome young man leaning against the wall could not be that boy with the acne and greasy hair whom I had known in high school.
   c. He lay under the ground knowing that the others thought he was dead, but the wet night had brought life to his dry and withered body.
   d. To my six-year-old eyes, the wheezing, rickety 1940 school bus was a yellow monster devouring yet another of its victims—me.
   e. As I sat with paper and pencil trying to hammer out words from a rusty mind, I could hear noises of children clamoring for Sugar Crisps and corn flakes; I put the task aside and went to find the cereal bowls.
   f. The waves erupted, pouring and splashing over the sand and engulfing my feet and ankles.
   g. As a method of preserving vegetables from a summer garden, freezing far surpasses canning in speed and efficiency.
   h. When I thought of the clothes I did not buy and the concerts I did not attend because of the hundreds of dollars I had spent on tropical fish, I realized my fondness for

angelfish and swordtails had vanished; I bought a two-dollar fishbowl and a few thirty-cent goldfish and walked out of the pet store.

i. The rocking chair, though old, still offered its owners a restful seat.

j. Having stolen the stapler from her mother's desk, the little girl gleefully pressed staples into all the sofa cushions.

2. Make a compound sentence out of the following pairs of sentences.
   a. The cottage was buried by the avalanche.
      The young boy could not get out.
   b. She was all woman.
      I was intrigued.
3. Make a complex sentence out of the following pairs of sentences.
   a. Drug pushers should be prosecuted severely.
      Drug users might then be helped more completely.
   b. Hard rockers and acid queens have set the mold for contemporary music.
      Jackson Browne's music still shines above the rest.
4. Make a compound-complex sentence out of the following pairs of sentences.
   a. I arrived in the kitchen.
      I found my cat lying on his back in the sink.
      He was playing with the faucet.
   b. Nuclear fission has great possibilities as a source of power.
      It produces highly radioactive wastes that must be disposed of or stored because of their high toxicity.
      This problem hinders its widespread application.
5. Write one brief and one longer example of each of the types of sentences: simple, compound, complex, and compound-complex. If you can, use the same basic thought in each as in the example of the old woman eating the potato chip.

Coordination and Subordination

In designing the thoughts that come together as the various types of sentences, you automatically *coordinate* and *subordinate*. While the words sound ominous, these two processes are the underpinnings of all sentences except the simple sentence. *Coordination* forms compound relationships, separate but equal. *Subordination* establishes dependent relationships. More importantly, each increases your options for expressing your ideas with exactly the right emphasis.

Coordination

Coordination shows ideas to be equal in importance or emphasis. To coordinate two independent clauses is to form a compound sentence, giving them equal stature in the sentence. Coordination balances each section so that no one part of the sentence commands more weight or more attention:

> The sand reflected the sun like a fiery mirror, and the salty spray stung our burnt bodies.

Both sides are equal; both are complete.

The most common ways to coordinate independent clauses within a sentence are to use a comma and one of the coordinate conjunctions (and/but/or/for/nor/yet) or semicolons. The coordinate conjunctions form a bridge between two related ideas:

> Put on your raincoat, **and** be on your way to school.
> I love her, **but** she loves brontosauruses and stegosauruses more.

The semicolon works in much the same way. Since it is used without the conjunction, though, it suggests a stronger, more emphatic pause between the two ideas:

> He pledged to give his life in the service of his country**;** he died, not six weeks later, in the foxholes of Verdun.

Careless compounds. Coordinating ideas is a natural tendency, but it sometimes creates problems. Occasionally we weave a few independent clauses together with *and*s and end up with a very loosely knit sentence:

> I picked up the telephone receiver, and it was my brother on the other end, and he told me to meet our mother at the airport at 2:30.
> She sat drinking Diet Rite Cola, and he sat drinking Molson's Ale, and they were both very quiet, and neither of them liked the situation very much.

The casual running together of thoughts in these sentences reduces their impact. When coordinated ideas add little to each other, they should either be made individual sentences separated by periods, made dependent clauses, or made part of the main clause:

> When I picked up the telephone receiver, my brother told me to meet our mother at the airport at 2:30.
>
> While she sat drinking Diet Rite Cola, he sat drinking Molson's Ale. They were both very quiet and neither of them liked the situation very much.

Good judgment and an ear for rhythm and meaning lie behind good compound sentences. While most often a careless string of compounds sounds awkward, sometimes running compounds together gives you exactly the effect you want. This sentence, for instance, works quite well:

> I have tales to tell, and I have songs to sing . . . but I have to fix dinner first.

Thought and circumstance determine effect. As always, apply the rule cautiously so that use does not become abuse.

Exercise

Improve the simple-minded compounds in the following sentences by making them into separate sentences or complex sentences.

a. There is a beautiful and fairly inexpensive way to decorate your home, and that is with houseplants.
b. He had been challenged to a shoot-out and had two choices, and that was to fight or to run like a scared jackrabbit.
c. It was morning and Brian was right about the directions and he had not led us astray.
d. In Andrew Wyeth's painting *Christina's World* a crippled girl is in a faded pink dress and her back is to us and she is dragging herself up a deserted hillside toward a farmhouse.

Parallel structure. A fine point of coordination is parallel structure. When we deal with thoughts of equal weight—whether as clauses, phrases, or single words—we tend to put them in the same form. Parallel structure lends logic to a series of items or thoughts in a sentence. In normal conversation, for instance, you would probably not say:

> I like fishing and to hunt.

Even if you did not know that *fishing* is a gerund and *to hunt* is an infinitive, the sentence would not sound natural to you. Instead, you would more likely say

> I like **fishing** and **hunting.** *(two gerunds)*
> or
> I like **to fish** and **to hunt.** *(two infinitives)*

In other words, the two objects are parallel in form. Parallel structure also gives punch to the following statement:

> Just out of spite, she picked the ugliest dress she could find. It had taffeta **ruffles,** a pink chiffon **bow,** and a **neckline** that touched her chin. *(three nouns)*

You can appreciate parallelism in many ways even though you may not have been aware of it as a grammatical structure. Think of the many verses in the Bible which ring familiar because of their natural parallelism:

> When I was a child,
> I spake as a child,
> I understood as a child,
> I thought as a child.
> 1 Corinthians

Professional writers use parallelism regularly. Alvin Toffler, for instance, uses parallel verbs in *Future Shock* to describe a wife's influence on the modular man/executive husband:

> Her friendships will rub off on him, color his judgments about the people under him, jeopardize his job.

You, too, as a writer, naturally form many parallel units. You create compound sentences with ease and often balance parts without knowing why you do so. When you put words in a series, you almost automatically give them parallel form:

> The little boy bought some fruit from the street vendor: an **apple,** a **banana,** a **tangerine,** and a **peach.** *(four nouns)*

The elephants, clad in hula skirts, **swayed, pranced,** and **bowed** as their trainer led them through the rings. *(three parallel, simple past verbs)*

Nonparallel verbs would interrupt the smoothness of that second sentence:

The elephants, clad in hula skirts, swayed, were prancing, and bowed, as their trainer led them through the rings.

Balancing a series of phrases or clauses can be a little more difficult. Sometimes beginning each parallel clause with the same word helps show the connection:

The press and the Congress disliked the Carter aides **because** of their youthful arrogance, **because** of their seeming disdain for traditional political networks and **because** of their hard-nosed and almost blind defense of President Carter's policies.

You can achieve the same effect without word repetition by repeating a grammatical form:

The woman stumbled up the stairs **crying** softly to herself and **hoping** to see her son one last time. *(two participles)*

Parallel structures also appear with the coordinating phrases either/or, not only/but also, both/and, first/second/third:

I will either **pass** this freshman composition course or **grow** arthritic trying. *(parallel verbs)*

Either I will pass this freshman composition course, **or I will grow** arthritic trying. *(parallel clauses)*

Exercise

Correct any nonparallel elements in the following sentences.

a. My cat's everyday activities include climbing walls and curtains, running frantically around the house, and playing with my toes.
b. It looked more like a country road: dirt, pebbles, no sidewalks, and just wide enough for one car.
c. A station wagon plunged into the back of my pick-up and shooting us across the median strip, like a bullet being shot from a gun.

d. The fire fighters must learn every hook-up, every hydrant, every street, and where all the alarm boxes are in their district.
e. In 1933, Germany witnessed the rise of Adolf Hitler and vibrated from the sound of tens of thousands of goose-stepping soldiers marching before enthusiastically cheering crowds.

Subordination

A "subordinate" is someone or something that is beneath, secondary to, or not as important as someone or something else. Children are usually the subordinates of their parents; privates are the subordinates of sergeants; laborers are the subordinates of their supervisors. Just as coordination makes things equal, subordination shows that one idea is not as important as another. In telling about your new watch, you would generally not say:

> I bought a new wristwatch. I bought it at Macy's.
> It is a Seiko.

Instead you would automatically *subordinate* the less important details to make one direct statement:

> I bought a new Seiko wristwatch at Macy's.

Subordination of dependent clauses, phrases, and words de-emphasizes one idea in order to emphasize another. Simultaneously, you can cut down on wasted words by reducing a thought to its smallest, most concrete level. The sentence about the wristwatch is now one simple sentence, with only one subject and one verb emphasized instead of three. The lesser details are subordinated and no longer have equal status with the more important one.

Here is a more elaborate example of the same process. Suppose on Saturday night you went to an Earth, Wind, and Fire concert with your brother because neither of you had a date. In describing the experience, you probably would not say:

> Earth, Wind, and Fire were giving a concert. It was on Saturday night. I didn't have a date for Saturday night. My brother didn't have a date for Saturday night either. So we went to the concert together.

You would neither speak nor write in such choppy sentences. But if we could not subordinate our ideas, our writing would be like that. All ideas would be equal and thus lack focus. In spite of a natural urge toward subordination, we occasionally write these stunted sentences which limp along like people in tight shoes. The cure lies in subordinating, in examining the relationships between our thoughts, and giving the less important ideas a less important position. Two possible revisions might be:

> Earth, Wind, and Fire gave a concert on Saturday night. Since neither my brother nor I had a date, we went to the concert together.
>
> Since neither my brother nor I had a date for Saturday night, we went to the Earth, Wind, and Fire concert together.

Each version emphasizes the same thought in the main clause, and each subordinates by putting lesser details in secondary places. What goes in the main clause depends on the writer, who puts the most important to him or her in the emphatic position in the sentence.

Methods of subordination. While you can sometimes subordinate one idea to another simply by omitting a few words, several actual devices help subordinate thoughts within a sentence. You might use a dependent clause, a subordinate phrase, or even a single word to distill several thoughts into one. The choice depends as much on rhythm as it does on meaning.

Dependent clauses. The three types of *dependent clauses* are adverb, adjective, and noun. As clauses, all three have subjects and verbs, yet none can stand alone as a sentence.

Adverb clauses answer the questions *when? where? why? how?* and *on what condition?* They are introduced by subordinating conjunctions:

> *when:* while, before, when, after, whenever, since, as, until
> *where:* where, wherever
> *why:* because, since, as, so that
> *how:* as if, as though
> *on what condition:* if, unless, though, although

The following two sentences are separate entities, each expressing a single idea:

> He rowed the canoe to the inlet. He saw a light.

To achieve the drama of terse description, two separate sentences might do nicely, yet their relationship to each other is somewhat vague. Choosing a suitable subordinating conjunction, you could make an adverb clause from one of the sentences to show the importance of one idea over the other:

> **As he rowed the canoe to the inlet,** he saw a light.
> or
> **Because he saw a light,** he rowed the canoe to the inlet.

To accent seeing the light, the rowing part can be subordinated by an adverb clause indicating "when." To highlight the rowing, seeing the light can become an adverb clause answering "why."

The adverb dependent clause gives you the same options with the next two sentences. On some occasions you may want to say:

> She put the new television set in the corner. It fit best there.

At other times subordination would condense the two ideas into one:

> She put the new television set where it fit best—in the corner.

This adverb clause showing "where" could not stand alone to state a complete thought of its own, but it helps synthesize and reduce the words needed to make the statement about locating the new television set.

Adjective clauses modify nouns or pronouns. They are introduced by relative pronouns: *who, whom, which, whose, that.* If you take the following two sentences and subordinate one of them with an adjective clause, you can pull both ideas into one strong complex sentence, sharpening the image of the weary runner:

> The marathon racer had grown tired of running. He slumped to the ground.
> The marathon racer**, who had grown tired of running,** slumped to the ground.

On some occasions, two sentences work best; more frequently, however, one subordinated sentence tightens and streamlines the thought. An adjective clause subordinates the next group of sentences also:

> The train came puffing up the track. It was an old steam train. It was a mirage from the past.
> The old steam train **that came puffing up the track** was a mirage from the past.

Noun clauses act as nouns and can thus function as subjects, direct and indirect objects, subject complements, or objects of prepositions. They are introduced by *who, whom, whose, which, that, what, whatever, whoever,* or *whichever.*

In the following sentence, the noun clause functions as the direct object:

> I know **who will be the next President of the United States.**

The entire clause acts as the direct object, exactly as any single noun would do in the same circumstance. In another sentence the noun clause can just as easily be the subject:

> **Who will be the next President of the United States** has been much discussed lately.

Subordinate phrases. Phrases do not have a subject and verb pairing; they are groups of words that modify nouns, pronouns, or verbs. Since they are not clauses, dependent or independent, subordinate phrases do not change the classification of a sentence; if added to a simple sentence, the sentence remains simple. Several types of phrases help subordinate ideas: a participial phrase, an adjective with a prepositional phrase, or an appositive.

A *participial phrase* uses the past or present participle of a verb to form a modifier:

> **Lifting her head,** she saw blood on her hands.

Again, the important thought forms the independent clause and the less important idea fits into a subordinating device. In this next example, subordinating with a participial phrase pulls several sentences into one:

> The Parthenon dominated the city. It looked like a ghostly image. It was in Athens. It was at night.

This awkward expression quickly becomes:

> The Parthenon**, looming like a ghostly image in the Athenian night,** dominated the city.

An *adjective with a prepositional phrase* also subordinates a lesser idea:

> **Angry at his mother,** the little boy stomped out of the kitchen.

The following three sentences give equal emphasis to the ideas in them:

> The zoo keeper finally had to resign. He was afraid of the lions. He was afraid of the gorillas also.

But by using an adjective and a prepositional phrase you can not only condense them into one sentence, you can subordinate the two lesser ideas to the main thought:

> **Afraid of the lions and the gorillas,** the zoo keeper finally had to resign.

The *appositive* is the third type of subordinating phrase. An appositive is a noun that tells more about another noun. It can form a very useful type of subordinating phrase, especially for streamlining description.

> Dr. Skinner was a wizened old philosophy professor. She shook her knobby finger and pronounced reality to be nonexistent.

Identifying Dr. Skinner quickly through an appositive phrase tightens the sentence:

> Dr. Skinner, **a wizened old philosophy professor,** shook her knobby finger and pronounced reality to be nonexistent.

The same effect occurs in the next example:

> Al Capone made Chicago infamous. He was finally jailed for income-tax evasion.

The appositive phrase shortens the description to:

> Al Capone, **the man who made Chicago infamous,** was finally jailed for income-tax evasion.

Subordinate words. Sometimes single words can be used to give lesser ideas less important emphasis. Appositives, adverbs, adjectives, and participials can all be used to capture a larger thought. You can easily subordinate one of the following ideas:

> The mail carrier was rushing to deliver the mail. He fell over the bicycle in the yard.

A participial conveys one of the ideas in a single word, so the main idea carries the emphasis, as it should:

> **Rushing,** the mail carrier fell over the bicycle in the yard.

You could write:

> Tchaikovsky's *Nutcracker Suite* is a lovely ballet for children. It is also liked by adults.

But you could use the one important word from the second sentence to subordinate in this way:

> Tchaikovsky's *Nutcracker Suite* is a lovely ballet for children **and adults.**

In each of the above cases, the dependent clause, phrase, or word helped the writer subordinate a less important detail to a more important one, as do the participial phrases in the pairs below:

> The man ran down the street after his windblown hat. He was a whirl of gyrating arms and legs.
> **Running down the street after his windblown hat,** the man was a whirl of gyrating arms and legs.

> The girl was drained of all energy after the Little League Championship game. She sipped Kool-Aid and munched on peanut-butter cookies.
> The girl, **drained of all energy after the Little League Championship game,** sipped Kool-Aid and munched on peanut-butter cookies.

One final example takes a paragraph of simple sentences and shows the radical improvement subordination can bring. The sentences on the right use various subordinating devices to tighten the writing and make it much more interesting.

I glance at my sons' room. It reminds me of something. The boys are beginning to grow up.	One glance at my sons' room reminds me that the boys are beginning to grow up.
Baseball gloves replace cars. Bats replace airplanes. They are on top of the toy box.	Baseball gloves and bats replace cars and airplanes on top of the toy box.

Hardy Boys books fill the book shelves. Superman comics do too. The book shelves once held Mickey Mouse comics. They also held *The Little Engine That Could.*	*Hardy Boys* books and Superman comics fill the book shelves that once held Mickey Mouse comics and *The Little Engine That Could.*
Records are in the record cabinet. They are by the Jackson Five.	Records by the Jackson Five are in the record cabinet.
Posters cover the walls. They are space posters.	Space posters cover the walls.
The boys are growing up. But there is still a sign. The sign proclaims "I Hate Girls." That sign is evidence. A few years of childhood remain.	The boys are growing up, but a sign proclaiming "I Hate Girls" is evidence that a few years of childhood remain.

Most of the subordinating in the paragraph above is achieved by eliminating excess words and relying upon one or two concrete words to communicate the relevant detail. However, dependent clauses and phrases also help sharpen and refine the revision. Skillful subordination makes writing concise, graceful, and easy to read; it is a sign of mature, focused, emphatic, and unified writing.

Exercise

Each of the items given below consists of several simple sentences. Combine them, through subordination, into one or two well-developed sentences. Alter the wording as necessary but include all of the details. Indicate what devices you use to achieve the subordination. Many combinations are possible.

a. For breakfast we had fried eggs.
We had country-fried ham.
The aroma filled the room.
I sat opposite my father.
I couldn't see his face.
I could only see a few stray hairs on the top of his head.
He was so involved in the newspaper.

b. I was sitting in the cafeteria between classes.
I was wolfing down a greasy, undersized cheeseburger.
I also had a paper plate full of French fries.

They were greasy also.
The jukebox blared Barry Manilow's "Mandy."

c. I am sitting at the dining-room table.
I am trying to do my math homework.
I have to do twenty-five differential equations for tomorrow.
My class is at 8:00 A.M.
The television is droning.
I can hear the dishwasher swishing.
The electric heater is humming.
It is hard to concentrate.

d. I watched a television special on Friday night.
It was a nostalgia festival.
It was aimed at all of us old-timers over twenty-five.
They showed reruns of "Mickey Mouse Club."
Then they showed an episode from "The Lone Ranger."
After that they showed a Hopalong Cassidy feature.
It was a fascinating return of childhood heroes.

e. A group of Cub Scouts are all wearing Washington Redskin jackets.
They are cheering madly.
They are holding hot dogs in one hand.
The hot dogs are laden with mustard.
In their other hand they are holding Cokes.
But the Cokes are watered down.

f. There were three hook-and-ladder trucks.
These trucks were followed by two pumpers.
That is another type of equipment which carries water in huge tanks.
They are built right onto the trucks.

g. I was getting out of the Navy.
I had to suffer through a time-consuming physical.
It was very thorough.
It was to see if I had been damaged by the Navy I guess.

Problems with subordination. Subordination is one of the most useful tools of writing, but it can cause problems if you are not careful. Good subordination requires that the subordinated parts be close to the words they modify. However, sometimes the subordination is unclear, or even amusing, because modifiers are *misplaced.* They are too far away from the words they are supposed to modify and thus modify the wrong word. At other times, the modifier has nothing at all to modify, making it a *dangling modifier.* While similar in effect, these two errors have somewhat different causes.

Misplaced modifier. If a modifier is misplaced, it is probably too far away from the word it modifies. Since it may seem to modify something else, the result may be either confusing or funny:

> Jingling the money in his pockets and whistling merrily, the neighbors chuckled as the little newsboy strutted down the street.

The neighbors seem to be doing the jingling and the whistling, as well as the chuckling, instead of the newsboy. The parts need rearranging to let the modifiers describe the right words.

> The neighbors chuckled as the little ***newsboy,*** **jingling** the money in his pockets and **whistling** merrily, strutted down the street.

This next example shows a double misplaced participle:

> The used-car dealer pushed the gabby mechanic into the garage having eased the eager teenager into his office wanting to buy his first car.

There is some doubt as to who is doing the easing and the wanting. If you rearrange the sentence, you can solve the problem:

> Having **pushed** the gabby mechanic back into the garage, the used-car ***dealer*** eased into his office the eager ***teenager*** **wanting** to buy his first car.

A misplaced prepositional phrase causes the same problem in the following sentence:

> After a month in the shop, I had the car for a couple of weeks when the drive train failed so back it went.

"I" was not in the shop; the "car" was. But the directional signals given in the sentence are confusing. Correcting the problem means adjusting the modifiers:

> **After the *car* was in the shop for a month,** I had it for a couple of weeks when the drive train failed; so back it went.

Dangling modifier. The dangling modifier does indeed just dangle; it has nothing to modify.

> Dancing through the streets in their hula skirts, the police officer was bedecked with roses.

Should the sentence be written this way, the police officer seems to be dancing in the streets because *police officer* is the noun closest to the modifying phrase. But police officers rarely wear hula skirts, so it is probable that someone else must be inserted to do the dancing.

> **Dancing** through the streets in their hula skirts, the Hawaiian ***girls*** in the parade bedecked the police officer with roses.

Another common variation of this problem occurs in a sentence such as this one:

> Reading the essay, it obviously has a point.

No one is present in the sentence to do the reading and the essay obviously does not read itself.

Students often argue about the injunctions against misplaced or dangling modifiers saying, "But you know what I really mean." However, the point to remember is that you the writer do not want your reader to either pause momentarily to decipher your meaning or laugh at the occasional humor in a modifier error, especially when your ideas are serious ones. Each pause—whether from confusion or humor—distracts the reader from the ideas. Good style does not call attention to itself; it enlivens your ideas. Bad style calls attention to itself and therefore calls attention away from your ideas.

All in all, the confusion created by the dangling or the misplaced modifier is simple to correct. You need only rearrange or add some words so that grammatically the right person is doing the right thing. Then, make sure the punctuation is correct. A few slight changes can help unscramble many distortions of meaning which occur from misplaced or dangling modifiers.

Exercise

Correct any dangling or misplaced modifiers you find in the following sentences.

a. Working at a drug store, good discounts on everything from aspirin to Whitman chocolates could be had.

b. Opening weary eyes, the gleaming sun streamed through the curtains, temporarily blinding me.

c. I looked with awe at those mountains, having only skied the now seemingly short and less treacherous hills around home.

d. Losing my wallet at the beach, hunger struck as we scoured the boardwalk.
e. Going up and down each long row of cars in the parking lot, the night grew steadily colder.

Nonsentences

Sometimes, amid the flurry of coordination and subordination, groups of words come together in ways that differ from normal sentences. Sometimes a sentence becomes fragmented; its thought is not complete.

> When I grew a beard.
> Trying to resist the Boston cream pie.

Sometimes a sentence runs on, jumbling several thoughts together without proper connections.

> It was Thursday I had a doctor's appointment.
> Marketing is the occupation to be in, my brother-in-law made $100,000 last year.

While nonsentences can, on occasion, be used with some effect, usually these forms produce confusion for the reader and red marks on the page for the student writer.

Fragments

A fragment is informal, much like colloquialism or slang. It is often a piece of a thought written as it might be spoken, in a casual, informal way. Either the subject or the verb of the main clause—and sometimes both—is left out. You might buy a pair of theater tickets by saying, in a fragment, "Two, please," when you really mean:

> I would like two tickets, please.

Or you might order your lunch by saying, "Two Big Macs and a Coke," instead of:

> I would like to order two Big Macs and a Coke.

Or you might mutter, "Uh huh," "No dice," or "Ciao." Any of these spoken fragments would be quite enough to pass on the kernel of an implied sentence.

Fragments work as spoken speech, and, under certain circumstances, some of them will work as written speech as well. When "Charlie's Angels" first appeared on television, a student began an essay about the program with two fragments used quite effectively:

> **Kate Jackson, Jaclyn Smith, Farrah Fawcett-Majors.** Do you know who these three ladies are? I didn't. **At least not until recently.** I became familiar with these names when the new season started on ABC this fall.

The piece is casual; the fragments create a stylistic effect to help pace the beginning briskly. Fragments can also be useful as an abrupt or succinct comment or afterthought:

> Did I learn a lesson after nearly drowning in twenty-eight feet of water trying to do a high dive? **Not I!** I went right back up and perched myself on the board again.
>
> Who's the best team in the American League? **The New York Yankees.** They have played in, and won, more World Series than any other team.
>
> The twentieth of August was a disaster for my mother. While she tried hard to forget it, for her that infamous day began a whole new set of numbers. **Forty!**

Although experienced writers sometimes use fragments with good effect, many student writers use fragments unintentionally. Instead of a single, well-placed fragment, students often create careless and random fragments because they are not quite sure of the structure of a sentence. A fragment will not work if it just teases the reader with a thought it never completes:

> When I first met my boyfriend.
>
> Tall, lanky Harvard boys wearing letter sweaters, waving pennants, and guzzling beer.
>
> Raced through the shower stall.

Each of these fragments is really just a part of a sentence, incomplete as it stands. The first is a dependent clause; the second has no verb, only participial phrases; the third has no subject. Even if you put one of these fragments into a written context, it would still not become a sentence:

> When I first met my boyfriend. He was wearing red platform shoes and I thought he was a first-class creep.

Simply inserting a fragment into a paragraph does not change the basic error. There are a number of ways to fix fragments. Some may need a subject. Others may need a verb. Still others, such as the adverb clause above, need to be attached to an independent clause:

> When I first met my boyfriend**, he** was wearing red platform shoes and I thought he was a first-class creep.

The other two fragments would need something added to make them sentences. The Harvard boys offer a subject, but the fragment has no verb. Changing at least one of the participles into a verb changes the incomplete statement into a real sentence:

> Tall, lanky Harvard boys **wear** letter sweaters as they **wave** pennants and **guzzle** beer.

The third fragment contains a suitable verb but it has no subject to do the racing. If you add some little boys, the sentence would be complete:

> The seven little **boys,** anxious to get into the swimming pool, raced through the shower stall.

Without such changes, these fragments are just confusing, unfinished comments.

Fragments dotting every page indicate carelessness or ignorance rather than flair. If you regularly write fragments, you may need help with basic sentence structure. You have to know how to write good sentences before you can use occasional, skillful fragments. Fragments often pose problems for your reader. They can also make a negative comment on your skill as a writer.

Run-on sentences and comma splices

Run-on sentences are the opposite of fragments. Instead of cutting a thought short or chopping it into pieces, the run-on sentence fuses two or more independent clauses without punctuation to keep them apart. The several ideas in each sentence run one into the next with no indication of where one stops and the other starts.

> Sinclair Lewis wrote *Main Street* he also wrote *Babbitt.*
>
> The glass elevator shuttled to the top of the building it clicked to a stop.
>
> The man drove up to the campus he saw his daughter standing among

a group of students dressed in Levis angrily he barked at the girl to get into the car then he drove frantically away.

The writer, secure in the knowledge of what he or she means, leaves the reader wondering just where one thought stops and another starts. If you were speaking to someone about the Lewis novels or the glass elevator or the angry father, you would automatically punctuate each thought with sufficient pause to plot out your meaning for your listener. But written this way, the run-on sentence literally does run things together. Other tacked-on, overlapping thoughts violate the main thought. Someone reading one of these sentences aloud, especially the third one, would be panting for breath long before the end of it.

Sometimes writers try to correct a run-on sentence by inserting a comma between the clauses. Instead of improving the problem, however, they create another one, the *comma splice.* A comma splice is the comma erroneously used to connect two or more independent clauses within one sentence:

Sinclair Lewis wrote *Main Street,* he also wrote *Babbitt.*

The glass elevator shuttled to the top of the building, it clicked to a stop.

The man drove up to the campus, he saw his daughter standing among a group of students dressed in Levis, angrily he barked at the girl to get into the car, then he drove frantically away.

The comma suggests a short pause, but it is not strong enough to join independent clauses. Splicing these clauses together with a weak comma is a little like an electrician splicing two wires together with a piece of Scotch tape. It just will not hold them together in a functional way. Occasionally, in an informal context, a comma might work to connect two very brief independent clauses. For stylistic quickness you might use something like this:

I cried, Mother cried. We both felt miserable.

This technique will not always work. Only when the clauses are brief enough to make the speed of the comma connection an asset to the prose should you think about using it. Usually a writing situation does not offer sufficient reason to use a comma splice since the comma will not be strong enough to hold two independent clauses tightly together.

The cure for both the run-on sentence and the comma splice is simple. The same tactics remedy both.

Run-on: Margaret reached for the flask she dropped it.
Comma splice: Margaret reached for the flask, she dropped it.

1. Separate the thoughts with a period and begin a new sentence, giving proper emphasis to each idea:
Margaret reached for the **flask. She** dropped it.

2. Separate the thoughts with a comma and a conjunction such as "but" or "and." In this way, you connect the thoughts but still keep some distance between them:
Margaret reached for the **flask, but** she dropped it.

3. Separate the thoughts with a semicolon to give a slightly stronger pause to thoughts closely related:
Margaret reached for the **flask; she** dropped it.

4. Subordinate one thought to another if you intend your reader to see one as actually less important:
When Margaret reached for the flask, she dropped it.

Depending on your intent, then, both the run-on sentence and the comma splice can be solved by any of the four methods: the period, the comma with coordinating conjunction, the semicolon, or the dependent clause. The sentences cited earlier as either run-on or comma-splice errors can all be corrected by simple adjustment of punctuation or dependency.

Sinclair Lewis wrote *Main Street*, **and** he also wrote *Babbitt. (comma + conjunction)*

The glass elevator shuttled to the top of the building**;** it clicked to a stop. *(semicolon)*

When the man drove up to the campus, he saw his daughter standing among a group of students dressed in **Levis. Angrily** he barked at the girl to get into the **car. Then** he drove frantically away. *(subordinate clause/period/new sentences)*

Run-on sentences are not always long sentences, and long sentences are not always run-on sentences. A run-on sentence can be as brief as

I slipped he fell.

A solid, correct sentence can be as long as fifty words or more. Proper punctuation keeps the parts tightly controlled.

My father, who is Archie Bunker personified in his splashy bowling shirt and baggy pants, cannot bear to have my boyfriend Max around the house; Max, who rides a snorting, metallic-red Harley Davidson, wears a leather jacket and blue jeans and ties his hair in a ponytail.

This one sentence might, on another occasion and for another purpose, be several shorter sentences. Long sentences can be useful occasionally, although too many of them can be just as troublesome as too many short sentences. But when you need one, punctuation serves the vital function of guiding your readers. It leads them through a maze of words showing them where to stop and where to turn. If your punctuation is careless, if your writing contains run-on sentences, comma splices, or fragments, your meaning will not be clear and your readers will be distracted and confused.

Exercises

1. If any of the following are fragments or run-on sentences, correct them.
   a. Tall pine trees shading families of picnickers like an awning on a scorching summer day.
   b. The once glistening silver fish was now muddy, with torn, bloody scales hanging from its abused body, it wearily slithered from the cold, dry beach toward the water, it wanted to die in the familiarity and comfort of home.
   c. The antique hurricane lamp was hand painted with blue and pink flowers it lay in the darkness of the cedar storage chest its fragile globe nestled in a fragment of an old quilt.
   d. Coffee spills, doughnuts crumble, books tumble, feet rush to class.
   e. Standing deserted, the old house, a rickety shell in the wilderness of trees.
   f. I wanted a small station wagon. One that I could park easily and drive around town without having too much trouble with its size.
   g. The wind was blowing, making a howling sound, no moon was anywhere to be seen.
   h. Suddenly, a series of lights flashed, the last was a green which triggered these "funny looking cars," they streaked endlessly down the runway leaving a flaming light traveling in their path.
2. Write a grammatically correct sentence of thirty to fifty words.

Creating the Concrete Sentence

Once you have some understanding of the internal structure of a good sentence, you might step back a moment and ponder the way mechanics and language work together. To control the mechanics well but to use language poorly is to waste energy. The shape and sound of your sentences determine your style. Some writers have a spare style, relying on little else besides nouns and verbs; others are more ornate. Either way, grammatical skills should be a quiet servant of clarity and grace.

To help balance language and mechanics, try, for a moment, to look at sentences from a basic perspective. If you start with a simple image—a simple subject and a simple verb—you can build a sentence, consciously adding subordinate clauses, participial phrases, adjectives, or adverbs to complete it. In this way you gain practice in manipulating sentence structure while flexing your own stylistic muscles.

A sentence can be as simple as this one:

The trees stood.
subject verb

This sentence is complete and appropriate to certain writing situations. Often, however, in refining an image, you want to be more specific. Therefore, you might consciously expand first the subject and then the verb. "The trees stood" becomes:

S V
The old trees stood against the shoreline.

The sentence is now more than a skeleton. A few modifiers expand the subject; a prepositional phrase extends the verb. And this version can grow further—still taut, firm, without flab but with more than bone. Carefully added modifiers can change the trees at random. They might become

gray trees
willow trees
trees bearded with cypress moss
strong, sprawling oak trees
full, green pine trees sighing softly
under the weight of heavy snow

While the bare noun "trees" can frequently be more powerful

than the tree of several words, at times you want a fuller image. To get it, you can subordinate or coordinate; but do so without becoming flashy or overdressed. For example, you may choose to introduce the trees with a prepositional phrase:

S
> Against the sprawling, rocky shoreline, the gaunt trees . . .

Once the subject is fixed, you would need to do the same with the verb. You might decide that the trees did any of the following:

> stood towering over craggy pines
> stood awaiting a crash of thunder
> stood swishing in the wind

Any of these additions could complete this particular sentence, the picture of these particular trees. But to settle on one for the sake of this example, you might use:

V
> . . . stood like an army of skeletons rattling in the cold north wind.

With subject and verb linked together, the whole sentence presents a strong image of gaunt trees shaking as the wind howls through their bare branches.

Each of the versions of the sentence from the original to the slightly expanded to the final rendition is a useful sentence in its own right:

> The trees stood.
> The old trees stood against the shoreline.
> Against the sprawling, rocky shoreline, the gaunt trees
> stood like an army of skeletons rattling in the cold north wind.

Often, such a conscious buildup of individual sentences helps create a strong and varied paragraph unit. But, as usual, exercise caution. While you do not ordinarily build every sentence you write from the ground up, a conscious rewriting of some of your sentences in the revision phase of your work will often improve the total effect. However, you must know when to start adding, when to stop adding, and when to add nothing. A cavalry officer shouting out his command "Charge!" needs no other words to communicate his message. So, too, the great power of the sentence "Jesus wept" would be destroyed if it were pulled and prodded to say more. If you knead and yank at

"The trees stood" too vigorously, you might well end up with something like this:

> Out of the forest, back against the sprawling, massive, tortuously rocky shoreline, etched clearly against the starry night, the gaunt, miserably bent, wizened trees stood eerily and stonily, bending and clattering like an army of skeletons rattling in the cold wind blowing in from the north.

There is a strange style in that sentence, but there is certainly no grace. The sentence lacks the tautness and firmness of good prose. The forty-six words, while correctly punctuated, are loosely fastened and clatter noisily through the sentence. The writing is forced, rigged. A reader would be hard pressed to make some visual sense out of that sentence, let alone find a meaning. It ends up being a bit silly and not at all believable or understandable.

Exercises

1. To each combination of subject and verb in the following list, add some concrete words to consciously build strong sentences.
   a. vampire clutched
   b. eagle swooped
   c. dress swishes
   d. Archie Manning performed
   e. lion prowled
   f. Boston Strangler attacked
   g. violin screeched
   h. butterfly fluttered
   i. boy laughed
   j. typewriter clattered
2. Comment on the effectiveness, or lack of it, in the following sentences. What would you recommend be left out of any sentence to improve it? Do you feel it necessary to alter some words?
   a. Life-giving blood, only hours before steadily flowing through the vibrant veins of the courageous young American, curdled on the muddy, body-strewn field of a land far from home.
   b. Scavenged from the car-trunk toolbox, the grimy, discarded cord, now the answer to our envisioned adventure, strangled the water-jugged, food-packed sled that careened its way to the snowy mountain paradise.
   c. Reflecting on pain of the past, the man, obsessed by seething rage and bitter anger, choked the glass in his blood-drained fingers until it shattered from his violent grip.

d. By the eerie, shadowy firelight of his ancient bat-infested cavern, the gray, expanding jelly-mass amoeba-like blob of a monster gorged his squealing, scampering, defenseless prey, absorbing them as though he were a gigantic sponge.

e. Vibrating violently from the earth tremor, the cracked glass bottle, sparkling, glistening antique that it was, splintered to the Italian marble floor, from its resting place on the ancient, hand-carved, curio cabinet shelf.

3. Take a piece of writing that you have done, either for this class or for another. Go through your finished paper sentence by sentence and identify the simple subject and simple verb of the independent clause(s) of each. Then read the skeletal subject/verb for each. If your paper is a series of sentences that begin "It is interesting . . ." and "There are . . ." or "This means . . . ," then your sentences are far from concrete. The subjects and verbs should be strong enough to convey most of the meaning behind your thought. Revise the sentences to correct this deficiency.

Sentence Variety

To combine sentences comfortably into a paragraph, you must consider the shape of each one. Some sentences should be long; some should be short. Some will be complex; some will be simple. A few writers turn out smoothly connected sentences naturally and freely, but many others need to take stock of the sentences within the paragraphs they have written. Sometimes paragraphs are crippled by strings of compound sentences. Sometimes they are hampered by rows of simple sentences which echo the Dick and Jane primers of our first-grade past. But if you let your thoughts sway and bend from compound to simple to complex, your writing will seem choreographed. Good control of coordination and subordination ensure a highly readable pattern.

Sentence variety should not become a complicated or forced exercise in changing just for the sake of change. Good sentence variety adds a subtle rhythm to a piece of writing, allowing a reader to move freely from beginning to end without being conscious of sentence structure.

Simple [A lonely object in the night, the silver bus flashed over the highway.] Among its load of passengers, I drowsed at ease, high on the freedom and excite-] *Simple*

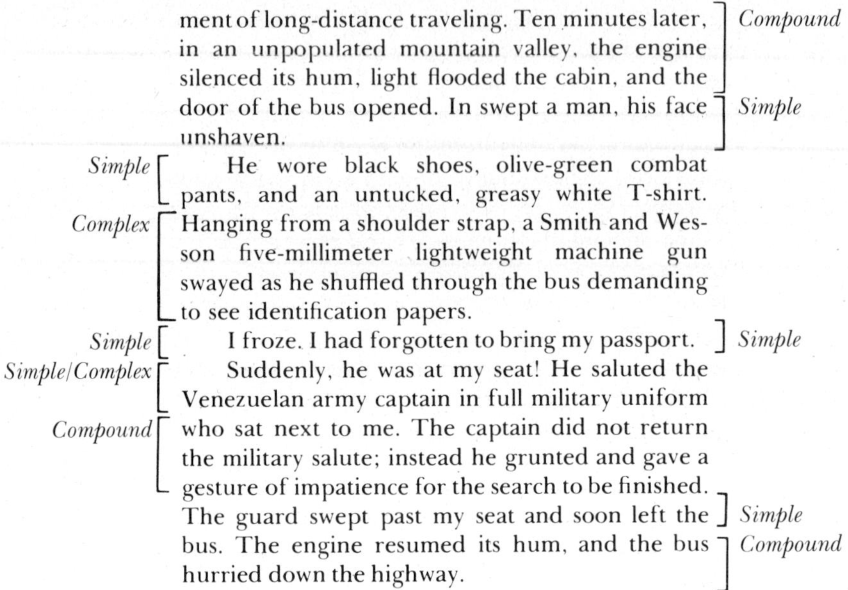

ment of long-distance traveling. Ten minutes later, in an unpopulated mountain valley, the engine silenced its hum, light flooded the cabin, and the door of the bus opened. In swept a man, his face unshaven.

He wore black shoes, olive-green combat pants, and an untucked, greasy white T-shirt. Hanging from a shoulder strap, a Smith and Wesson five-millimeter lightweight machine gun swayed as he shuffled through the bus demanding to see identification papers.

I froze. I had forgotten to bring my passport.

Suddenly, he was at my seat! He saluted the Venezuelan army captain in full military uniform who sat next to me. The captain did not return the military salute; instead he grunted and gave a gesture of impatience for the search to be finished. The guard swept past my seat and soon left the bus. The engine resumed its hum, and the bus hurried down the highway.

Gaining good sentence variety is not just a matter of snipping and rearranging clauses and punctuation marks. The rhythm of the piece, created largely by the structure of the sentences, will vary according to what you are trying to say. Many long, complicated, compound-complex sentences belong to more formal writing. Passages of simple sentences fit the informal language of personal experiences, letters, diaries, and such. Mixing several kinds of sentences will usually achieve a balance among the thoughts, subordinating the lesser ones to the major ones and giving appropriate energy to your ideas.

Exercises

1. Examine the following passage and be prepared to describe and discuss the effectiveness of its variety of sentence structure. Label each of the sentences simple, compound, complex, or compound-complex. Try to make some statement about either the negative or positive impact such structure has upon the thought. Be prepared also to comment on the language of the sentences. Is the paragraph overwritten? Can the language be toned down?
   My first attempt at conjuring up a gourmet dish resulted in a disaster which is still a source of embarrassment. I made a chocolate *bombe* . . . that bombed! I loomed over the stove,

staring at the muddy brown serpent twitching and writhing in the pan. Suddenly, in defiance of the heat, the snakelike ooze leapt up; it poured its thick length over the edge of its prison. Slithering to the cliff of the stove, it hesitated in a tight coil before slinking down the front. I watched in mute horror. At the crevice of the oven door, the creature wagged its molten head, surveying the trail ahead. Then, as if controlled by a mystic impulse, it moved again, only to disintegrate on the ledge into pools of liquid that dripped down slowly, forming a quiet pool of chocolate on the floor.

2. Examine some paragraphs of your own for both variety and length of sentences. Rewrite the pieces as necessary to establish good sentence variety, or if you feel the variety is already effective, explain why.

Chapter Exercises

1. Examine any structural problems in the following paragraphs. Use the list given below to help you in your analysis.
   - coordination problems
   - faulty parallelism
   - subordination problems
   - dangling modifiers
   - misplaced modifiers
   - faulty sentence structure (fragments, run-on sentences, or comma splices)
   - inadequate sentence variety

   Revise the sentences so that the paragraphs read smoothly and correctly. Make any adjustments in language which you feel might improve the original.

   a. Getting six kids off to school at my mother's house. It is a mass confusion. Mother is screaming for Chip to cut off the television set. She wants him to come up from the basement. He has to brush his teeth. Michelle is doing the latest dance. That is the hustle. Jamie is doing it with her. They are dancing in the middle of the kitchen floor. While dancing, last night's dinner is being warmed by them for breakfast. We had spaghetti. Maria is weeping because she doesn't like the dress that mother had pressed for her to wear. Mother pressed the dress last night. Rita is chasing Molly. Molly has sneaked into Rita's purse. She swiped Rita's last stick of gum. Believe it or not! They make it out of the house on time. To catch the bus.

b. The few remaining students left in the college cafeteria. It is 5:30 P.M. They look like survivors of the Great Battle of Lunch. It went on earlier. A janitor trudges from table to table. He is weary. He lugs his trash can behind him. He sighs at the Grand Funk Railroad record moaning and whines out of the two loudspeakers. The music is deafeningly loud. He also shakes his head. A wilting "Ski Quebec" poster is reaching for the floor. It once proudly clung to the brick wall. It is losing its grip. A half-eaten apple rests on a bed of ashes and cigarettes in a foil ashtray. Its overhanging skin curls around the browning, emaciated insides. Two cigarette butts protrude from a plastic dish of cemented pudding on another table. They look like antennae. Scattered chairs back off from the plastic tables. The tables are covered with grease and salty. A French fry is dying in its own ketchup blood. It looks like a worm. The chairs were originally in a circle around each table. The vending machines are ominously silent and empty. They stare out at the cafeteria which is deserted. Their PLEASE MAKE ANOTHER SELECTION lights are the only clue to their earlier activity.

c. A year ago last night. We drove home from a party loaded with alcohol. Driving home, the car went out of control, ended up on someone's lawn. I veered to the right to escape further damage, and I floored it, and we went across to yet another lawn. Hitting the sewer grating between the two properties. Blowing out three of my tires. While my three tires were losing air, my front end was bulldozing a wooden fence, as also they were a two hundred dollar tree. I was trying to flee the scene on three flat tires. I was boxed in by startled neighbors. They were in their cars. By that time, the police had arrived, and it was over. In the final analysis, I was slapped with eight points, a one-hundred dollar fine, and given a ferocious headache the next morning.

2. Write a short paragraph in which you concentrate on sentence structure. Mix concrete language with carefully expanded sentences that have good variety, good subordination, and good parallelism.

Chapter Checklist

1. A sentence should be a natural expression of your thought. The words you use to express it and the structure you give it

depend on the tone, the meaning, the context, and the audience. You must choose what works best.

2. Consider coordination as a way to express thoughts of equal importance. Keep words or thoughts in a series parallel.
3. Subordinate to keep your thoughts balanced in importance. Avoid giving lesser details undue importance.
4. Watch out for dangling or misplaced modifiers.
5. Be careful to check for fragments, run-on sentences, and comma splices. Avoid these errors except when you have a justifiable stylistic effect in mind.
6. Strike a balance between the mechanics of a good sentence and the concrete elements of good writing.
7. Unless you are striving for a certain effect, vary the types of sentences you use in a paragraph.

Organizing Paragraphs

A paragraph cements several sentences into a block of information. While it is often a small part of a still larger whole, the paragraph is also a finished unit in itself. It can be a description of a piece of scrimshaw, a complaint against the trash collector, a critical comment on a book. A paragraph is any one of a thousand subjects neatly discussed, analyzed, explained, or described on a small scale in one cluster of sentences.

If you listen carefully to two people talking—in a restaurant, on a beach blanket, around a fireplace—you hear a kind of natural paragraphing. The give and take of their conversation creates this grouping of thoughts. They pass from subject to subject—the grouchy waiter at the Pizza Hut, the beautiful roses growing in a nearby garden, a new tapestry on someone's apartment wall—as whim or pause or suggestion permits or demands. Sometimes these comments are delivered in careful, polished English. Sometimes they are mumbled in fragments linked by "um" and "like" and "ya know"; sometimes they are interrupted by an occasional "My nose itches" or "Go ahead; the light turned green." Whatever the style, the conversational flow often forms natural units of thoughts, discussing one subject and then moving on to the next.

It is more difficult to capture units of thought on paper. You can not write down your ideas just as you are thinking them, letting one flow after another. There is no room for an itchy nose in the middle of a paragraph about salamanders or IBM computers. Written thoughts must be tauter, firmer, more compact than spoken ones. A paragraph must be more than a few lines divided by random indentations. Paragraphing is a practical way of showing where one thought ends and another begins.

Focusing a Paragraph

Walking out of a classroom after taking a difficult exam, you might say to your friend, "Man, that was the hardest test I've ever taken in my life." And you would go on to describe how difficult it was. Sitting in the pub later, you might say, "This summer, I'm going to get a really great job in Alaska." Then, you would excitedly discuss becoming a lumberjack or a pipefitter or a paramedic with an Eskimo tribe.

A reaction, a feeling, an event, a circumstance—any of these can generate an attitude and a comment. Without saying "Now I am going to talk about ——," we just talk. Many times during a day or week we will say something like, "Guess what I did today?" and then tell about jogging an incredible eight miles or eating a monumental banana split. Or we will say, "That game yesterday was fantastic" and enthusiastically comment on the 37 to 7 score, the three quarterback sacks, and the ninety-two–yard run. If you wrote down these thoughts, you would have the semblance of a paragraph. Each has a focus—fantastic game, monumental banana split, incredible eight miles, great job, hardest test—and each presumably has related development to explain it.

The assurance of conversational ease often abandons us, however, when we start to write our own paragraphs. We wonder where to start and what to write about. While finding a subject should not be a problem, it often seems to be. Sometimes your teacher will supply a topic; sometimes your boss will hand out a specific assignment. Sometimes a miscalculated telephone bill or an unfinished roof repair job will prompt you to pick up a pencil and pad. At other times you may just have to look around the room or poke in a magazine to find an idea. While some subjects, such as government inefficiency or human cloning, may be too big for a paragraph, you can actually write a paragraph about almost anything, as long as you set some limits to restrict its development of thoughts.

Topic sentence

Once the subject is set, determining what to say about it is the next task. While you may not realize it, you form an opinion about most subjects even before you write about them. If your topic is to be Labrador retrievers, your opinion may already range from impossible dogs to the very best of family pets. Before you write about paying state income taxes, you may already feel that such taxes are either criminal, tolerable, necessary, or just plain highway robbery. Antique furniture may be dust-collecting junk or valuable treasure; Mexican fast food might vary from tasty to awful to bland or delicious. You can use any of these attitudes to direct a paragraph by casting them into a focused topic sentence. You could say:

> Labrador retrievers are impossible dogs.
> Mexican fast food tastes awful.

Words such as "impossible" and "awful" are only vague references, but they catch the essence of a writer's attitude. Then, in the interests of making your writing as concrete as possible, you should try to expand on the general attitude to make those sentences as specifically suggestive as possible. For example, the "impossible dog" could become:

> Although she is a beautiful animal, **my Labrador retriever would never win a blue ribbon for good behavior.**

With such a revision, you could suggest the "impossible dog" character without having to be quite so blunt or unimaginative as to stop at "impossible dog." The "awful" Mexican fast food statement might mature into something like this:

> **The enchiladas and tamales at Pedro's Taco Palace could burn blisters into the tongue of a non-native diner.**

Making both the food and the impact a little more specific transforms the original statement into a sprightly opinion.

The topic sentence, then, expresses a writer's attitude about a subject. This attitude is a generalization based upon certain specifics which the writer has observed. If your Labrador retriever leaps on visitors, drags bones through the house, and occasionally forgets she is housebroken, you conclude from these specifics that the Labrador retriever—or at least yours—is an impossible dog. If you happen to be someone who does not enjoy gulping huge glasses of water and wiping tearing eyes while you are eating, you might decide that for you Mexican food is awful. The topic sentence tells the reader what the paragraph is to be about. The rest of the paragraph fills in the specifics.

To focus a paragraph, then, the topic sentence should reflect a writer's attitude or point of view toward a subject. It should not be a statement of fact. Once you have made a statement of fact, there is not much left to say:

> My uncle is fifty-five years old.
>
> The Takoma Park Elementary School was built in 1892.
>
> His name was Reginald P. Downing.

"Fifty-five years old," "built in 1892," and "Reginald P. Downing" are not generalizations; they can neither be extended nor developed. A topic sentence for each of these subjects should be a statement that indicates where the paragraph is going, what kinds of details will follow:

> **My fifty-five-year-old uncle,** who claims to have dined with Rockefeller and played golf with Dwight Eisenhower, **is the world's best liar.**
>
> The grand, Victorian structure that was the old Takoma Park Elementary School had to be torn down, they said . . . and **they had their reasons.**
>
> His name was Reginald P. Downing; **he was a skid-row derelict with a flair as aristocratic as his name.**

In contrast to the original statements, the controlling focus in each of these sentences is a generalization – an opinion, an attitude, or an interpretation: the best liar, tearing down an impressive old building, a derelict with style. The rest of the sentences in these paragraphs would develop the specifics: examples of the uncle's fanciful escapades, questionable reasons for tearing down a community landmark, a description of the befuddled airs of an old wino.

Depending on your overall design, once you are satisfied with a focus, you can put a topic sentence almost anywhere in the paragraph. Ordinarily, the topic sentence begins a paragraph, announcing or summarizing a main thought to be developed by the following sentences. For instance, you could begin a paragraph with a topic sentence such as this one:

> **Not even rainy weather could spoil our Acapulco vacation.**

The rest of the paragraph would then show the fun despite the rain: surfing in the Pacific Ocean during rain showers; regal dinners at posh hotels while thunderstorms raged; a rainy day spent winning $300 in a casino.

On other occasions, the topic sentence ends the paragraph. Having the details build up to the focus can create a step-by-step progression; establish a special mood, such as an air of suspense; or provide a strong wrap-up statement to pull together previous information. In a paragraph discussing a new book about the John Kennedy assassination, for example, you might analyze the book's thesis of conspiracy and then conclude the paragraph with a topic sentence such as this one:

> Overall, **this new book on the Kennedy assassination sheds new and valuable light on the double-bullet theory.**

Under certain circumstances, a topic sentence fits into places other than beginnings and ends. You can slip a topic sentence somewhere into the middle of a paragraph, offering a few sentences of background or detail before focusing the thought. If you were writing a paragraph about Sacco and Vanzetti, you could easily put the topic sentence in the middle. A few sentences establishing their identity, their crime, and their fate would be a logical beginning before focusing the paragraph with a simple transitional topic sentence such as this one:

> **Sacco and Vanzetti did not deserve their fate.**

The rest of the paragraph would offer reasons for making a claim for the pair's innocence.

There is also a further refinement of topic sentence placement—to imply the controlling thought rather than to state it outright. In this way a paragraph could suggest, for example, the horror of a freeway collision or the agony of the defeated weight lifter or swimmer without ever actually pronouncing horror or agony. This tactic is not for the inexperienced or the lazy writer since it demands some skill in making a strong enough implication to convince a reader of the paragraph's unity.

Exercises

1. Which of the following sentences might serve as the focusing topic sentence for a paragraph?
   a. Smoking a cigarette and strolling down the avenue, I felt super.

b. The view from the patio is breathtaking.
c. I live at 1732 Pine View Avenue.
d. Hester Prynne is a character in the *Scarlet Letter.*
e. Having a baby by natural childbirth can be frightening as well as rewarding.
f. I am having a difficult time writing a paragraph.
g. Growing houseplants is easy if you know how.
h. The ancient box was made of beaten gold.
i. The increasingly popular sport of skiing is one of the most exhilarating as well as one of the safest pastimes one can have.
j. Seventeen Goya paintings are in the Prado.

2. Write a workable topic sentence for one item from each of the following subject lists.
   a. something new which you have recently bought: a refrigerator, a camera, knapsack, a pair of Levis.
   b. a person you know (friend or foe): mother, father, bowling partner, school crossing guard.
   c. an event you have participated in: swimming meet, Easter egg hunt, soccer game.
   d. a lamentable situation you have experienced: losing your car keys, contracting measles two days before a high-school prom, buying a "lemon" instead of a used car.
   e. a happy situation you have experienced: catching the biggest fish, buying a new pair of water skis, getting the highest grade on a test.

Framing a Paragraph

Every night we would climb into her soft, inviting lap, which somehow was always able to hold the three of us. I would undo her braided white hair and brush it to its full length beneath her still small waist. Then, she would reach into her apron pocket and pull out her pipe. An Irish country doctor had prescribed it as an antidote to her grief at the loss of her husband. She would then cock her head and begin those stories we loved so well. Her voice was clear, but the brogue was unmistakably Celtic. When her eyes twinkled and she flashed her toothless grin—she wore teeth only for company—then we knew the story would be comical. But when she pulled out her worn black beads, we knew that our story time was over and that she had more important people to talk to. **I will cherish the times we spent with my grandmother long after she is only a memory.**

This is a finished paragraph. It has a topic sentence. It has ample development. It is a concrete, varied discussion of a specific experience. But the paragraph did not just happen. As brief as it is, it is the product of a labored writing process: picking a topic, focusing it, sketching out a plan for it, and then writing it. Your process will be similar. Once you are satisfied with topic and focus, you are ready to lay out a framework to transfer the thought into a functioning paragraph like the one above.

Unity

A good paragraph often starts as a collection of random jottings, but it can not remain that way. In finished form, a paragraph must have *unity*. In other words, the paragraph must be a tightly knit unit of sentences all aimed at developing the topic sentence focus. If you start describing your experience of buying a new Volvo and end up talking about dating the charming dealer instead, you have a problem with unity. If you try to analyze no-fault automobile insurance and spend three sentences out of twelve railing against the uninsured driver, you have a problem with unity. When a paragraph has unity, all of its parts contribute to the whole. All of the sentences in the paragraph about the grandmother contribute to the description of the warm memory of the story hour. Each sentence builds upon the topic sentence focus. When a paragraph lacks unity, some of its sentences talk about other things. The grandmother paragraph does not have room for an aside about the St. Louis suburb in which the children might live or a reference to the ship which brought the grandmother to America. These details may belong in other discussions of the grandmother, but they do not belong in this one. To put them here would violate the unity.

The best way to guarantee unity in a paragraph is to sketch a simple working outline for it before you start to write. You could jot down the focus as a few words or even as a complete topic sentence. Then, you could make a quick list of some of the points which you feel will support it. These are called *major supports*. If you are describing a white-water canoe trip, write down some details which made it exciting: rocks, rapids, falling overboard, for example; if you are comparing two airlines, make a list of some of the differences you want to cite: reliability, equipment, staff, size, service. The subject itself will usually guide you. You might then wish to add some *minor supports*, smaller points which expand the major ones: a specific description of one especially violent section of rapids, the type of aircraft an airline has.

Everything on the list should relate to the one topic sentence focus without digressing into other subjects. Such a skeletal pattern looks like this:

Topic Sentence Focus
  Major Support
    Minor Support
    Minor Support
  Major Support
  Major Support
    Minor Support
    Minor Support
    Minor Support

This sketch is not meant to be a true outline; it is more of a guide. You can use a formal outline structure if you wish, but realistically, you need a flexible writing plan which captures the essence of your thought without the intrusion of worrying about Roman numerals and capital letters. This list should be flexible enough to let you move things around if you have to. You should also be able to test a paragraph's unity just by glancing at the supporting elements. You may see the ones that do not belong there more clearly this way than when they are fully developed sentences.

To illustrate how such a sketch can take you from idea to paragraph, here is the plan and the product of a student who wrote about a nostalgic visit to the historic seaport town of Annapolis, Maryland. Her general impression of her trip was that in many ways it was like returning to the past. So she used that thought as a controlling focus and formed it into a topic sentence:

A visit to the docks of Annapolis is, in many ways, like returning to the past.

Then, she made a list of some of the details that gave her that impression:

Oystermen
Crabbers
Fishmonger
Vegetable cart
Minister's wife selling baked goods

To this list she added a few smaller details as minor supports and ended up with this pre-writing plan:

Focus: **Visiting Annapolis is like returning to the past.**

Major Supports / ***Minor Supports***

- Oystermen
  - Skipjacks
  - Antique designs
- Crabbers
  - Weathered faces
  - Instruct the young
- Fishmonger
  - Sing-song voice
  - Contrast to frozen food
- Vegetable cart
  - Horse-drawn
  - Roams square
- Minister's wife selling baked goods
  - Lucky customer

This rough sketch lists supports that are all related to the topic sentence focus: returning to the past. The oystermen, the crabbers, the fishmongers, the vegetable cart, and the minister's wife selling baked goods all seem to belong to an older time. Discussing the tourists who visit the Naval Academy or the expensive yachts that moor at the dock would not fit the focus. Each point in the list can withstand the unity test. Each point can go from rough outline to actual paragraph with ease as a complete and concrete sentence.

Major Supports		***Minor Supports***
	A visit to the docks of Annapolis is, in many	
Oystermen	**ways, like returning to the past.** Oystermen, remi-	
	niscent of days past deftly steer their skipjacks into	*skipjacks*
	the harbor waters. Their boats' graceful lines boast	
	the handiwork of a long-forgotten shipbuilder's	*antique designs*
	dedication and masterful touch. Weathered old	*weathered faces*
Crabbers	men of the sea lower their crab nets and lines,	
	giving pointers on this time-honored craft to	
Fishmonger	eager young hands. The sing-song of the fish-	*instruct the young*
	monger's voice is almost an anachronism in this	
	day of flash-frozen seafood. A horse-drawn	*contrast to frozen*
Vegetable cart	vegetable cart roams the nearby square with	*food/horse-drawn*
	hooves and wheels echoing musically on the	*roams square*
Minister's wife	cobblestones. One local retired minister's wife	
	often sells home-baked goods. Anyone lucky	*lucky customer*

> enough to purchase her delicious delicacies will savor the delights of spicy apple pie still warm from the oven. One can easily visualize the "good old days" and experience them, in a sense, just by visiting this old town and strolling around its harbor area.

Thus the idea moves from plan to paragraph. Although this planning process may seem wooden, it is an excellent way to organize your thoughts to avoid stumbling and stammering when writing them. In this way you can test your idea. With a good focus and with several strong major and minor supports, your paragraph should be unified.

Exercises

1. Choose one of the topic sentences that you created for exercise two on page 89. Develop a rough sketch for it which you can use to write a paragraph. Check the list of supports for unity.
2. Write the paragraph which you outlined in exercise one. Be careful to carry each support from a few words to an actual sentence.
3. Select a textbook you think you can not understand. Outline several paragraphs from a chapter you find especially difficult by creating a simple focus/support sketch. Now analyze the paragraphs. Could the author have subdivided the support statements to clarify the subject further? Does the topic sentence really tell you what the paragraph is about? Can you write a clearer topic sentence?
4. Identify the topic sentence in the following paragraphs as well as the major supports and any minor supports. Suggest any revisions that you might make to improve either focus or development.

   a. The small, foreign car was dwarfed by the huge, long tractor trailers on the highway. Its boxlike shape, rounded on the corners, made it seem like a child's toy found on the kitchen floor. The car's dark British royal blue paint shone like a mirror reflecting the broken white lines etched into the pavement. Its long strips of shiny chrome highlighted the dark blue background, giving the car a dashing appearance as it roared down the highway. The tightly stretched, black convertible top accented the shining trim smartly, as if the car were on its way to a fashion show. Wire rims, like those found on a bicycle, held the mighty radial tires on the axle with a huge, chrome wing nut securing them tightly.

b. An amateur astronomer can determine whether a light in the sky is a galaxy, planet, or star by the brightness and steadiness of the light emitted. A galaxy is the hardest of the three to recognize. It usually consists of a tight clump of barely visible stars. Sometimes you have to look slightly to one side to study a galaxy. A planet, being brighter than a galaxy, is easier to distinguish. Some planets are brighter than others, but they all have the property of giving off steady light. The brightest planet, Venus, which is seen at dawn, can be as bright as the moon. Planets are known to shine, stars to twinkle. All stars give off light erratically, but their individual brightness does not vary. Some stars are brighter than others, due to their proximity to the earth. Antares, a star outside our galaxy, is 290 times larger than our sun. It seems no larger than the rest of the stars in the night sky.

c. Standing distant from the main routes of the touring buses, Launch Pad #5 survived another day of neglect. Once reflecting Florida sunshine, the tall silver structure now stands encased in discolored gray paint. Droppings from neighboring birds seem to flow down the long vertical columns of rust. Long rubber hoses, once encasing vital electrical wiring, now swing loose, wrapping and unwrapping around the long horizontal supports. Rabbit pellets seem to smother the collapsing concrete floor. The whole structure leans, twists, and moans from the constant stress. It accepts this and goes into another night without recognition.

Coherence

Once you are satisfied that all the parts of the paragraph form a unified whole, you can push further toward creating a polished paragraph by testing their coherence, how well they stick together. Coherence is the logical transition between the parts inside the paragraph. This connection springs both from content (the parts you choose and the way you arrange them) and from the use of various mechanical devices. Coherence is necessary. Unity without coherence results in a second-class paragraph.

Coherence through subordination and coordination. One of the easiest ways to form a coherent link between sentences within a paragraph is through coordination and subordination. All sentences are, of course, subordinate to the topic sentence. Subordination shows how some thoughts are secondary to others while coordination shows how thoughts are equal. The balancing of ideas in a varied, rhythmic pattern provides a smooth flow from sentence to sentence within a paragraph. Without careful subordination and coordination, the paragraph sometimes dwindles to a list of simple sentences or a series of compounds bumping one into the next. These few sentences illustrate the jagged effect of that unrelieved sentence pattern:

> Amtrak is a huge train system. It is languishing. It is large. Perhaps it is as large as some of the great systems in the history of rail passenger service. The company is floundering.

Varied coordination and subordination would help that passage read more smoothly:

> Amtrak is a huge **but languishing** train system. It is large, perhaps as large as some of the great systems in the history of rail passenger service. **But despite its scope,** the company is floundering.

Coherence through tense and pronoun agreement. Another way to gain coherence is to keep verb tenses and pronoun number consistent within the paragraph. Blatant shifts in time or person startle your reader. If you begin a discussion in the present tense, do not jump to the past tense in the next sentence. These two sentences show the confusion caused by shifting tenses:

> Cold and alone, he turned on the gas stove. He dies in his sleep.

The shift in tense within the description immediately confuses the time intended. You want all the parts to cohere, to make sense, as they pass from one to the next. Mixed pronouns create the same problem. Unless you are careful, you may find yourself back and forth between singular and plural or between first, second, and third person pronouns. A reader can get into quite a muddle about just who is doing something if you begin with "I," slip next to "you," and switch over to "he" or "she." Notice how such a shift occurs in this example:

> Legally, as doctors and nurses, we must do what we can to extend life. Life must be extended even if you prolong suffering.

Sometimes both problems occur in the same passage:

> Upon entering the rickety beach house, you had to play hopscotch to avoid falling through the rotting floorboards. Going to the old-fashioned kitchen sink is a delight since you could get a taste-tempting treat of all the salted, rusty water one could drink. After a refreshing dip in the ocean, you can drag your sand-covered body to the mildewed shower stall.

Try to be consistent. If you want to tell a story in past tense, stick with past tense. If you want to discuss a situation with third person, use third person regularly; don't shift back and forth to second.

Coherence through transitional words and phrases. A common way to link parts of a whole is to use transitional markers to help one sentence glide into another. Words such as "in addition," "however," "moreover," "although," "first/second/third" pull related thoughts more tightly together and show their relationship more clearly. Two versions of the passage below show the value of transitional devices in forming a tighter relationship between sentences:

> In the mid-1970s, the Minnesota Vikings were a very well-built team because of the draft and some big trades. In 1973, the Vikings acquired Fran Tarkenton from the New York Giants, and they picked up Chuck Foreman through the college draft. The Vikings were probably the most evenly balanced team in professional football at that time.

This series of largely simple sentences is too stiffly arranged. With a little subordination and some transition, it will read more smoothly:

> In the mid-1970s, the Minnesota Vikings were a very well-built team because of the draft and some big trades. **For example,** they picked up players like Chuck Foreman through the college draft. **But perhaps more importantly,** they pulled off some coups, like the Tarkenton trade in 1973. **Undoubtedly,** the Vikings were the most evenly balanced team in professional football in the mid-1970s.

Coherence through repetition of key words. Repeating words important to the sense of a paragraph's message also helps coherence Such repetition emphasizes a word, weaving it through several sentences to tie them together internally. Sometimes, however, repetition becomes boring and monotonous. Do not allow the repeated words to dominate so as to become irritants. Such is the problem in this passage in which a student discussed a collection of old trains he had sold. Midway through the paragraph he wrote:

> I had a freight set, slightly more common than the passenger set but still worth about $250 for the whole set. The freight set consisted of five freight cars. A Hudson steam locomotive completed the set.

Such repetition adds nothing to the sense of the paragraph; rather than pulling thoughts together more effectively, the repeating of "freight" and "set" seem clumsily echoed. A simple revision would be:

> I had a **freight set,** slightly more common than the passenger **train** but still worth about $250. It had five **freight** cars and a Hudson steam locomotive.

Coherence through parallel structure. Parallel structure, discussed in Chapter 3, can also serve as a transitional device. Whole sentences sometimes reflect parallel structure to endow a paragraph with a rhythmic transition from one thought to another or minor support to major support. For example:

> We all sat quietly enjoying the evening. **Ian was writing** a book. **I was reading** one. And **Jerry was working** on the income tax.

Repeating the subject/verb pattern in the three explanatory sentences arranges an internal transition which is subtle but definite.

Exercises

1. To practice using devices that help gain coherence, work through the following. Use any subject or topic you wish.
   a. Write a series of a few simple sentences, and then rewrite those same sentences subordinating and coordinating appropriate ideas. Which set is more effective?
   b. Write a few sentences in which you shift pronouns and tenses. Then, revise the sentences so that pronouns and tenses are correct and consistent.
   c. Write a few sentences using transitional words effectively. Remove the transitions and comment on the change.
   d. Write a few sentences showing inappropriate repetition of words. Then, revise to show how those same thoughts might

be presented through effective repetition, possibly coupled with other devices.

e. Write a few sentences using parallel structure between sentences to gain coherence.

2. Examine the coherence of the paragraph you wrote in the previous set of exercises. Be prepared to identify the devices you used to achieve internal coherence. Revise the paragraph if lack of coherence seems to be a problem, commenting on the transitions you insert.

Order

There are times when content will arrange the coherence for you. Often that is due to the natural order of the paragraph. The most common order, already illustrated in several paragraphs, is *deductive order,* topic sentence first followed by supports. The reverse of that is *inductive order,* supports first and topic sentence last. There are also some special ways to order your ideas.

When you tell a story or narrate an event you usually order your details by moving from beginning to middle to end. You use *chronological order,* arranging the parts as they occur in time.

> Opening the bedroom door ever so slightly, I could hear the rattle of the chain on the door below. My first instinct was to call the police . . . but predictably there was no answer. I took out the revolver and stood there shivering, terrified. The clack of the chain continued. Then, it stopped.

The several parts of this event must be ordered in exactly the way they happened. If you take out the revolver before the chain ever rattles to suggest someone is trying to break in, something goes awry in the ordering of the parts. When retelling an incident, you want all the parts to follow as they occurred, rather than confuse the reader by going back later to include points you may have left out.

Spatial order lets you arrange details by moving from place to place. In describing a room, for instance, or a car or a hotel or a space module, you should go from one side to the other, from inside to outside, from front to back. Moving back and forth at random can create visual chaos for the reader. Careful spatial order streamlines a description as you reconstruct an object, a place, a person, etc., as faithfully as possible.

> The cherrywood fireplace stood against the solid oak paneling. Resting on the mantle was a brass tea caddy and a beautiful ivory clock. On each wall hung watercolor prints, two of which had been done years ago by the mistress of the house. The rug on the floor picked up the hues of the wood surrounding it.

This description moves from the fireplace against the wall to the clock on the mantle to the watercolors on the wall. Finally, it touches the floor and the rug that picks up the tones of the wood around it. To have gone from wall to floor to mantle to watercolors to fireplace to rug would have created an order problem.

For matters other than description or narration, there is also the *logical order* necessary to develop a subject. Occasionally, you can comment on a new play or a proposal or a case chronologically or spatially; more often, however, you try to define the most logical form possible. You might list reasons, make suggestions, itemize problems, make comparisons, and such. The most important information usually fits at the end, although sometimes the most powerful argument must come first to generate immediate interest. The following paragraph presents a logical order of discussion for the rise in popularity of racquetball.

> Racquetball, a game similar to tennis, is the fastest growing sport in America. Racquetball is very easy to learn, and, once the initial cost is spent, it is very inexpensive. Unlike other sports, the courts for racquetball are small, and many outside or inside courts can fit into small areas. For middle-aged people, racquetball offers an excellent physical activity, since the game relies on coordination and stamina rather than strength. Anyone who can play racquetball for more than two hours is in better than average shape. The game exercises all muscles equally, unlike jogging which primarily works the legs. Some of the best competition between friends is on the racquetball courts.

The order of the supports in this paragraph follows the logical sequence of moving from ease of learning to cost to playing area to benefits, a sensible way to discuss the game.

Exercise

Identify the order you used in the paragraphs which you wrote for the previous exercises. Revise if you feel some improvement can be made in the existing ordering of supports.

Length

After considering the ways to arrange and to link the supports which build a focus into a paragraph, we might come back to the issue of length. Just how long should a paragraph be? When is it complete? In one way the answer is simple: When you have finished one idea, begin a new one in a new paragraph. At times, however, that is easier to say than to do. Judging length is often a problem for beginning writers, whose paragraphs are sometimes too short or sometimes too long.

A page of short paragraphs usually indicates stunted development; you cannot say very much in a paragraph of one or two sentences. Also, the jagged pattern that short paragraphs make is often visually jarring for your reader. More importantly, the undeveloped thought makes understanding the message a real problem. You can see this comprehension problem in these five paragraphs taken from a paper contrasting high-school and college experiences.

> The normal high-school class will cover the same material for three or four days. In addition, high schools have many rules about tardiness and absenteeism. They usually demand notes.
>
> College is very different.
>
> College teachers are more concerned about teaching the material and not wasting class time trying to catch skippers.
>
> The high school also has a problem with the dress code issue.
>
> Colleges rarely bother their students about what they wear. They can wear blue jeans or suits and ties. It doesn't matter.

The thoughts in that brief essay are so undeveloped and strewn about that they are hard to follow. The writer put each new thought in a new paragraph but did not develop any of them. The short paragraphs lack focus and internal development.

Sometimes the short paragraph does have a function. Paragraphs in fictional dialogue change when speakers do; frequently that means paragraphs of a line or two.

> Clyde lifted his hand to strike the girl's tear-splotched face. "Why," he asked in a rage, "why did you stay at the bar when I asked you to leave?"
>
> She mumbled an answer, but the hand in front of her face hid it from him.
>
> "Speak louder if you expect me to hear you." He lowered his hand. She wasn't worth his anger.

Newspapers and magazines regularly start new paragraphs every few sentences to visually break the narrow column of solid print.

> Crime. That's something that happens to the other guy—or is it?
>
> As crime increases, so do your chances of being a victim of robbery, burglary, aggravated assault or car theft.
>
> For a Pittston Township resident crime "hit home" on July 5.

In an essay, a short paragraph in the midst of several long ones can give a refreshing pause and rhythmic break. The short paragraph can be a good transition between longer thoughts. For the most part, however, paragraphs in an essay have to be longer than one or two sentences or they simply will not be able to develop what they have to say.

Paragraphs that are too long can be just as troublesome as those that are too short. A paragraph continuing for two or three pages should be broken up, probably into several parts. Sometimes a writer tries to cover every possible relevant detail; sometimes he or she just gauges poorly where one thought ends and another should begin. Such a solid block of text is hard to read, and a reader has to work hard to sift out meaning. Paragraphing gives your readers a ready grasp of changes in thought. To read and absorb the thought quickly, they should be able to skim through the whole piece, touching on the first sentences (usually the topic sentences) of each paragraph. If one paragraph stretches too far, it may mean that you did not know where to stop or that the focus is too broad.

You will of course find some legitimate long paragraphs. Frequently, a formal discussion of a research project involving numerous elements of support will demand long, complicated paragraphs. Often statistics, quotations, and facts take up considerable space within such a paragraph. But most often, the really long paragraph does not find its way into student essays.

How, then, can you know how long to make a paragraph? There is no actual standard of paragraph length other than the one given earlier—new paragraph for new thought. As you become a more skilled writer, you will develop a sense of judgment which helps you determine when you have said enough without saying too much. A topic sentence with four, five, or six major supporting sentences and perhaps a few minor supports should be enough to develop most thoughts. There are times when you must say more; there are times when you must say less. You need to be flexible. Just as sentences need variety, so, too, do paragraphs. The size of the paragraph depends on the thought and the effect you wish to achieve.

Exercise

Once more look at the paragraph you wrote for the earlier exercise. This time assess it for its quality of completeness. Is it long enough to develop the stated idea? Is there more that could or should be said within the paragraph?

Creating the Concrete Paragraph

The success of any piece of writing ultimately depends upon how well it suits audience and purpose. But the finished, final form of that piece of writing is not necessarily the way the sentences first hit the page. Focusing, sketching, and writing a paragraph form a very individual process. Some people write middles first, sketching out details and then firming up the topic sentence; others stride confidently forward knowing what they want to say right from the start. Whether you need two drafts or seven depends a lot on your skill, your style, your work habits, the importance of what you're doing, and the time available. What works for one person will not work for another. What works on one occasion will not work on another. As long as you are flexible enough to add, delete, condense, or expand as the need arises, the paragraph has a chance to reach its best form.

Firming up that best form is what revision is all about. After you have carefully structured a paragraph for unity, coherence, and order, you have to look critically at content, mechanics, and form. You do not want to sabotage an otherwise well-written paragraph from within by poor spelling or comma splices and sentence fragments. Variety, language, length, and shape, all of these elements contribute to the well-formed paragraph. In addition, each sentence—from first to last—should be as specific as use, purpose, and audience will allow. You are writing for a reader; make the paragraph both interesting and concrete.

Concern for final touches can make a difference in the quality of a paragraph which is technically correct but suffering from blandness. To illustrate, here is a first-draft paragraph by a student:

> The young woman was only twenty-eight years old, but she had done many things in her lifetime. She had been a Care Nurse for a while in Central America, where she worked in the poorer villages. Later she went to the Dominican Republic, where she helped the people greatly, although she at the same time became a tool of political factions. Later, she came to Washington, D.C., where she was helped by close friends through an unwanted pregnancy and the ultimate unhappiness of giving the baby up for adoption.

Technically, the paragraph works to develop its topic sentence focus of the woman's having done many things in her brief lifetime. She had intense experiences in Central America, the Dominican Republic, and finally in Washington, D.C. The sentences are all grammatically correct, although some are wordy. A few concrete images dot the paragraph, but basically it is flat. The student rewrote the paragraph to make it more interesting. He tightened up the topic sentence. He made each support a sharper, more specific statement by making nouns and verbs work harder. He knew more details; he had just not included them earlier. He also streamlined some of the sentences through subordination, thus improving sentence variety, and he made better use of transitions. When the student finished revising the paragraph, it looked like this:

> The woman, although young, had managed to compress several lifetimes within her twenty-eight years. For two years she had worked as a Care Nurse in the remote villages of Honduras and San Salvador, where she saw many lives begin and many more ended by the Four Horsemen. Her year in the Dominican Republic had shown her love from parents as she treated their children and hatred from political rivals as they tried to use her as a tool in their power struggles. And finally, in Washington, D.C., close friends helped her through an unwanted pregnancy: through the months of watching her body change, through the too-short joys of childbirth, and through the ultimate torture of giving her child up for adoption.

This second paragraph is a more specific, more informative picture of the woman and her experiences. The quality of the improvement comes largely from the student's going beyond the basic demands of paragraph structure and superimposing a concern for individual words and sentences on top of basic content and form. The effort is worth the time it takes; the dividends are clarity, grace, and concreteness.

Exercise

Revise one of the following paragraphs in the manner of the example just above. Use the checklist at the end of the chapter to guide your effort.

a. Because of inflation consumers now have to pay more for nearly everything they purchase. Candy bars are much more expensive. A cup of coffee now costs thirty cents or more. A gallon of gas has become very costly. The price of a ticket to the movies was once a dime and now is several dollars. A gallon of milk is unbelievable in price. Who knows what it will cost the consumer tomorrow.

b. It is very easy to tell the time period in which most songs were written. The sixties' music was harsh and serious. Guitars dominated. Later, in the seventies, other fads replaced rock and roll. This music had different accent, beat, lyrics, and subject matter.

Chapter Exercises

1. Here are a few student paragraphs presented as they were turned in. Pretend that you are the one who must grade them. Analyze the paragraphs by considering the following facets of good paragraph structure:

   effective focus
   unity
   order
   coherence
   length
   good sentence structure
   good mechanics
   sentence variety
   concrete language

a. An overwhelming sense of peace and serenity came over me that autumn day as I sat at the edge of the lake. Everything seemed to be standing still, not a ripple in the water or a breeze in the air. The lake was a smooth piece of glass. It reflected perfectly the reds, yellows, and oranges of the surrounding trees, like an upside-down photograph. The late afternoon sun, setting on the nearby hill, acted as a giant spotlight on this spectacle of nature. Silently, I applauded and then went on my way.

b. Julius Erving is a fantastic basketball player. In a game against the Seattle Supersonics, the Dr. scored forty-eight points, grabbed twenty-five rebounds, and passed off for ten assists. While playing against New York, he dunked the ball eight straight times, leaving the Knicks completely helpless against his fabulous moves. In Buffalo, he single-handedly destroyed the Braves by pouring in fifty-six points. According to the newspapers and sports magazines, Erving is praised as the greatest basketball player of all time.

c. As a method of preserving vegetables from the summer garden, freezing far surpasses canning in speed and efficiency. Freezing is accomplished quickly and easily by blanching vegetables in boiling water for two or three minutes, cooling them in ice water for the same amount of time, and packing them into plastic bags. Canning, by comparison, involves the lengthy process of packing vegetables into special glass jars, with mouths too small for the vegetables you're trying to force in; screwing on sealing lids and rings; and pressure cooking for, sometimes, forty-five minutes. The jars must then be checked for proper sealing. Freezing is fool-proof in that there are no worries about sealing or leakage. One last point to consider is the fact that freezing works well for the small amounts picked by the home gardener every few days as opposed to the large amount of produce needed to fill one batch of canning jars, which is seven pints or quarts. Needless to say, there is no question in my mind which I prefer.

2. Examine some of your own previous writing, either from this class or another. Check the unity, coherence, order, and completeness of your paragraphs. Pick one or two paragraphs and revise them.
3. Examine a few paragraphs from various magazine articles or from your textbooks for structure. Determine, if you can, what the topic sentence is and where the major supports begin and end. Discuss the means by which these writers achieve coherence if you feel they do. Talk also about the quality of the language.
4. Write a well-developed paragraph containing four or five major supports and a topic sentence. Try to include several minor supports as well. Check the paragraph against the checklist at the end of the chapter. Pick one of the following topics or choose one of your own. Narrow it appropriately to fit into a paragraph-sized unit and devise a suitable focus for it.
   a. an unpopular law
   b. a miracle cure
   c. a pleasant experience
   d. a new shopping mall
   e. a trip

Chapter Checklist

1. Focus each paragraph with a topic sentence, an expression of attitude about a subject. A topic sentence is not a statement of fact.
2. A paragraph has unity only when all the major supports

relate directly to the topic sentence focus. Minor supports amplify the major ones.

3. A paragraph has coherence only when there is a logical connection between all the sentences. Coherence can be achieved through coordination/subordination, tense/pronoun agreement, transitional words and phrases, cautious repetition of key words, and parallel structure.
4. A paragraph is well ordered only when each supporting sentence follows the other in one of several patterns: deductive, inductive, chronological, spatial, or logical.
5. Paragraph length should be determined by content. When you finish discussing one idea, begin the next one in a new paragraph.
6. Revise each paragraph for unity, coherence, order, length, mechanics, and diction.

Developing Paragraphs

Ideas flow into paragraphs in many different ways. Much of the decision of how to assemble the supports of a paragraph depends upon your purpose. When you are trying to make a point, you usually design a strategy to suit your needs. To explain why you should be allowed to stay out until 3:00 A.M., you might offer several *reasons* why as well as give a few *examples* of friends who are allowed to do so. If you are thinking of buying a typewriter, you might *compare and contrast* a Smith Corona Automatic and an IBM Selectric. *Describing* your new stereo set would call for a different technique. Showing *cause* for being late for work needs yet another approach. You use different strategies—sometimes separately, sometimes together—when you are writing, just as when you are speaking. While the essence of a well-written paragraph remains constant, different strategies supply you with alternatives for fleshing out the middles. Later they will serve you just as well in writing an essay. The task is to use these tactics to your best advantage. To describe, to illustrate, to compare and contrast, or to analyze, you build a paragraph's supports in different ways. Each strategy demands a slightly different technique.

Description and Details

Describing is not only a natural impulse; it is also an easy, yet effective, way to structure a paragraph. When you describe, you observe and arrange details in such a way that they *show* something to your reader.

With one type of detail, you could describe an object, a person, a place, or an event: a Suzuki 600, a grandmother, the Cape Hatteras lighthouse, or a Super Bowl game. With another kind of detail, you can describe a process: how to change the points on a 1957 Chevy, how to make a soufflé, how to filet a fish, or how to paint a house. Another type of detail helps you narrate or record an experience: how you fell down a moving escalator or how you won a tennis match in straight sets, finally.

While good use of detail is vital to all writing, it is especially important to description. The heart of good description rests in its use of detail. But, as already discussed in Chapter 3, the details in our world are so plentiful that we often take them for granted. We are so used to hearing whirrs and zings, seeing the redness of an apple or the roundness of a clock face, or feeling the chill of an ice cube or the slip of a satin bathrobe that we often forget to mention these details when we describe something. Instead we say only, "An ugly lamp stood in the corner" or "Refinishing a desk is easy." We omit the vital statistics of color, size, shape, movement, sound, and texture because they are familiar to us. *Showing* the ugliness of the lamp needs the specific detail of the ivory dolphin sitting at the base, the scarlet, fluted shade, and the yellow, porcelain rosettes climbing up the lamp's stem. Maintaining that "refinishing a desk is easy" does not *show* anything until you lay out the steps of stripping, scraping, sanding, and staining. These details need not be extensive; they just need to be concrete and relevant.

Whether you are describing a wrinkled face, how to build a model ship, or the night you were mugged, the supports should be details which relate directly to the paragraph's focus.

Focus

Supports
- Detail 1
- Detail 2
- Detail 3
- Detail 4

Using this basic plan, a student described an old, deserted house she had seen. She made a list of the major details which she had noted:

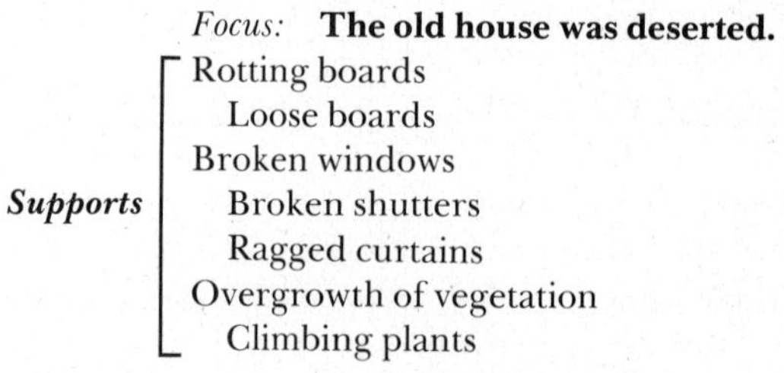

Then, she expanded these points into a paragraph:

Major Supports		***Minor Supports***
	The old house was deserted, a rickety shell in the midst of a wilderness of weeds. The rotten,	
Rotting boards	peeling boards, dull with age and weather, hung loosely on the frame of the empty house like clothes on a skeleton. The loose boards flapped desolately	*loose boards*
Broken windows	in the chattering breeze. Broken shards of window glass jutted from the splintery window frames, making the windows appear to grin at the world.	
	Squeaky shutters clacked to and fro, dangling	*broken shutters*
	crazily by single hinges. A faded rag of curtain,	*ragged curtain*
	waving at sunlit fields, fluttered at the vacant eye	
Overgrowth of vegetation	of a window. Here and there, grasses and ferns grew in the cracks of the walls, roof and chimney.	
	The lusty green plants spiraled and curled their way over the house as if to swallow it in a voracious blanket of growth. The house didn't seem to mind. It squatted, ramshackle yet graceful, in the sun-spattered field.	*climbing plants*

The structure of this paragraph is strong. The picture of the rickety old house is clear. Its rotting boards and broken windows and overgrown vegetation come to life through the well-chosen detail which describes it. The paragraph presents a wealth of specific details which distinguish this particular old house from other old houses; that is why it works so well.

Description needs sharp details, but it also relies heavily on a logical order of those details to avoid creating a clumsy picture. The details could advance from place to place. In describing a boxing arena, a railroad station, a patio, or a glove compartment, *spatial order* lets you move from one side to the other, from inside to outside, from front to back. Describe your Mercedes by looking first inside or first outside, but do not move from the wooden dashboard inside, to the Michelin tires outside, and then back to the plush carpeting on the interior floor. The description of the old, deserted house illustrates good spatial order. Concentrating on the exterior, it shows first the boards then the windows and finally the vegetation.

Details can also move chronologically. When you tell a story, relay a process, or narrate an event, you should order the details by moving from beginning to middle to end. This *chronological order* arranges the parts as they occur. Start at the beginning of the New Year's Eve party and move progressively to its end. Describe the process of giving a dog a bath step by step. Do not put him in the tub before you have turned on the water or rooted through the cupboard to find the dog shampoo.

The essence of good description lies ultimately in the quality and arrangement of the supporting details; the picture will only be as sharp and as orderly as they are. Words such as *overcooked, rainy,* or *noisy* work well to focus a topic sentence, but they do not provide a concrete picture of a supporting detail. *Show* these impressions with specific details that let your reader smell the burnt toast or feel the stinging pellets of rain or hear the clang of kitchen pots. Use strong nouns and active verbs to carry the description; use metaphors, similes, and allusions to dress it up further. Let the moving detail of someone raising an eyebrow or wringing his hands work just as hard for you as the more static detail of the color green or the shoe size 15½.

Exercises

1. Pick one or several of the following subjects and make a rough sketch for its development as a descriptive paragraph.
   a. a slippery sidewalk
   b. a frail old woman
   c. a hard time getting up in the morning
   d. a thrilling detective show on television
   e. how to fix something
2. Write a descriptive paragraph of your own. Use one of the subjects from the previous exercise or devise one you like better. Make a rough sketch of its contents. Remember, to be effective, you must get your reader to understand what you mean: to see the picture you wish to draw, to hear the tale you wish to tell, or to follow the process you wish to describe.
3. Bring to class an example of effective description from a newspaper or magazine. Be prepared to discuss its language and descriptive structure.
4. Here are two descriptive paragraphs. Read them over and comment on why you think they are effective or ineffective.
   a. The air was cold and damp. The chilled, salty mist was blowing in my face like sand in a strong breeze. As I walked along the beach, my feet turned blue from the cold water of the Atlantic Ocean. My wet suit would keep my body, arms, and legs warm, but my face and hands began to feel the numbing my feet encountered. These are the feelings of the winter surfer.

b. We simply couldn't be lost, but it looked like we were. In our VW, we had percolated along for four hundred miles through completely alien territory without a hitch. Now, having escaped the clutches of the expressway at last, we were hopelessly lost in the mazes of suburbia not two blocks from Jeremy's house. Logically, we puttered into a gas station for directions. The station manager frowned horribly, and his directions, given in a Southwestern drawl a little louder than a snail's whisper, were long and complicated. After I had frantically scrawled his instructions on an old envelope trailing over my knee, we set off bravely into the sunset once more to wander in confusion until Jeremy himself breezed by us on his ten-speed bike. With a shriek of relief, Tom pounded the horn, and I shot out of the sunroof and screamed. Happily, we trailed along at ten miles per hour behind Jeremy, home to Cedarwood Knolls, in the heart of beautiful, downtown suburbia.

Illustrating

Examples, like details, enrich your writing. Whereas details help describe something, someone, or someplace, examples illustrate a point. They offer a "for instance," a specific to illustrate the general statement. Sometimes, examples are woven into a paragraph as minor supports for major supports; sometimes, the examples themselves are important enough to become major supports.

If you want your parents to send you to Europe for the summer, you might illustrate your position by mentioning the benefits to several friends who have gone: Vicki learned to speak Spanish, Josh got a job with the Dutch embassy, Lucas earned six credits toward his B.A. degree. If you were writing an article about widespread welfare fraud occurring in large urban areas, you might let one paragraph cite examples of several specific big cities and the percentage of welfare fraud found in each.

The plan for writing a paragraph of illustration is fairly simple. The major supports would be several examples developed to illustrate the topic sentence generalization.

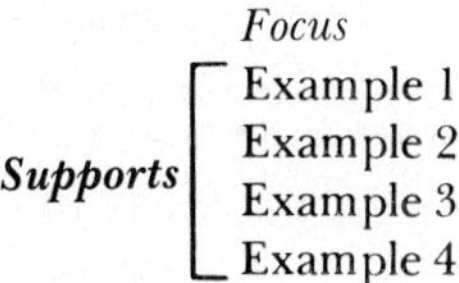

There will be times as well when you could use one long, extended example to serve your needs more fully than several shorter ones.

To develop a paragraph of illustration, a student who had been a Marine in Viet Nam made the claim that his experience there had made him so familiar with various weapons that he could identify them just by listening to the sounds of their firing. He proved his point by listing a few weapons and imitating their sounds:

Focus: **Experienced Marine can identify weapons by sounds.**

Supports

- M-14, M-60=Roar
- M-16=Buzz saw
- 50 caliber machine gun=Pounding
- AK47=Metallic hammering
- 12.6 millimeter machine gun=Pile-driver smash

His boast became this paragraph illustrating his claim:

Major Supports		***Minor Supports***
	The experienced combat Marine can always tell what weapons are being fired—friendly or enemy—just by the sounds they make. The American M-14 rifle and the M-60 machine gun are	
M-14, M-60=Roar	easily recognizable because of the deep roar/slam their large 7.62 millimeter NATO lead bullets	
M-16=Buzz saw	make. The newer M-16 is known as the "buzz saw" because of the sound its much smaller 223 caliber	
50 Caliber= Pounding	bullets make. A team of circus workers driving tent pegs with wood mallets is the closest description of the distinctive sound of the 50 caliber heavy machine gun. The Communist automatic rifle, AK47,	
AK47=Metallic hammering	is known to every Marine by its sharp, destructive cracks, like the rapid hammering of a ten-penny nail. The Russian 12.6 millimeter machine gun	
12.6 Machine gun=Pile-driver smash	would be recognized by veterans of every war of this century as the German Marine, which it copies by its slow, slamming pile-driver smashes. The experienced Marine can sit in the middle of a jungle in the dark of night and analyze the surrounding fire fight by its sounds.	

The supports in this paragraph are all examples of weapons and sounds which *illustrate* the generalization the student felt to be true:

The experienced Marine can identify weapons by listening to them. The paragraph makes no attempt to *explain why* the Marine has this talent; it merely gives examples of his ability. That is the way examples work. They further a point by illustrating it. Often, as in the example above, minor supports aren't necessary; other means achieve the same results.

Providing several examples of the types of people who read *Cosmopolitan* would *illustrate* the variety of people who read the magazine; it would not *explain why* they do. Using the problems of Oklahoma as an example of the effects of serious drought on the economy of western states would let you explain the impact of drought more specifically than if you tried to discuss all the problems of all the states affected.

Whether you have one long or several brief examples, arrange them in an order logical to the subject. If you are giving examples of the benefits or the drawbacks of the Equal Rights Amendment, you might quickly cite a few short ones and work up to the lengthier, more complicated illustrations. Or you might let less important examples precede the more important ones. For a different subject, say the impact of inflation on the cost of consumer goods, you might go from the rising cost of basic necessities, such as beef and coffee, to the increased expense of frills, such as tennis racquets and jewelry; you could also reverse that order.

But keep your examples relevant. Do not include a danger of ERA if you really wish to show its benefits. Save that for another paragraph. If you are illustrating rising costs, do not include something that has not increased in price or something that actually costs less than it did a year ago. Let your good sense guide you on which examples to include and how to order those included.

Specific, concrete examples can be a strong plus to any piece of writing. They can add a dimension of believability which is otherwise missing. Examples depend on the economic use of detail; be as specific as circumstances and length will allow. If you are trying to show that riding a motorcycle without a helmet can be dangerous, illustrate with specific accidents, citing the place, the time, the person, and the type of injury to the helmetless rider. If you are discussing the monetary rewards of stamp collecting, give some examples of famous stamps which have made their owners wealthy, or even just slightly richer, by including the details of years, names, colors, and, of course, dollar amounts. Details serve examples by making them clear and precise, and strong nouns and active verbs are just as vital in illustrating as in describing.

Exercises

1. Pick one or several of the following subjects and make a rough sketch for its development as an illustrative paragraph.
   a. Best-sellers which are poor/good literature
   b. Antiques your grandmother uses as her regular furniture
   c. Government agencies which seem ineffective
   d. Scenic spots in a certain state or area
   e. Drugs which can be dangerous
2. Write a paragraph of illustration of your own. Use your own subject or pick one from the previous exercise. Make a rough outline for it. Remember, you are *illustrating* a concept, idea, action, etc., not explaining or justifying it.
3. Bring to class an example of effective illustration, either several short illustrations or one extended example, from a newspaper or magazine. Be prepared to discuss the use and effectiveness of the example.
4. Here are two illustrative paragraphs. Read them over and comment on why you think they are effective or ineffective.

   a. The turbulent crowd surged to its feet to watch the action on the playing field as the enraged fans protested the umpire's decision. A bald, red-faced man roared like an elephant and threw his cigar at the field. The woman next to him, with arms as big as prime Virginia hams, energetically shook her fist and swore at the umpire. Two red-headed twins hurled their popcorn to the field, precipitating a rain of paper cups and plates, wads of paper and sticky gum, and hunks of food that swirled down to cover the playing field like a painting of surrealistic trash.

   b. Contrary to the many criticisms of rock music, it is a field that is vast and expanding. Joni Mitchell's work, for instance, is mostly soft rock. She is well-known for her stirring ballads with their moving lyrics. Or there is Chicago. The whole foundation for their music is a brass section which they sometimes spice up with a Latin beat. The Beach Boys playing a fast-paced, bouncy beat are continuously advocating the good life of "California Girls," sleek cars, and "Surfin' Safaris." Hard-driving primitive rock has been Kiss's specialty, concentrating more on flashy visual effects than on musical ability. But even this group with its basic music level has put out a song with a symphonic orchestra in the

> background. Another variation of rock is electronic music. Groups like Yes with their keyboards plugged into synthesizers have an infinite number of sounds at their disposal. Rock music not only changes from group to group, but it is also diversified within each group.

Comparison and Contrast

Comparing and contrasting are common ways of presenting parallel ideas. If you want to buy a dishwasher or cast a vote or go to a movie, you compare and contrast two or three machines or politicians or films before you make your decision. As a student you might be asked to write an essay in which you compare and contrast the characters of Macbeth and Lady Macbeth or show the differences between the decades of the 1920s and the 1930s.

Strictly speaking, to compare shows *likenesses;* to contrast shows *differences.* Usually we do both when we are considering the merit of two items. We can use a *point-by-point* comparison which allows the comparison/contrast to become visible immediately. The points of comparison, for the dishwasher for instance, act as major supports: cost, durability, service, gadgetry. Each of the subjects—specific dishwashers such as Maytag and Kitchenaid—is then a minor support related to one point at a time.

Focus

Supports

- Point 1
  - Subject A
  - Subject B
- Point 2
  - Subject A
  - Subject B
- Point 3
  - Subject A
  - Subject B

A student who had twin sons decided to write a comparison/contrast paragraph about her children. Although they looked alike, one was a rascal, and one was an angel. So, she first made a list of the ways in which they differed and decided that a point-by-point comparison would make the differences more immediate, hence more striking.

Focus: **Twin boys – similar in appearance, different in personality**

Supports

Difference: personality
  Patrick
  Kevin
Difference: eating habits
  Patrick
  Kevin
Difference: sleeping habits
  Patrick
  Kevin

Later, when she finally wrote the paragraph, she began with a few sentences that quickly showed similarities and then let the comparative points highlight the sharp contrasts between the children. She also put Kevin before Patrick in two of the supports just for variety.

Major Supports		***Minor Supports***
	The scruffy blue overalls are identical. The blue-striped T-shirts are a matched set. Both pair of tennis shoes that clad their tiny, fat feet are exactly the same size. A golden cap of springy curls adorns each of their heads; even the cowlicks are in the same place. Merry blue eyes shine in faces that are perfect copies of each other. However,	
Differences	physical appearance is where the similarities end.	
Personality	Patrick is the acrobat, clown, and one-man show in our house. His daring antics have resulted in three trips to the hospital emergency room for repair	*Patrick*
	work. Kevin is docile, easygoing, and gentle; he delights in being Patrick's audience. In fact he seems quite content in the role of innocent by-	*Kevin*
Eating habits	stander. Kevin waits patiently for his meals while	*Kevin*
	Patrick lords over the table banging his fists and	*Patrick*
	shouting until his food is set in front of him. Kevin's	*Kevin*
Sleeping habits	sleeping habits are such that even Dr. Spock would	
	be impressed. Patrick, on the other hand, thinks any reason is sufficient excuse to keep us running up and down the stairs for hours. **In physical appearance these sons of mine are identical; their personalities, however, are strictly individual for one could never replace the other.**	*Patrick*

Another way to structure a comparison/contrast is with a *subject-by-subject* pattern. In this way you can take a longer look at each subject by itself. You would first discuss one of the subjects – the Maytag dishwasher perhaps—saying all that needs to be said about the way it relates to the comparative points: cost, durability, service, gadgetry. Then you would discuss the other, relating it to the same basic points.

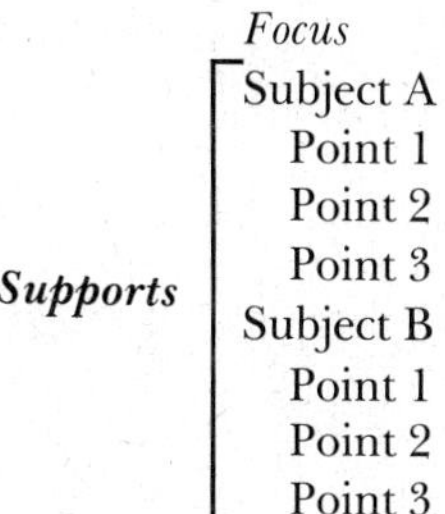

A student who wanted to show the marked differences in her experiences with each of two young men she had been dating, Harlan and Ken, structured the paragraph in a subject-by-subject fashion. She wanted to describe each man separately to draw a very complete and distinct picture of the taste and style of each one. A subject-by-subject comparison let her first discuss Harlan and then Ken by comparing them against the same points. In this way, she made the contrast between them very clear and yet slightly more subtle than alternating points would permit.

Focus: **Dating two different types can prove interesting**

Supports

- Harlan
  - Job
  - Clothing
  - Automobile
  - Apartment
  - Entertainment
- Ken
  - Job
  - Clothing
  - Automobile
  - Apartment
  - Entertainment

Her paragraph filled out like this:

Major Supports — ***Minor Supports***

Harlan — **Dating two opposite men at once can be an interesting experience for any woman.** Harlan is the white-collar worker, branch manager of *job* Sloane's Furniture Store and quite accustomed to the so-called "good life." He dresses in nothing but Pierre Cardin suits and always trails a faint *clothing* scent of Aramis. A new Corvette transports him *automobile* from his high-rise condominium to parties, clubs, *apartment* and restaurants where he drinks nothing but Chevas Regal or Courvoisier. To indulge in his *entertainment* love for jazz and blues, he has bought a $2,500 quad unit complete with the most sensitive listening and recording equipment. On the other hand, *Ken* Ken is a telephone installer, the ordinary blue- *job* collar worker. This guy can do anything with his hands . . . whether it is sanding a boat or building a generator. Trucking about in his flannel *clothing* shirt and blue jeans, he chugs to and fro in a 1966 *automobile* Ford pickup truck which he tunes regularly. He lives in a room in the basement of his parents' *apartment* home with his tools and new projects piled high around him. Ken is a blue-grass fan. While relax- *entertainment* ing with a can of Schlitz, he can pick out a song by ear on his guitar or make his harmonica sound like a train whistle. How incredibly strange to be in a sexy, backless halter dress one night and grubbing around in a pair of ragged jeans and T-shirt the next.

Although the two students followed different methods, they each ended up with very tightly written comparison/contrast paragraphs. You can easily do the same by adhering closely to one structure or the other once you begin it. Choosing which method to use—point by point or subject by subject depends a lot on the emphasis you wish to achieve. You can emphasize contrasting points with the first; with the second you can put more stress on the integrity of each subject.

Whichever method you select, a good comparison/contrast paragraph depends upon a workable subject. Compare and contrast items, events, things, or people of equal stature: a Volkswagen to a Ford Pinto or a Cadillac to a Continental. Unless you are being satiric or clever, do not compare and contrast a Volkswagen and a Cadillac. They are two different types of automobiles designed to meet two different needs.

Once you decide on a subject, develop each item equally. Judge them against the same points of comparison. The woman who contrasted her sons could not speak of the physical appearance and personality of Kevin without doing the same for Patrick; to discuss Patrick's hobbies or childhood diseases instead would destroy the contrast. The same would be true for Harlan and Ken. Talking about

Harlan's fraternity brothers without at least mentioning Ken's bowling buddies would distort the comparison. If the subjects do not relate to the same points, they become mere description rather than comparison/contrast.

Finally, keep the language of the comparison/contrast specific and concrete. Details and examples find their way into differences and likenesses. Careful use of nouns, verbs, and modifiers will show your readers one boy with blonde hair and another with brown. Or it can show one orchestra with ten violinists and another with only four. Also, use to your advantage words and phrases such as "likewise" and "on the other hand." They underlie the comparison/contrast and guide your readers through the paragraph to show them where points and subjects begin and end.

Exercises

1. Pick one or several of the following subjects and make a rough sketch for its development as a comparison/contrast paragraph.
   a. two books
   b. two desserts
   c. two color television sets
   d. two relatives
   e. two quarterbacks, goalies, halfbacks, defensive guards
2. Write a comparison/contrast paragraph of your own. Use your own subject or pick one from the previous exercise. Make a rough outline for it. Use either a point-by-point comparison or a subject-by-subject comparison.
3. Bring to class an example of effective comparison/contrast from a newspaper or magazine. Be prepared to discuss the effectiveness and the order of the comparison/contrast.
4. Here are some comparison/contrast paragraphs. Read them over and comment on why you think they are effective or ineffective.

   a. Although my friend Rudy and I purchased our Volkswagen buses at about the same time, one would not believe that they were bought in the same year. The paint on my bus is still shiny and even from careful washing and waxing; Rudy's bus is suffering a terminal illness, the cancerous rot of rust. My engine, with ninety-one thousand miles on it, still has the steady sewing machine clatter that is a purr to a Volkswagen owner; but wherever Rudy drives, he is followed by a trail of thick, blue smoke. The under-inflated, bald doughnuts that Rudy has have become dangerous to drive on, while my tough-skinned steel-belted radials with twenty-thousand miles on them are quite capable of another twenty thousand. Long after Rudy's bus is haunting a metal graveyard, mine will still be chugging down the road.

b. Two very attractive and easy to care for plants are the spider plant and the beehive cactus. The hanging spider plant has long grasslike blades, some of which are white-margined. The cactus is oval shaped and stands about two feet tall. The cactus is covered with long thornlike protrusions. The spider plant has large white roots which require that the plant be repotted every eighteen months to two years. The cactus has short roots which should be repotted every two or three years, mainly for a fresh soil change. Propagations for the spider plant are produced at the end of long curved stems, which are readily cut and potted in soil. The cactus propagations have to be cut directly from the plant then dried out completely before rooting in sand. The spider plant's soil should be kept moist, while cactus need a dry growing medium. As for lighting, a spider plant can be hung in a window or out on a patio. The cactus needs indirect sunlight, which means finding a favorable floor space for it. Although the cactus is easier to care for, both are ideal domestic plants.

c. When offered a choice between oil paints and acrylics, most art afficionados would choose oils. Oils are mixed with turpentine and linseed oil, which makes the medium easy to spread with the brush or palette knife, whichever tool is preferred. Acrylics must be mixed with either water or a mixing medium, which retards drying only long enough for a few quick strokes of color by an experienced artist. Oil colors can be adjusted right on the canvas, while acrylics usually are available in such strident hues that the painter is quite literally stuck with what's there. Finally, while oil paints leave the artist time to make corrections, fast-drying acrylics nearly always force a rebeginning.

Analysis

Analysis digs behind generalizations. It probes beliefs and attitudes and frequently determines the causes or effects of certain phenomena to find the essential explanation lying hidden at its core. Sometimes we seek reasons; sometimes we trace causes and effects. We analyze in order to *explain why*.

Reason analysis

If you have been late for class, you offer reasons to explain why. If you disagree with the President's stand on Soviet relations, you offer reasons to explain why. If you wish to buy a $350 movie camera rather than a $95 one, you justify that decision with some reasons to explain why. Analyzing by exploring the reasons behind a statement, a belief, or a phenomenon involves a simple skeletal framework such as this:

Focus

Supports
- Reason 1
- Reason 2
- Reason 3
- Reason 4

In other words, the topic sentence and the major supports form a Why/Because relationship: The topic sentence is true because of reasons 1, 2, 3, and 4.

Since reason analysis is such a common process, a conversation between two students can illustrate the ease with which such a paragraph can be written. The students were discussing their tropical fish aquariums. One said he was considering adding a "kissing fish" (Helostoma Temmincki) to his collection. The other, who had already had a bad experience with a kissing fish, tried to talk the first out of his decision by saying that the kissing fish did disastrous things to a community aquarium. It was a bully; it was a glutton; and it was extremely unsociable. Later, when this student had to write a reason paragraph, he recalled this discussion and translated it into this sketch:

Focus: **H. T. unsuitable for community aquarium**

Supports
- Fights with other fish
- Eats all the food
- Uproots plants

Developing these reasons into a paragraph, then, was very easy:

Major Supports | ***Minor Supports***

Despite the popularity of the Helostoma Temmincki or "kissing fish," it is an unsuitable occupant of any community aquarium. While this fish is added to most hobbyists' collections because of its peculiar habit of "kissing" with its thick stoma-like lips, this kiss is actually a tug of war. This fish

Fights with other fish

is a psychopathic bully. Since in its natural habitat, it can grow twelve inches long, it is constantly nipping and chasing the smaller fish in the community. The Helostoma Temmincki also has a tendency to be a selfish feeder. It gulps down any and all food and chases other fish to the far corners of the aquarium much like a blue jay among a group of small sparrows. Another of H. Temmincki's annoying habits is the destruction of any plants in the neighborhood. It will maliciously uproot any type of aquatic garden. Because of these less than endearing qualities, anyone purchasing this fish with the hopes of a welcomed addition to a community aquarium will be in for an eye-opening surprise.

Eats all the food

Uproots plants

This paragraph about the kissing fish has good unity. The reasons firmly establish why the kissing fish is not a wise addition to an aquarium which contains other fish:

Why? Because it is a bully.
Why? Because it is a glutton.
Why? Because it is destructive.

The arrangement of these reasons involves some logical ordering for best effect. Sometimes you can put the strongest point first and taper off with the less important ones. If you were explaining the reasons behind a traffic accident, you might want to say, first, that the main reason for it was that the driver had been drinking. Possibly then you would add that the pavement was slick from rain or that a child was crying in the back seat or that the traffic light was not working. The alcohol which blurred the driver's impulses, and hence ability to handle these other circumstances, would then be emphasized as the strongest reason why the tragedy occurred.

At other times, you put the weaker reasons first, building up climactically to the most important. If you want to explain why you think mental institutions should be built within the community and not be hidden away in secluded areas, you could list the reasons why such a change would be good for the patients: to give them a chance to shop or eat in restaurants occasionally or just to take walks in favorite places. Then you could list some reasons why the change would help the relatives: to make visiting easier, cheaper, and more frequent. Finally, you could build up to what might be the most important reason: the community would learn that most mental patients are neither dangerous nor criminal, thus helping reduce the stigma of mental illness.

At still other times, the reasons will be more or less equal in importance. Explaining why Holland is a popular country with tourists, you could mention the historic attractions, the beaches, the flowers, or the quaintness in almost any order. Ultimately, in ordering the reasons, you have to use your own good judgment. Put related ones close together and order them according to the emphasis you want to achieve, the rhythm of the paragraph, or the coherence of the parts.

Analysis in a reason paragraph should have this kind of tight structure. If you are giving reasons why you want to buy a house in a particular suburb, do not pause to talk about the real-estate agent's Cadillac or another client's bad manners. Make your reasons also be concrete statements, not just vague or general references to abstract ideas. Do not say you would like to buy a certain house because it is in a "nice neighborhood." To develop this reason, the "nice neighborhood" should be complete with oaks lining the curb, brick houses, well-trimmed yards. Then "nice neighborhood" becomes a meaningful reason in the way you intend it to. Your readers will not necessarily understand or perceive it that way unless you tell them.

Exercises

1. Pick one or several of the following subjects and make a rough sketch for its development as a paragraph of reason analysis.
   a. Picking a particular school
   b. Liking a certain opera singer, rock group, musician, etc.
   c. Wearing a certain outfit to a particular function
   d. Approving or disapproving a particular local, state, or federal decision
   e. Living in a certain neighborhood
2. Write a paragraph of reason analysis of your own. Use your own subject or pick one from the previous exercise. Make a rough outline for it. Develop a tight Why/Because relationship between the topic sentence and the supports.
3. Bring to class an example of effective reason analysis from a newspaper or magazine. Be prepared to discuss the process as it is illustrated in the piece.
4. Here are two reason-analysis paragraphs. Read them over and comment on why you think they are effective or ineffective.

a. Sixty percent of all the eligible voters in the United States will not vote in the next presidential election. Some of these nonvoters won't care enough for any of the candidates running for office, while others won't be able to decide for whom to cast a ballot. There will be those who feel their choice will win (or lose) regardless of whether they vote or not. A portion may not bother to vote thinking the real election is by the electoral college and the popular vote means nothing. Of course, there will be those who have never registered to vote and thus will never be able to partake in the almost exclusively American privilege, the vote.

b. Deale, Maryland, a small town located in the southern part of Anne Arundel County, is a tourist attraction during the summer months. Freedom of spirit and exciting sport is attained by renting boats for a day on the Chesapeake Bay. Everyone likes to get away from the hustle and bustle of everyday living. Fishing boats, rowboats, speedboats, and canoes are available from a large number of local marinas. The fishing is plentiful. Many a tired but happy fisherman reels in dozens of Blues and Rock, large enough to bring a smile to the weariest face. Crabs are usually plentiful during July and August. However, if the rainfall has been excessive, too much fresh water enters the bay and crabs will be scarce. During a good season, empty plastic bleach bottles and bobbers dot the waves, indicating crab traps floating below. At low tide, people can be seen near the shoreline with long-handled nets. Crabs are dipped from the water and thrown into baskets attached to floating inner tubes. Many people own summer homes, their escape from pollution, noise, and stress. They spend the entire summer here, returning to their city dwellings after Labor Day. Weekends bring friends or relatives desiring relaxation and fun. Many backyards are filled with the smells of delicious foods sizzling on charcoal grills. The sight and sound of happy, relaxing sun-worshipers is everywhere.

Causal analysis

Another kind of analysis traces causes and effects. Causal analysis helps show how causes and effects generate one another. A cause leads to an effect; the effect, in turn, gradually becomes the cause of yet another effect. On and on this chain reaction goes. Your car breaks down as you drive to work; therefore, you are late. Because you are late, you miss an important telephone call. Because you miss the telephone call, you lose a sale. Because you lose the sale, you do not get a bonus. Each cause leads to an effect which in turn becomes a cause leading to a new effect.

There are numerous ways of following through on such an analysis, since not all cause/effect explanation is chain reaction. Much of it concerns parallel causes and effects. You could focus on the causes, a process similar in some ways to assigning reasons. Then, you might show how a job at McDonald's, nightly visits to the Pizza Shack, and a love for Bridge Mix candy transformed you over the summer into a buxom creature who was twenty pounds overweight. The effect (becoming overweight) is cited, but the causes will get the paragraph's attention:

Focus: C + C + C → E

Supports
- Cause 1
- Cause 2
- Cause 3

You can also focus on effects as the main concern of the paragraph. If you said that wild, inebriated celebrating after your high-school graduation resulted in two speeding tickets, a twenty-dollar debt to fix a broken bowling machine, a wine-stained baby-blue tuxedo, and an incredible headache, you would be placing the emphasis of the supporting development on the effects of that action. A sketch would translate that pattern into this:

Focus: C → E + E + E

Supports
- Effect 1
- Effect 2
- Effect 3

There are other times when you must make a distinction between immediate causes or effects, those which are recent in action, and long-range causes or effects, those which are more distant. For instance, the immediate cause of the Nixon administration's attempt to make John Dean a scapegoat for Watergate resulted in the immediate effect of Dean's implicating almost everyone in the White House. The long-range effect of that same action was the eventual resignation of a President. The immediate cause of World War I was the assassination of the Archduke Francis Ferdinand; the long-range cause, which reached back into a previous decade, was the complicated web of entangling alliances entered into by the countries of the world, particularly the Baltic states.

To illustrate the process of causal analysis on a more simple level, here is a paragraph written by a student who had sold his automobile and bought a motorcycle. In addition to saving on expenses, as he had anticipated, there were some unexpected effects of his action: He abandoned the warmth and comfort of automobile driving for the somewhat dubious pleasure—it turned out—of driving a motorcycle. The sketch he outlined to analyze the effects looked like this:

Focus: **Selling my car and buying a motorcycle created some unforeseen hardships.**

Supports
- No heat in cold weather
- No protection from rain
- Oil and gas spatters on clothes

The paragraph which developed looked like this:

Major Supports		***Minor Supports***
	Selling my car and buying a motorcycle created hardships that I wish I could have more fully foreseen. As I ride through freezing, biting winter	
No heat in cold weather	air that numbs my whole body, I recall the warm comfort my automobile used to supply on demand. I also remember when a heavy rain meant no more	*freeze in winter*
No protection from rain	than a quick sprint from my car to a dry shelter. Now when I ride in the rain, even with a raincoat, I usually arrive a wet, sopping mess with three inches of water sloshing about in my boots. Know-	*usually get soaked*
Oil and gas spatters	ing the value of gas and oil, my generous machine seems inclined to want to share its wealth with me. Its generosity has reduced my clothes to blots of greasy oil smelling of premium gasoline. A little foresight could have saved me a great deal of misery.	*soiled clothes*

The student's paragraph analyzes the plight which he now feels his lack of foresight brought upon him. Each effect of his action is presented in a nicely specific, concrete statement.

Causal analysis is a useful process for attempting to make sense out of some of the things that happen around us. Why were the seventies calmer than the sixties? What will happen to Taiwan? Will fuel conservation methods have an impact on future automobile design? Do children who skip grades at school suffer any ill effects? While causal analysis may not be as clear-cut as some of these examples suggest, ultimately, you have many options open to you to investigate them: many causes, few effects; one cause, many effects; immediate causes, immediate effects; long-range causes, long-range effects.

Whatever the connection you eventually make, let the topic sentence state the focus and give the supports a logical order. Although such order is frequently chronological, do not assume that something is necessarily a cause or an effect just because it comes before or after something else. The sun rises after the rooster crows, but the rooster's crowing certainly does not make the sun rise.

Be careful, also, not to oversimplify causes and effects. To say that the present economic recession is caused by the crooked politicians who run this country may be overstating the case just a bit. Obviously, the situation is far more complicated than that. Let your causes and effects be sensible manifestations of the analysis you undertake. Present them in strong, concrete language that will let you say the murderer slew six beautiful, young girls because his girlfriend abandoned him, rather than because he had an emotional problem. By staying within these restrictions, you should be able to present a useful causal analysis of almost any situation.

Exercises

1. Pick one or several of the following subjects and make a rough sketch for its development as a causal-analysis paragraph.
   a. Missing an important exam
   b. The fifty-five-mile-an-hour national speed limit
   c. Going on a blind date
   d. Eating too much of a particular food additive
   e. Trying a new sport or hobby
2. Write a causal-analysis paragraph of your own. Use one of the subjects from the previous exercise or devise one you like better. Make a rough sketch of its contents. Carefully draw the cause/effect relationship in the topic sentence.
3. Bring to class an example of effective causal analysis from a newspaper or magazine. Be prepared to discuss its cause/effect connections.
4. Here are two causal-analysis paragraphs. Read them over and comment on why you think they are effective or ineffective.

   a. My using birth-control pills as a contraceptive led to many complications. I became depressed and would cry without having any specific reasons. I was increasingly argumentative with my husband. Eventually, I was stricken with an illness called thrombophlebitis, which is a blood clot in a vein of the leg. Because of this illness, I was hospitalized for ten days. I am no longer able to use birth-control pills due to the serious side effects I encountered.

b. The decrease in judicial authority in the courts has made the battle for controlling crime almost a losing one. Several years ago, the felony of rape carried a sentence of life imprisonment. Now it is the harassed victim who must be put on trial in the courtroom. Statistics show an increase in murder in almost every major city in the United States. According to the latest FBI report, a murder is committed every seventeen seconds and only a quarter of the murderers are ever apprehended. If the offenders *are* ever apprehended and if they *are* formally convicted and if they *do* receive any type of sentence, the prisoner is eligible for parole within seven years. I think it is about time the taxpayers, who support the overcrowded prisons and make it possible for the law enforcement department to receive a payroll, should have the right to protect themselves by legislating harsher prison sentences to keep the thought of committing an offense just a thought.

Combining Methods

As you prepare to write, unless you have a specific assignment to describe something or to compare and contrast some other things, you frequently do not think in terms of all details or all reasons. You think instead of the relevant items that must be covered to convey your point—some reasons, some examples, some details, and so on. When everything falls into place, you may or may not have pure *reason/analysis* or *description* or *comparison/contrast.* Therefore, these patterns of description, illustration, comparison/contrast, reason analysis, and causal analysis, given as they are here in isolation, may be a little misleading. You will have many occasions to use these methods separately; you will also have many occasions that require combining methods. While good descriptive detail is basic to all writing, you will need examples to help trace causes and effects; you will need description to show a sharp comparison/contrast. Sometimes you will have to slip in reasons to help explain a process; at other times you will use details, reasons, and examples in an extended causal analysis which demands considerable development to be convincing. And sometimes when you do a longer piece of writing, one paragraph will explain reasons while another whole paragraph will just give examples of how these reasons work.

By way of illustrating the kind of give and take that occurs when you try to explain something, here is a paragraph taken out of the context of a larger essay. The student who wrote it was comparing real female police officers with their television counterparts and used a mix of tactics to convey her idea of the phony glamour tacked onto the televised heroines. In this paragraph she was comparing and contrasting the two kinds of officers on three basic points: appearance, status, and impact on police departments. Woven into this paragraph were reasons, examples, and descriptive details:

Television policewomen differ greatly from policewomen in the real world. In the fantasy world of television, the typical policewoman is usu-
Description ally a slender, blonde, and attractive detective who, although the only female in the entire division, receives the highest respect from her male cohorts. Her mere presence seems to transform even the most vulgar, crude, and repulsive policeman into a meek, mild altar boy. In the real world, however, the average policewoman is not a detective, but a
Reason Analysis patrol officer. But then, the main reason most TV policewomen are detectives is that cases carried by patrol officers never have endings. After a patrol officer pulls a routine investigation on a call, the case, if there is probable cause, will be turned over
Examples to the proper division. Juvenile gets a twelve-year-old vandal; Homicide picks up on the murders; Vice follows up the leads about a prostitution ring. Also, the presence of a policewoman does not change the atmosphere or the attitudes in a police department, but rather the department changes
Examples the policewoman. In a study conducted by the St. Louis County Police Department in Missouri, several policewomen commented that they had been forced to sacrifice some of their femininity in order to gain acceptance from their colleagues. The real policewoman has to contend with verbal abuse, not only from citizens who do not appreciate or understand the existence of female law-enforcement agents, but also from their male co-workers who cannot accept the arrival of women in a once male-dominated profession.

This paragraph shows you how several strategies can work together. Confronting the separate paragraph patterns not only gives you several valuable tactics for presenting your ideas but also helps underscore the lessons about paragraph structure, re-emphasizing the value of well-planned unity and coherence. These lessons will expand later to develop whole essays or parts of essays. Yet, writers should not be slaves to molded forms; their thoughts should have room to grow. The tactics discussed in this chapter will say something very specific when you need that something said; at other times, a combination of methods will convey your message just as effectively.

Chapter Exercises

Following are several paragraphs. Read them over and determine which method of development is primarily used in each one. Discuss also the general merits of each paragraph: unity, coherence, order, and completeness.

a. The bomb runs of an F-4 "Phantom" flying beach support are truly spectacular to witness. Sitting in the relative safety of an assault craft, you can hear the mighty silver bird long before you can see it approaching the beach. As the Phantom screams overhead, you clamber for a space along the rail where you will be able to see as well as hear the ballet of destruction about to unfold before you. The warrior of the air approaches his target almost casually before wiggling his wings slightly and entering into the preliminary dive of his dance of death. The bombs tumble, almost skip, from their racks before racing each other to see which will be the first to disintegrate upon the beach in a cloud of flying sand, billowing smoke, belching flame, and a roar of defiance to all who care to listen. The Phantom, the major part of its performance complete, finishes the display by rudely spitting several bursts of leaden death at the beach's inhabitants before climbing skyward again and indifferently turning his back on the bruised and injured strip of sand which once again closely hugs the soothing sea. As you return to your place in the assault craft, all you can think to do is thank a merciful God that you were not on that beach watching the spectacle from a slightly different perspective.

b. Because of the strenuous workouts, year-round training, and severely strict diets, bodybuilders must be mentally tougher than most athletes. They must work out six days a week, sometimes twice a day, for an exhausting three hours. These workouts are so strenuous and so intense that they could actually burst the heart of the average person if they were attempted. Unlike most sports, bodybuilding has no off-season. The contests are held year-round, and you must train year round to keep pace with the high caliber of competition. Once they have left the gym, bodybuilders become concerned with diet. They know no junk food, and everything is eaten for nutritional purposes only. Protein is the basis of the diet, both solid and liquid. Close to the time of the contest, the bodybuilder subsists on only liquid protein. You have to have a great mental attitude just to force yourself to drink this concoction which tastes like sawdust. Because of these factors, one must say the bodybuilder is a rare breed of determination and will power.

c. The way people walk down the stairs can identify them as well as fingerprints. Wayne, the businessman in Apartment C gallops like a horse with springs on his feet. His wife, Kathy, the clog lady, walks like she's wearing cement bricks. Amalie, the baby in Apartment C clops with one lead foot and taps down with her second. You would think she was a peg-legged pirate instead of a toddler. Tim walks down two steps, stops, taps down three more, stops, then continues on. You get the impression of a young Mr. Bojangles tapping his way down the staircase to school.

d. Every night I would put my small hand in his large, calloused one and gently tug until he realized what I was waiting for. We would stroll down the cobblestone sidewalks, past Leon's Italian market and D'Archangelo's Pizza House until we arrived in the center of the small town of Wimber, Pennsylvania. Everyone we passed on the street would wave and say hello or stop to chat for a while. Finally, he would pull two shiny quarters from his pockets, and we would play my favorite game, "Guess which hand it's in." Although he led me to believe I won fair and square, I always knew he put one coin in each hand. He was such a soft touch. He would usher me into Weilan's ice-cream parlor and order my favorite treat, a banana split piled high with hot fudge sauce and mounds of whipped cream and nuts. After I had gorged myself to the brim, we would start on our journey home. Stopping on every street corner, we would peer through the shop windows to see what treats they had to offer. Our trip would not be complete though without venturing into

Anderson's penny-candy store where for fifty cents I could obtain enough treats to last for a week. I will long remember those evening walks with my Uncle Alfred, even though he is only a fond memory now.

e. The old gray ship sat in the misty harbor with its guns silent. Rust had shown its face through the old weather-worn gray paint on its decks. The empty and well-built compartments appeared to be like a hollow grave with the hatch open as if inviting strangers in. Old Glory, all battered and torn, waved from the stern boldly as a reminder of the destructive power of the ship's mighty guns. Only the whisper of the wind can now be heard in the steel cables that stretch out and upward to the antennae that seem to touch the sky. The now deadened engines that once controlled the mighty rush of the waves against her steel sides sit silent like mere bumps on a log. Nothing now but echoes of the wind and the birds playing on the mast can be heard aboard the once great "Man of War."

f. My four-year-old daughter Jennifer is a precocious little lady who never lets me forget that she is around. When I am trying to catch up on some much-needed sleep, she slips into my room and whispers that pancakes and eggs would be nice for breakfast. After she succeeds in getting me out of bed, her appetite vanishes while she rummages through her dresser drawers searching for an outfit to wear. Jenni is a regular fashion plate. Her clothes must match from her hair ribbon all the way down to her ruffly socks and red, white, and blue sneakers. She is such an expert on today's fashions that she helps me pick out the clothes I wear. When I am putting on make-up or polishing my nails, my little shadow is right next to me, patiently waiting to have herself made beautiful also. She thinks nothing of recklessly searching through my jewelry box, adorning herself with bracelets and rings, or rooting through my chest of drawers, snagging my new pantyhose. The real treat does not begin, though, until it is time to get ready for bed. We argue over what type of shampoo to use and which pajamas to wear. Finally, with the little tyke settled, I prepare for my hard-earned evening of privacy and relaxation. Just as I turn on the television and make myself comfortable, Jenni patters down the hallway, darts into the living room, leaps onto my lap, and exclaims, "I thought I would come out and keep you company."

Chapter Checklist

Describing

1. Details need not be extensive, but they should be concrete. They should let the reader see, hear, taste, or feel the images you are transmitting.
2. Be sparing in your use of vague or abstract words such as "happy" and "sad."
3. Use a logical order in arranging details: spatial or chronological, whichever fits better.
4. Be selective; not everything is important enough to mention. When images are strong, economy of detail works well.

Illustrating

1. Use examples to illustrate a point, not explain it.
2. Be selective; choose examples which will be directly relevant to your point.
3. Arrange examples in a logical order: most important to least important, least important to more important, and so on.
4. Use several, concrete examples or one long, extended example.
5. Use concrete detail to make examples as specific as possible.

Comparing and Contrasting

1. Use a point-by-point comparison or a subject-by-subject comparison, but be consistent.
2. Let the topic sentence indicate whether you are showing likenesses or differences or both.
3. Balance the comparison/contrast. Pick subjects that are equal in stature and consider them against the same points equally.
4. Use concrete detail to develop each side of the comparison.
5. Use transitional guide words such as "likewise" or "on the other hand."

Reason Analysis

1. Be selective in choosing reasons; make them relevant through a direct Why/Because relationship between supports and topic sentence focus.
2. Use concrete language to express reasons.
3. Use a logical order in arranging reasons: most important to least important, least important to most important, etc.

Causal Analysis

1. Almost everything fits into a cause/effect chain. Be careful to assess causes and effects as they relate to each other.
2. Include all relevant factors, but do not include causes or effects simply because they come before or after a particular phenomenon. They may be unrelated.
3. Do not oversimplify causes or effects.
4. Distinguish as necessary between immediate and long-range causes and effects.
5. Use concrete language to express both causes and effects as specifically as possible.

6

Organizing Essays

Most of us are quite good at expressing opinions—especially if we do not have to write them down. We can groan about the rate of inflation when we buy a carton of cola or a bucket of fried chicken for twenty cents more than we paid a week before. We can grumble about bureaucratic inefficiency when we have to wait in line for three hours to get a hunting license or to pay a tax bill. We can rail about the potholes in the road or the twenty-mile-per-hour speed limit or the stray dogs that wander through the neighborhood. We can be quite articulate when talking about these things to husbands or wives or friends. But for some reason we tighten up at the thought of having to *write* an essay. Our minds switch to serious subjects such as capitalism or Communism or democracy; our language becomes stilted and phony; we get rigid and tense because we fear we may have nothing important to say.

Actually, much of that choking up may be unnecessary. If you can write a paragraph, you can write an essay. The basic skills of focus and development are very similar. An essay is just a longer form to give order to your ideas. It offers a larger forum, more room to make your point. An essay, for the most part, is a statement of its writer's opinions. If you write down your thoughts about the speed limit, the stray dogs, or the potholes, you will have written a simple essay. While most essays will be more complicated than a complaint about an expensive carton of cola or a three-hour wait in line, the essence remains the same. Whether their purpose is to pick a fight, sway an opinion, or simply share information, all essays are alike in one way—they focus on and express a point of view.

An essay, however, is defined not only by its writer's ideas. Writers inevitably confront readers—teachers, classmates, uncles, friends, foes. These readers not only have reactions to what they are reading; they also have their own viewpoints. Think of how many times you have read something with which you have disagreed: an article advocating vegetarianism, a support of television as a baby-sitter, a review panning the best film you have ever seen. So it will be with your reader. While you are scolding the oil companies for realizing enormous profits from high prices at the gas pumps, your reader may have lost money when the price of oil stock went down. While you are cheering the Israelis, your reader may support the Arabs. While you are unhappy with the type of jobs open to women, your reader might be a man who is quite content to have his wife at home.

Your task, then, when you write an essay is dual. You offer your thoughts and opinions, but you must also provide the specifics that support them—facts, details, logical reasons. To assert with fiery rhetoric, "This country is on the skids," or "Women definitely belong in the kitchen," is not sufficient. No matter how much energy you put into your words, no matter how high your soapbox, you will not do much persuading unless you can offer some proof that what you say has some truth to it. While your readers still may not agree, perhaps you can win from them a grudging, "Well, I don't really think you are right, but I must admit you do have a point."

To make that point, an essay must have shape. It must have structure—either natural or formal. It must be more than a collection of random ideas strewn across the page with no directing force or control. For all too many of us, this organizing process is our downfall. We have dozens of ideas which languish for want of some sure method to assemble them. Professional writers do not practice some mystical craft beyond our grasp. They do, in a sophisticated way, what most of us can learn to do by following a few simple steps.

Starting Out

Finding a subject

What happens before you start to write is just as important as what happens afterwards. Before you can concentrate seriously on the shape of your writing, you must have something to say. You need a point, a reason to write. Sometimes the point is clearly drawn for you. An instructor may say, "Discuss the problem of teenage alcoholism" or "Contrast the two Shakespearean villains Iago and Edmund." At other times, circumstances define the point. You have the specifics; you need the focus. Sloppy automobile repair work may prompt you to write a complaint to the Better Business Bureau. Problems with a new hiring procedure may require you to write a memo to your boss. Or you may just want to write a letter to your brother congratulating him on his high-school graduation. A sociology teacher might say only, "Write an essay about a major urban problem." Your ancient history professor may say, "Examine some phase of Athenian culture." You must then make the decision whether you will write about rent control or the failure of rapid transit, Aeschylean drama or Plato's Cave. In short, whether your subject is one that is given to you or one you have total freedom to select, you have to have something to write about before you get started.

Narrowing the subject

A natural way to refine a topic would be to start with the general subject you want to write about. When you have the choice, pick a subject that interests you. If you are a sports fan, for instance, you might like to write a paper about athletes. But soccer players and swimmers and boxers and weight lifters, all athletes, need different skills to perform different feats. The notion of "athlete" is simply too big. Therefore, you could narrow it down to one type of athlete—perhaps the football player. But since there are at least twenty-two kinds of football players, twenty-eight NFL teams, a large number of semiprofessional teams, and uncountable numbers of college, high-school, Little League, and backyard sandlot teams, you have to narrow even further to one position, one problem, one phenomenon, or one player:

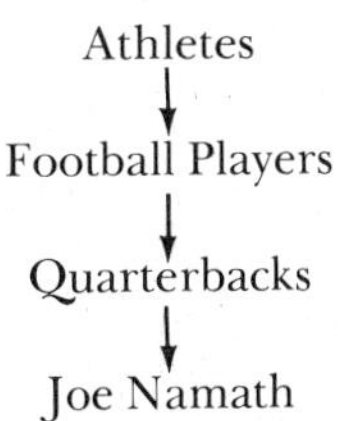

Tracing the subject from general to specific lets you come to grips with a workable subject, one that is tight enough to do justice to the typical 500-word college essay.

If you are a movie nut, you could think about films in the same way, narrowing a topic from the general to the more specific. You can not just write a paper about movies. From *Birth of a Nation* to *Dr. Jekyll and Mr. Hyde,* from Charlie Chaplin to Gary Cooper, there are too many titles, too many actors, too many categories of films to talk about. The subject must be smaller. You might go from films to types of films to particular titles, actors, or directors. For example:

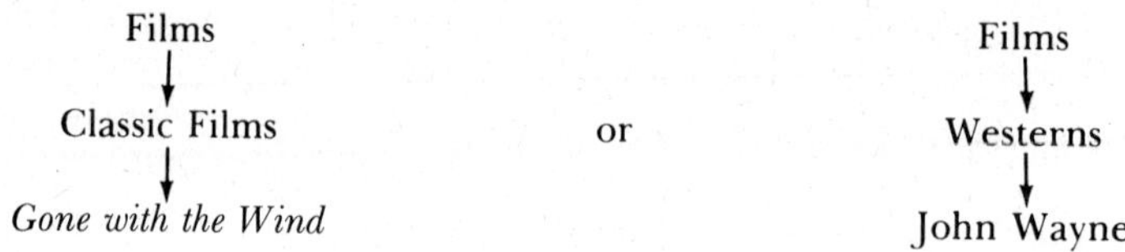

If you stop to think about it, how specific could you be about athletes or films? How specific could you be about government agencies or resorts or trains or architects or mental hospitals? You have to have a sensible plan for shaping a topic. You cannot write a five-hundred-word paper about South African apartheid or the world economy or the American involvement in Iran or Vietnam. There is simply too much to say about each of those topics. Unless you narrow them down to smaller units, they are better subjects for books than they are for five-hundred-word essays.

Focusing the subject

Once you have the subject, you have to ask yourself what you want to say about it. Just as a paragraph needs a focus, so does an essay. Frequently, you have an opinion about a subject when you select it—a basic attitude of approval, disapproval, fear, awe, concern, horror, delight. You should be able to turn this attitude into a focus for your essay. If you disapprove of handguns, you could write an essay advocating banning them. If you are sympathetic to ecologists fighting to protect baby seals, you could write an essay urging an end to such slaughter. If you choose to write about athletes, you could narrow athlete to quarterback and write an essay arguing that good passing skill is the most important ability of a good quarterback. If you go one step further and decide to discuss the specific quarterback Joe Namath, you could write about your respect for his talent as a quarterback despite his many injuries and his colorful, off-the-field personality. If you write about film, your attitude toward *Gone with the Wind* could develop into one paper criticizing its treatment of the Civil War or another praising its memorable casting. John Wayne could prompt an essay on the archetypal western hero just as easily as he could inspire a discussion of his long career as the fulfillment of the American Dream.

Thesis statement. Once you have sharpened your focus, the easiest way to convey it to your readers is to tell them what it is as soon as possible. A paragraph has a topic sentence to focus it; an essay needs a *thesis statement.* (Review Chapter 4's comments on the topic sentence.) A thesis statement is a sentence in the introduction—often the last one—which tells what the essay will be about. It does not simply announce a topic as in, "I would like to talk about Joe Namath." Instead the thesis statement expresses the writer's attitude about the subject. Like the topic sentence, it is a generalization; it cannot be a statement of fact. Declaring that the real name of the asparagus fern is *Asparagus Plumosus* or that Charles Goodyear was the inventor of vulcanized rubber will not focus an essay. The thesis statement makes a generalization, and it presents the attitude which the following paragraphs will develop.

If you have the topic sufficiently narrowed, the thesis statement will sometimes form itself. If you saw *Gone with the Wind* and were impressed with the casting of Clark Gable, Vivien Leigh, Olivia DeHaviland, Leslie Howard, and some others, you might come away thinking:

> *Gone with the Wind* had superb casting.

That thought becomes the basis of a good thesis statement. Later, when you write the essay, as you fuse this sentence with others in the introduction, you could make it stronger or more colorful, paying some heed to concrete language. For example:

> Superb casting contributes to the reputation of *Gone with the Wind* as the greatest movie ever made.

John Wayne's role in westerns leads to a thesis statement in the same way:

> John Wayne is the archetypal western hero.

That sentence would be sufficient to focus an essay. Later, with some polishing, that thesis statement can become:

> In a career that started in the 1930s, John Wayne, maturing from baby-faced ranchhand to craggy, leathery cowboy, has become the archetypal western hero.

The quarterback topics work in the same way:

> The most important skill for a quarterback to have is excellent passing ability.

That basic focus can grow to:

> Although scrambling ability can be a virtue for a quarterback, if he is really to be the engineer of his team's success, a quarterback needs excellent passing ability.

Awe of Joe Namath's abilities as a quarterback may start as:

> Joe Namath was a good quarterback despite his bad knees and his "Broadway Joe" nickname.

But it may later be refined to become:

> Despite a pair of wobbly knees and a playboy reputation, which earned him the nickname "Broadway Joe," Joe Namath managed to become a great NFL quarterback.

Basically, as you focus a paper, try to strike a good balance between an overly general and an overly specific thesis statement. Do not let the thesis statement get so broad so that you try to do too much; do not let it get so narrow that you won't be able to do enough. If you want to write about popular music, you would need to say something more specific than this:

> There are lots of exciting things happening in contemporary music.

In five hundred words, you could not include all you might want to say about disco beats, Moog synthesizers, the Rolling Stones, Olivia Newton-John, and everybody and everything else deserving mention. Yet that same paper focused by this narrow thesis statement would be equally difficult to write:

> Elvis Presley first sang "You Ain't Nothin' but a Hound Dog" in the 1950s.

This statement is a fact; you can't take it much further than this. But you could talk about some phase of popular music by settling on one performer and dealing with one aspect of his or her style or career:

John Denver's natural performing style and his country-boy lyrics made him a favorite American singer of the 1970s.

The great value of any thesis statement is that it fixes the focus for both you and your readers. It plainly tells not only what your subject will be but, almost more importantly, your attitude toward it as well. If you approve of compulsory driver's training or deplore the Panama Canal Treaties, say so right at the beginning. Your thoughts will be sharper and more easily controlled if they have a clear-cut focus crisply presented in the introduction. A well-balanced thesis statement serves as a good springboard into the body of an essay.

Exercises

1. Listed below are several topics which may be too broad for an essay. Examine each one and suggest ways to limit it to become a suitable subject for a five-hundred-word essay.
   a. battleship
   b. light bulb
   c. pollution
   d. food
   e. problems in education
2. Here are several thesis statements. Comment on their effectiveness as concrete, workable thesis statements for a five-hundred-word essay. Rewrite any of them you consider poor.
   a. There is a good reason why the bobcat, found mainly in Montana and the western Rocky Mountains, is being classified as an endangered species.
   b. St. Elizabeth's Hospital is in Washington, D.C.
   c. For a race car driver to be competitive, she must have a loyal and skilled crew before, during, and after the race.
   d. Watergate has had a tremendous economic, social, and political impact on this nation and the world.
   e. The exceptional overall play of the Rams' defense saved them from an embarrassing defeat by the Pittsburgh Steelers.
   f. The federal government should become more involved in the preservation of our nation's historic landmarks.
   g. President Kennedy's actions of the early 1960s must ultimately be blamed for the terrorist activities of Corru, the Cuban secret army based in Miami in the late 1970s.
   h. There are 61,000 Vietnam refugees in America.
   i. The abused child's mother was a waitress.
3. Write thesis statements for the topics you refined in Exercise

1. Try to create a concrete as well as a well-focused statement for each one.
4. Look at some professional essays either in an essay collection or in some current magazines. Try to find the statement of focus in these essays. Be prepared to discuss in class how the author achieved a focus, where it can be found, how specific it is, etc.

Sketching a Framework

Once you have settled on a focus, you can plan the development of the essay. Thinking through a topic is as important as actually writing about it. A good essay needs a good focus backed up with specific evidence. When you wrote paragraphs, you focused each one with a topic sentence and then made a rough list of ideas to support it. The list warned you if you were straying from the focus or if you had insufficient support. (See Chapter 4.) You can build an essay in the same way. You know you have a workable thesis statement when you can make a list of supporting ideas which will develop the focus. Each of these major supports will become a separate paragraph when the essay is developed.

The quality of the essay depends in part on the quality of the support you can muster. To illustrate, suppose, as you casually sauntered into your house one day, your mother confronted you with, "Get upstairs and clean your room; it's a mess!" Convinced of your innocence, you go upstairs, grumbling and muttering. The one "messy" thing you see is an unmade bed. You would challenge that definition of "mess." An unmade bed is hardly enough support for an angry scolding. If you reset the scene another way, it would make a different point. Suppose this time as you sauntered into the house hearing your mother cry out, "Get upstairs and clean your room; it's a mess!" you actually found a "mess"! The bed is unmade, Coke bottles line the dresser, underwear pokes out of dresser drawers, a pair of wet blue jeans muddies up a corner, dirty socks sprawl on the rug, and school books mound high on a cluttered desk. While you may disagree about whether this "mess" needs to be cleaned up, you would have a harder time denying that the room is a mess. This time your mother has lots of support.

If she recorded these opinions, your mother would actually be presenting simple essays; she would be expressing opinions based on a certain measure of support. In the first case, she has too little support for her conclusion:

Focus: **The room is a mess.**
Support Unmade bed

The second time, she has much better support:

Focus: **The room is a mess.**

Supports
- Unmade bed
- Coke bottles on the dresser
- Underwear hanging out of drawers
- Wet blue jeans in the corner
- Dirty socks on the rug
- Books on a cluttered desk

The second position seems more reasonable, more supportable.

Here is another simple illustration. If you own a Honda Civic and are pleased with its economy, you may try to convince your friends to give up their big cars to buy one, too. You might be sitting on your patio or in a bar or a restaurant talking to them, but your conversation could be the rudimentary form of an essay. The thesis statement would be your boast:

My Honda Civic is a fantastically economical car.

As you talk, you would line up the proof. You might rave about the car's good gas mileage, relatively low purchase price, and few repair bills. If you were to jot down the points you made, you would see how naturally an essay can sometimes organize itself. The generalization about the car's overall economy becomes the thesis statement; the list of supports demonstrating that economy becomes the basis for several paragraphs which make up the body of the paper.

Focus: **The Honda Civic is an economical car.**

Supports
- Low initial cost for basic models
  - Price $4500
  - Many accessories included
  - Inexpensive accessories
- Good gas mileage
  - 40 mpg
  - Regular gas
- Low oil consumption
  - 3 quarts/10,000 miles
- Good repair record
  - Low repair rate
  - Easy owner repair
- Low insurance premium

While this example is only a rough listing of supporting ideas for the general focus of "economical," it is a unified discussion of the car's economy. Nothing is out of place; everything furthers the focus of "economy." The generalization has solid support. The unity is tight. There are no digressions about Pintos or Fiats or Volkswagens.

Supporting material, then, joins *focus* as a vital element of an essay. Once you have settled on a subject, jot down some ideas to develop it. These ideas will become the major supports, the body paragraphs which will flesh out the essay. A rough sketch of an essay's content will keep you from slipping into an analysis of characters in Tennessee Williams' *Streetcar Named Desire* if you are trying to write about Laura, the daughter in *The Glass Menagerie.* A sketch would keep you from writing a paper about the poor quality of Sony television sets based on the single bad experience you may have had with one. A list could warn you if the content looks flimsy before you struggle to put it into essay form.

These examples are simple ones, but their purpose is to show that writing an essay can be an easier task if you take some care before you begin to write. Thinking through the topic before you write about it can save you time and anguish later. Although it may seem mechanical and wooden, a sketch will help you give form to your thoughts as individual paragraphs and thus as a whole essay.

Exercises

1. Look back at the topics you narrowed for exercise 1 on page 141, pick two, and develop a rough sketch for each one as an essay.
2. Pick several of the thesis statements in exercise 2 on page 141 and sketch a rough plan for a possible development of each one.
3. Look back at one of the essays you found for exercise 4 on page 142 and make a sketch of the plan of development you think the writer followed.
4. Choose a subject you might be interested in developing into an essay. Develop both a focus and a rough sketch for writing the essay.

Moving from Sketch to Essay

Common sense as much as formal logic says that an essay needs a beginning, a middle, and an end. The quick sketch that you make to convert idea to essay gives you two of these three parts: beginning and middle. The focus fits into the introductory paragraph; the major supports flesh out the body as each one translates into a paragraph. The ending can be a concluding paragraph added to tie up the thoughts which have gone before. A finished essay should actually fit snugly into this structural chart:

Introduction

The introduction frequently begins with a broad generalization and works down to the thesis statement, which focuses the whole essay. See Chapter 7 for introductory strategies.

Body

Paragraph I
- Topic Sentence
  - Major Support
  - Major Support
  - Major Support
  - Major Support

Each paragraph should contain as many *major supports* as are necessary to develop the thought put forth by the topic sentence and as many *minor supports* as are required to amplify the major supports.

Paragraph II
- Topic Sentence
  - Major Support
  - Major Support
  - Major Support

Paragraph III
- Topic Sentence
  - Major Support
  - Major Support
  - Major Support

Continue with as many paragraphs as you need to develop the idea presented in the thesis statement. The topic sentences of the paragraphs should contain the general supports for the thesis statement of the paper.

Conclusion

The conclusion rounds out the essay—perhaps through restatement of the thesis or a summary. See Chapter 7 for some suggestions for concluding an essay.

A working sketch can easily grow into an essay no matter what the simplicity or complexity of the subject. For example, one student wanted to write about some lessons in economics he had learned after buying an old "Bathtub Porsche." He was struck by the irony that he had greedily bought the car because it was such a bargain only to find that it was so expensive to repair and maintain that it was keeping him too poor to enjoy it. He made a list of his major expenses, grouped them together, and used that as a basic sketch for writing the paper.

Focus: **My old "Bathtub Porsche" costs me too much for me to enjoy it.**

Expensive major repairs
Engine $1000
Transmission $800
Car rental during repairs $200
Expensive basic maintenance
Tune-up 10,000 mi. $250
Oil change 5000 mi. 6 cans at $1.00 can
Gas consumption 15 mpg premium
Expensive additional repairs

Muffler/tail pipe	$200
Tires/alignment	$300
Brakes	$200
Paint job	$800

All this expense is keeping me too poor to enjoy the car.

Armed with this sketch, the student was ready to write an essay recounting his experience. The parts of his sketch fit neatly into the larger pattern of an essay in this way:

Introduction Paragraph 1
(Thesis Statement) Focus: **My old "Bathtub Porsche" costs too much for me to enjoy it.**

Body

First Major Support: Paragraph 2
(Topic Sentence) Focus: **Expensive major repairs**
Engine work $1000
Transmission $800
Car rental during repairs $200

Second Major Support: Paragraph 3
(Topic Sentence) Focus: **Expensive basic maintenance**
Tune-up 10,000 mi. $250
Oil change 5000 mi. 6 cans at $1.00 can
Gas consumption 15 mpg premium

Body

Third Major Support: Paragraph 4
(Topic Sentence) Focus: **Expensive additional repairs**

Muffler/tail pipe	$200
Tires/alignment	$300
Brakes	$200
Paint job	$800

Conclusion Paragraph 5
All of this expense is keeping me too poor to enjoy the car.

A reasonable first draft grew out of this rough sketch. After some polishing, the student handed in the following finished essay. Marginal comments highlight the basic parts to show how a carefully sketched writing plan can turn into a nicely structured essay.

Introduction

Last winter Kenny, my mechanic brother-in-law, discovered the "buy of the century" for me. My Ford Falcon had limped its last few miles to the junkyard, and I needed a replacement—fast. He had a friend . . . who had a friend . . . who gave me a "really good deal" on an old yellow "Bathtub Porsche," more properly known as a 1956 Porsche Cabriolet. It was an irresistible item to a foreign car freak like me. Without thinking twice, I bought the car for $1,000. ***Now, one year later, I have discovered, much to my dismay, that trying to maintain this grand old car is an incredible drain on the funds of an impoverished college freshman.*** *(Thesis Statement)*

Body

First Major Support

Soon after I bought the car, I found that my thousand dollar investment in classic car wheels would be totally wasted if I did not replace its engine and transmission. *(Topic Sentence)* Grudgingly, I turned the car over to Kenny who tackled the engine first. *(engine work)* He tinkered and puttered and in two weeks handed me a bill for $1000. But that was just the beginning. The car still could not run very fast or very far without having its transmission rebuilt. *(transmission)* Again, Kenny buried himself under the hood. And again, in two weeks, he reemerged. This time, though, he not only gave me a bill (just $800 this time), but he also gave me the keys to a car that ran beautifully. Of course I still had to pay the $200 it cost me to rent a car while Kenny was repairing my "new one." *(car rental)*

Second Major Support

My delight in my golden chariot was short-lived. **Now that the car was running smoothly, I had another lesson to learn about Porsches—the cost of maintenance.** A tune-up every 10,000 miles is not unusual, but a tune-up for a Porsche is. What with platinum spark plugs and special points, my regular tune-up bill is $250. Also, I have to change the oil every 5000 miles. Six cans of oil at $1.00 a can quickly add up to more than I would like—even if I buy the oil by the case. And one can't overlook the gasoline that the car gobbles with far too much regularity. Fifteen miles per gallon on premium gasoline keeps me feeding my dates hamburgers instead of steaks.

Topic Sentence — *tune-up* — *oil change* — *gas consumption*

Third Major Support

Perhaps the most painful part of my experience is that it is not yet over. **If I am to keep my beloved car, I cannot run it much longer without plunging into the list of additional repairs which my good brother-in-law has kindly itemized for me.** It badly needs a new muffler and tail pipe, no doubt at least a $200 job. The car not only sounds like a dragster, it leaks carbon monoxide. Fortunately summer is still here, and I can keep the windows open. Before next winter comes I also need four new tires to replace the bald doughnuts on which I now skid around. Between tires and alignment, I will spend another $300. Then there are the new brakes, another priority item at $200. And if I am really going to make all of this worthwhile, I guess I will have to break down and get the car a new paint job. That alone is a cool $600.

Topic Sentence — *muffler/tail pipe* — *tires/alignment* — *brakes* — *paint job*

Conclusion

Overall, I am not sure that my great bargain was worth the money. Since I am a full-time student, my part-time income of $50 a week is regularly burnt up by the pressing needs of my Porsche just to keep it sputtering about. Adding up the $1000 I paid to buy it, the $400-a-year insurance premium I pay to drive it, the $2000 I spent to repair it, the $1500 I have yet to invest to guarantee that it will haul me about safely, I have already spent $4900 for a car that is probably more of a status symbol than I need at this point in my life. I keep telling Kenny that I should have bought a used Pinto or something, but he just smiles. To be quite honest, I can't quite tell whether he is smiling with pleasure at the fact that there is now a very collectible car in the family or at the fact that he has just bought a new motorcycle with all the money he has earned from me. The only thing I am sure of is that **putting all of this money into this old relic is keeping me too poor to enjoy it.**

Some Qualities of a Good Essay

Although its subject is simple, the essay about the Porsche exhibits many of the basic qualities of a good essay. Structure and content work together to present a tightly organized discussion. Its general structure is clear cut. The introduction sets the scene recounting the purchase of the car with *who* and *why* and leading up to the problem of owning an expensive Porsche; the thesis statement clearly makes the point that the writer will talk about: how the car is a drain on his finances. The individual paragraphs of the body develop different aspects; each paragraph supports the thesis statement. The conclusion offers a wrap-up summary which totals everything in dollar signs and fixes the perspective of the full-time student with a part-time job trying to support an expensive car.

The paragraph structure in the essay is key to its being well developed as an essay. Good paragraphs make good essays. Each of the body paragraphs is well developed. Each has a focusing topic sentence limiting its discussion to one of the three areas of expense—major repairs, basic maintenance, and extra repairs. Each offers very specific support for its focus with engines and transmissions, tune-ups and oil changes, and tires and brakes. If each paragraph has a strong topic sentence and strong major supports which further the essay's thesis statement, the body of the essay will be solid and well developed.

The language of this essay is also striking in its economy and specificity. The diction is slightly informal, which fits the subject and the writer well. Words and phrases are concrete. Many strong nouns laced with modifiers—*Ford Falcon, platinum spark plugs,* and *bald doughnuts*—work with strong verbs such as *limped, tinkered,* and *skid* to carry the images. Specific details and examples fill the paragraphs to reconstruct this experience as the student perceived it and not as the reader necessarily would wish it.

Finally, the mechanical elements of the essay are quite respectable. The paragraphs have good sentence variety and ample subordination. The sentences are grammatically correct with no fragments, run-on sentences, or comma splices. Grammar and punctuation problems are not a visible concern in the essay and do not interrupt the essay with misspellings or dangling particples.

This essay is just one of many kinds of essays that you can write, but its structure is basic to almost any writing assignment you may undertake. Your essay should reflect the same several levels of structure that this one meets: essay, paragraph, sentence, language, and mechanics. If your essay does a good job on each of those levels, you will probably have a very effective piece of writing.

Exercises

1. Examine the professional essays you selected for earlier exercises for some of the organizational qualities of a good essay. Examine each for general essay structure, paragraph structure, sentence structure, language, and mechanics.
2. Choose one of the subjects for which you had prepared a rough sketch in an earlier exercise and expand that sketch into an actual essay.
3. Be prepared to comment upon the manner in which your own essay meets the criteria of structure of essay, paragraphs, and sentences. In class swap papers with another student and judge each other's papers for these organizational qualities.

Chapter Exercises

1. Look at the following rough sketches which have been used to write essays. Either individually or in a small group, discuss the focus and supports to determine whether or not a well-developed essay could grow out of the sketch as it is offered. Do the supports seem to fill out the focus; is the focus adequate for expansion into an essay? If necessary, suggest how to make these sketches more functional.

   a. *Focus:* **A well-planned move can save time, money, and a lot of headaches**

      Preparation
      - Putting small things in boxes
      - Wrapping fragile things well
      - Breaking down anything that can be reduced to smaller pieces
      - Packing and marking boxes

      General advice
      - Stay out of movers' way
      - Bring small things yourself

Notice scratches, etc., before moving
Make sure walkways, etc., are cleared
Arrival in new home
Know where furniture should go
Create storage space for boxes
Know where boxes should go to be available as needed

b. *Focus:* **Performing as a concert pianist**
Very demanding
A lot of dedication and desire
Mental and physical drain
No social life

c. *Focus:* **Working for director who casts two actors in the same roles**
Have less time for each person
Have less time to help individual
Have less time to help group
People start to fight
Need no understudy
Fewer performances

2. Either separately or in a small group, cast yourself in the role of teacher/grader and analyze the effectiveness of the short essays presented here for the quality of their focus and development. Use the Chapter Checklist to recall the main points of structure. Make suggestions of what should be done to solve the problems of form and development in the papers. You might also comment on any other strengths or weaknesses in paragraph and sentence structure, language use, and mechanics.

a. Gym has always been one of my best subjects in school, especially now that my class is on volleyball. And everyone is friendly, interesting, and nice to be with.

The students in class blend nicely and are well-mannered. They vary in ages and curriculums. Most of them are students that just came out of high school and there are others that came back to college because they couldn't finish attending school for some reason or people that are almost finished. I've always admired people who came back or go back to school to get a higher education even though if one of the classes they're coming to is just a gym class.

Even though I'm not the most athletic or the best volleyball player, I still love playing it. Since this class was designed for better skills and more knowledge or understanding of the rules, I feel like I'm getting better. I've learned more rules that I didn't know before, and my arm muscles are stronger. Now I can say that I serve, bump, and set the ball the way it's supposed to be done.

The team I'm on is made up of beautiful and interesting people, especially John who is very talented young man. He is a very athletic guy and knows how to do everything there is to do in a volleyball game. For a guy who is not over 5 ft. 10 inches tall and not big, he can spike so hard people couldn't tell what had happened. Whenever he wears yellow it makes him look even better because it blends in well with his light brown curly hair and dark brown eyes. One can see if he is upset with something because he is always smiling. He is a very friendly person, it's easy to like him.

I'm going to miss all of the people in my volleyball class when the semester is over. And I hope I see them again in the future. But I'm still going to like and play volleyball in school. It gives me something to look forward to after Sunday is gone.

b. For many years Americans have avoided the problems of the elderly. We have focused our attentions on what we thought to be more important matters. We seem to have forgotten who has kept this country in existence. But more important, where our heritage came from. Today, we find this problem an ever growing one.

Because of their age, the elderly are forced to retire. To live on a fixed income established by our Social Security System. Many of which are still able to work. Most of the elderly own their own home. Society tells them unless the home meets "our standards of suitable living conditions," it will be condemned. Many of them have little or no money for these repairs. They are sometimes forced to sell.

Children lack respect for the elderly. In the family environment, they are often regarded as senile and their advice is usually disregarded. Since they are unable to protect and defend themselves, we find them victims of crime. Kids especially enjoy stealing from them.

No one knows better than the elderly how it feels to be lonely. We have taught them that once they reach a certain age. Life stops! No longer is it important for us to visit that mother or grandmother. We have classified and forgotten them.

It is time we realized the place of the elderly. Because of

their wisdom, knowledge, and many years of experience they are the backbone of this country. Taking advantage of these qualities would provide our younger generations with a sense of pride and direction. Wake up America! The elderly have paid their dues. Let us pay ours.

c. The white smoke curled upwards from the apostolic palace at St. Peter's square in Rome, announcing the election of a new pope. This was October 16, 1978, and by now most of the people of the world have come to recognize the face of the new pope. For the first time in four hundred fifty-seven years, a non-Italian pope has been elected. His name is Karol Wojtyla, a Pole Cardinal who took the name of Pope John Paul II. Pope John Paul II is a man with many facets to his character, a man who is so versatile that he is now being called a "Renaissance Pope."

To call him a "Renaissance Pope" is a great compliment, but it is given to a man who truly deserves it. Pope John Paul II is a poet in his own right with his books being published in both English and Polish! Long-playing records of his songs are selling so fast, that the shops are having a hard time keeping them in stock! Karol Wojtyla has been an actor, a playwright, a stone-quarry worker, an athlete, a philosopher, and a pastor. All these attributes have now fused together to "produce" a man who will long be remembered in history.

By sheer strength of personality, Pope John Paul II has proved to be one of the best leaders the world has ever seen. He is respected by many. Proof of this is his invitation to speak at the United Nations. There, in the fall of 1979, he gave a soul-searching talk by telling the nations of the world to be more conscious of their role in this world. Pope John Paul II told these nations to take a more realistic approach to the poor of the world. He also acted as a peace mediator when he went to Ireland to try to help bring this divided country to the path of peace. Karol Wojtyla proved his courage when he went to his native country, to Poland, where he spoke out against any system of government which inhibits the religious freedom of the people. There, he let the world and the Polish people get a glimpse of the vulnerability, or rather love, he has for his native Poland.

As seen, Karol Wojtyla has played many roles in his life, but without any doubt the greatest role he has ever been asked to take is to be the Shepherd to his Christian flock. The greatest impact he has made is with the Catholics of the world. Finally, the Catholics have found a leader whom they can look up to. Pope John Paul II has inspired in his followers a new sense of faith. He has not made any revolutionary changes in the church; rather he has enforced what is already there. He is using discipline tempered with love. At last a pope can be seen as a human being with feelings, not just a figurehead locked up in the Vatican fortress. Pope John Paul II has come out amongst the people of the world. He has come out like the Shepherd did, thousands of years ago in Jerusalem. Pope Wojtyla preaches love and shows it on every occasion especially with the young and helpless. These are the people who need the most guidance and something to believe in. Not only Catholics have come to revere and respect this great pope but also people of other faiths like the Jews and the Protestants. The Catholic church is receiving the "shaking" it needed. From now on Catholics are going to find out that being a Catholic is not an easy thing. They are going to have to make sacrifices for their faith.

I had great personal satisfaction when this pope was elected. To me, the Catholic Church had reached a crucial time, where some change was needed. I felt that this was the time this "change" was going to happen. I was right. I felt overjoyed! Karol Wojtyla was elected! For better or for worse, things were going to start happening! When I heard that the pope was coming to my "doorstep," so to speak, I could not resist the temptation to go and see him. I was not disappointed. Hallelujah God has at last noticed our predicament and decided to do something about it! Hallelujah AGAIN!

3. As a class or as a small group, select a topic suitable for a five-hundred-word essay. Together, devise a focus for it and sketch a possible body to develop the paper. Then, let each individual in the group develop the paper as he or she sees fit while following the basic, agreed-upon format. Compare development later to see how the essays differ internally.
4. Choose one of the simple topics suggested below and write an essay of your own. Narrow the subject, frame a thesis statement, sketch a rough outline for the body, and write the paper. Be sure to end up with at least five paragraphs of at least five sentences each. Pay attention to the points listed in the Chapter Checklist. Make marginal comments as were made on the essay on the "Bathtub Porsche" to indicate

thesis statement, topic sentences, supports, and also methods of development.
a. Describe the personality or the physical features of someone you know well. Try to make the reader see the person as you perceive him or her.
b. Discuss the singing style or performing style of a rock group, individual singer, actor, athlete. For example, Mick Jagger, Aretha Franklin, Paul Newman.
c. Explain why you liked some film, book, or television program you have seen recently.
d. Do a causal analysis of the success or failure of your favorite professional or college football, basketball, or baseball team during its last season: offense, defense, strengths, and weaknesses.
e. Write a paper in which you describe the kind of training you need to become something specialized—anything from doctor to lawyer to bulldozer operator.

Chapter Checklist

1. Narrow the subject sufficiently to allow it to be concretely developed in the space allotted—two hundred, five hundred, or a thousand words.
2. Include a beginning, a middle, and an end: introduction, body, and conclusion.
3. Express the focus of an essay in a thesis statement, usually at the end of the introduction, to sum up your attitude or point of view toward your subject.
4. The body of an essay should contain several well-developed paragraphs, each containing a topic sentence, several major supporting sentences, and minor supporting sentences as needed.
5. Conclude an essay with a suitable finish that ties up all the trains of thought presented in the introduction and body.

Strengthening Essays

Essays emerge in different ways—sometimes carefully thought out, sometimes hastily or clumsily jotted. No matter what your individual style, the preceding chapter presented the germ of good essay form, advice to nurture both confidence and skill. The narrowed subject and the working sketch translate into a rough but definable essay. The eventual power of an essay will depend mightily on the quality of these basic parts.

But an essay's vitality also depends on the brisk pace of the introduction, the smooth coherence of the middle section, and the decisive cutting off of a thought once it has reached proper proportions. This chapter will go beyond the basics—to refine and polish the separate pieces, to smooth out the edges. Such refining requires that you have a conscious awareness of the subtle touches that will heighten your focus and development. Beginnings, middles, and endings, all important parts of a paper, rely on different tactics for different effects. Conscious selection of one strategy over another is part of your decision of the best means of making your message clear and convincing; effective delivery depends on the manner in which the supports are structured. Then, in revising, individual paragraphs must be fussed with and worried over to get the message just right. The result of this careful attention will be a powerful statement, a strengthened essay that does justice to the ideas that set it in motion in the first place.

Starting, Connecting, Stopping

Beginnings and endings of papers are important, often neglected, parts, but they are not mere tricks of padding. And since paragraphs do not automatically connect, transitions between them are important too; they are not just cosmetic ornaments. Each part serves a useful purpose—to introduce, to connect, to conclude. Everything you write should help your readers, but a poor start can lose them, missing connections may confuse them, and a flat conclusion may leave them with an unfinished, so-what feeling.

Beginnings

Preach to your readers, scold them, or make them laugh, but give yourself a fighting chance to get their attention. Not only does an essay need a beginning, it needs a strong beginning. Too often we take our readers for granted and write as if they weren't even there. Not every introduction has to be a masterpiece of zinging prose. There are many times when you will not want to be humorous or cute. But the introduction that carries its weight well is the one that contains concrete language and a sharp focus no matter what the mood. And a good introduction is limited; it just introduces, without plunging into the content of the body. With a little care, a dose of imagination, and some concrete language, a good introduction will give your essay a vigorous start.

The inverted paragraph. The *inverted,* or *funnel, paragraph* is so common that it is almost a cliché as far as introductions go. It is, however, a workhorse that gets the job done. The inverted paragraph begins with a generalization and narrows down to the more specific focus of the essay.

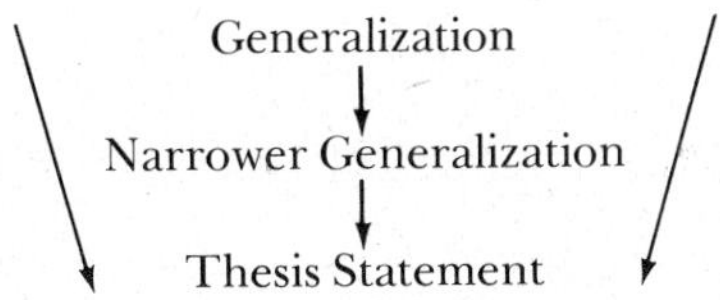

The following introduction to a comparison/contrast essay about Alice Cooper and Kiss is an example of the inverted paragraph.

> Some rock stars have established themselves more as showmen than as musical artists. To fill concert halls or arenas, these groups and

> individuals have relied more on flashy visual effects than on their ability to produce coherent music. This practice has attracted many critics, but it has also attracted people who are willing to pay a lot of money to watch and sometimes listen. Alice Cooper was one of the first rock stars to do this, and he has been doing it for about ten years now. Kiss, a group that has been around a few years, has also been very successful with their rock show. **But these two rock phenomena present their rock shows very differently.**

As you can see, the introduction begins with the generalization:

> Some rock stars have established themselves more as showmen than as musical artists.

It narrows further to the statements about the two performers to be compared:

> Alice Cooper was one of the first. . . . Kiss . . . has also been very successful. . . .

It then proceeds to the thesis statement itself:

> **But these two rock phenomena present their rock shows very differently.**

This process of narrowing down to a focus is similar to the one you use to select a topic for the essay initially. To discuss the worth of the new Dodge pickup, you could begin by mentioning America's truck craze; narrow that down to pickups in general; and then focus on the Dodge pickup in particular. If you wish to talk about the catacombs crumbling in Rome, start the introduction with a broader reference to the lives of the early Christians; move on to their reasons for using catacombs; and then focus the essay with your comment about the catacombs today. The process is a simple matter of reduction:

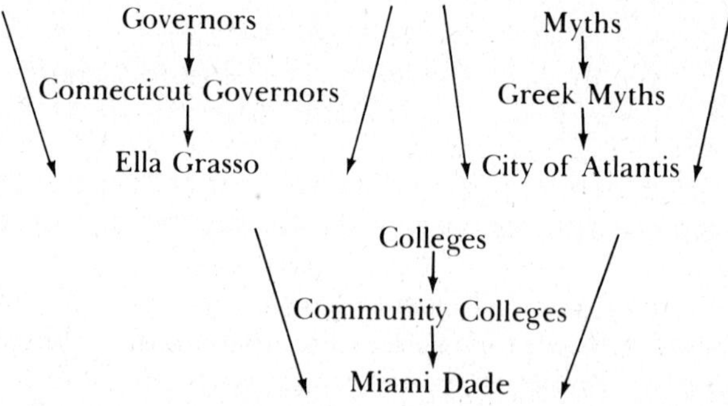

The funnel paragraph can get boring if you overuse it, but its ease of structure makes it a common, workable approach to organizing an introduction. It is especially valuable for the beginning writer looking for a proven formula. Sometimes, though, the generalizations threaten the inverted paragraph with vagueness or dullness. In that case, some conscious dressing up can keep it an effective tactic. Two versions of the same introduction can illustrate this difference.

Both opening paragraphs below introduce an essay about the gimmicks and tricks cigarette advertisers use to con people into buying their products. The original looked like this:

> Manufacturers advertise to sell their products. Most of the time, their ads are deceptive. They use logical fallacies to get the public to buy their products. **Cigarette manufacturers are no exception; they use statistics, slogans, and technical jargon to sell their cigarettes.**

The basic structure is adequate. The introduction begins with a generalization about manufacturers and narrows down to the more specific focus of cigarette ads. But the paragraph is flat, vague, and uninteresting—barely hinting at the richness of the subject of advertisers as con artists. Revised with the special intent of making it more concrete, this paragraph grows fuller and more interesting:

> Manufacturers must advertise to sell their products. Each one, from the makers of panty hose to hair dye to cat food, plies us with bright colors and pretty faces to form ads which are, from time to time, deceptive. Sometimes the hapless consumer is besieged by the "un-Cola" or sometimes by Morris the Cat or sometimes by the impressive sounding statistics of 99 percent fewer cavities. Whatever insults to our collective logic are found in the gimmicks, these ads work to convince us, the moneyed public, to buy something we often do not need. **Banned from television, cigarette manufacturers fill the pages of magazines with statistics, slogans, and technical jargon to sell their products.**

Like the original, the revision is sound in structure. It moves from the generalization about most advertisers down to the more specific focus of deception in cigarette ads. But this introduction uses details and examples to fill out the original generalizations. Un-Cola and cat food have a lot in common: They are both concrete images which help the reader see what the writer has in mind when accusing advertisers of betraying the public. Used moderately, the details add flavor to this introduction without disturbing its basic function.

Whatever the content, the standard introductory format of the inverted paragraph will serve you well as a solid standby. When you feel more confident, though, to give your introductions more flair or greater depth, you might try any of the several other devices given below. Keep in mind, however, that concrete language is the backbone of any introduction, no matter what the format.

A surprising, interesting, shocking, or amusing fact. Starting the paper with a startling or striking fact about the topic or some closely related subject can give a needed jolt to a beginning. For instance, an essay dealing with relationships between men and women might start with a statement such as:

> Dr. Samuel Vega-Romero has found that in a male-female relationship, the man starts nine out of every eleven arguments.

A paper about the decline or the reemergence of religion might begin with this fact:

> There are 950,550,000 Christians in the world.

An argument debating capital punishment might start with a detail such as:

> The first electrocution of a criminal took place in Auburn Prison in Auburn, New York, on August 6, 1890.

Facts such as these catch a reader's interest. This introduction to an essay about Thomas Jefferson's ideas on slavery gives an example:

> Thomas Jefferson was the father of several illegitimate children borne by a slave girl. So says Fawn Brodie, author of a respected biography of Jefferson. If this is true, it is difficult, at the distance of two centuries later, to understand the basic dichotomy that lies behind that fact. Thomas Jefferson was the Father of the Declaration of Independence and the Constitution, and he favored the abolition of slavery—in theory. **In practice he was still very much a southern slaveholder exercising the master's right of property over the people he owned.**

An appropriate quotation. Citing a pertinent quotation, either as a lead in to the introduction or in the midst of it, is another good way to begin an essay. A paper on the irony of the American involvement in Vietnam might begin with this quotation from one of Lyndon Johnson's 1964 presidential campaign speeches:

> We don't want our American boys to do the fighting for Asian boys.

An essay about the role of monarchy in the modern world might begin with the Shakespearean quote:

> Uneasy lies the head that wears the crown.

A review of a play might start with a quotation from the play or from a critic's response to it. If you were to write a critical paper about Shaw's *Mrs. Warren's Profession,* you might begin with some comments from the *New York Herald*'s 1905 review of the play:

> "The lid" was lifted by Mr. Arnold Daly and "the limit" of stage indecency reached last night in the Garrick Theatre in the performance of one of Mr. George Bernard Shaw's "unpleasant comedies" called *Mrs. Warren's Profession.*

A quotation can be slipped into an introduction easily. For example, here is the beginning of a paper discussing the American space program:

> "One small step for a man, one giant leap for mankind." On a summer's eve in 1969, Neil Armstrong's words echoed to us as we were watering our lawns, playing tennis, or eating French fries at a fast-food restaurant. The United States had achieved the impossible, the incredible. We had placed a man on the moon. But now that a decade has passed, the space program is languishing. Cape Kennedy and the Houston Space Center have wound down. Highly trained engineers and technicians are unemployed. **Our space program, the charmed offspring of the Eisenhower and Kennedy administrations, is in serious trouble.**

Quotations can work just as well after the introduction begins:

> The Mamas and the Papas, the Moody Blues, and Johnny Ray were once all common household words as familiar as Ajax and Brillo. As Andy Warhol once said, though, "In the world of popular music, everybody is famous for just fifteen minutes." But sometimes a Bing Crosby or a Frank Sinatra will fix himself firmly in our musical imaginations. Such was the case with Elvis Presley, the king of rock and roll for twenty-two years. From his part-time singing days as a Memphis truck driver to the undisputed sway he held in the world of rock music, **Elvis Presley gyrated and crooned his way into our hearts and our souls with a style that no rival could ever equal.**

An anecdote. Recounting an anecdote, whether comic, satiric, or serious, can also launch a good introduction. An anecdote is a very short account of an incident or event. While it is longer than most quotations or facts, the anecdote would blend into an introduction in the same way. Here, for example, is an introduction built on an anecdote:

> My sister and I, ages eight and six, walked down to the market one evening and found a cardboard box filled with cupcakes and fruit pies sitting outside the store. Never suspecting that the pies were simply waiting to be carried *inside,* we assumed that such booty was *outside* awaiting its fate on the trash truck. Gleefully, we stuffed our mouths with chocolate and blueberry. We had no sooner returned home and walked in the front door, when our mother, standing by the telephone talking to the storekeeper, inspected our sticky fingers and the brown and blue smudges on our lips. Needless to say, with reddened bottoms, we marched back to that store with our next three weeks' allowances to pay for the pilfered goods. We were aghast to learn that our logical deduction hadn't been so logical after all. In the eyes of the world we were thieves. Such was the discipline of times past. **Now, beleaguered by the advice of Spock, Gesell, Dodson Fitzhugh, and *Better Homes and Gardens,* I wonder, as the mother of two young children, what should be the discipline of times present.**

This next example uses an extended jest in an anecdotal way:

> Once a rabbi, on a certain wondrous occasion, actually saw God. On his return, the people and the press clamored to be told what God looked like. For a while, he resisted all attempts to pry his secret knowledge out of him, but finally, reluctantly, he agreed to tell them. "Well . . . ," he said, "to begin with . . . she's black." While we laugh at the joke, behind it is something not quite so laughable. **This jokester found a very effective way to challenge religious, racial, and sexual stereotypes all at one time.**

A stereotype. Using an exaggerated or stereotypic version of an idea, a concept, or a person to begin a paper lets you point out its illogic boldly and clearly, thus making it easier for you to demolish. For example:

> The motorcycle rider is a perverted and sinister Hell's Angel with no manliness other than that drawn from his chrome and metal monster, his leather jacket, his swagger, his swearing, and his tatooed arms. He swings tire chains with great proficiency, rapes old ladies for sport, and drinks rotgut whiskey straight from the bottle. He is of a violent breed dedicated to wreaking havoc upon the otherwise orderly progression of normal people's lives. But this villainous rogue is not alone

> on his snorting steed. He now has lots of competition. **Because of the energy crisis, an army of mild-mannered men in suits and ties have parked their Ford station wagons and mounted motorcycles.**

Here is another example using the same technique:

> The pregnant woman is thought to be a fragile piece of china and is treated as if she were a pariah of some sort. She shouldn't ski or ride bicycles or climb mountains or paint furniture in preparation for the blessed event. She is counseled by well-meaning persons of both sexes to eat for two, to lounge about watching television, and, in general, to turn into a blimp with two wobbly stumps for legs. She should become, in short, Sylvia Plath's "melon with two tendrils." But except for a few hardship cases, this frailty is a myth. **The pregnant woman is capable of doing almost anything the nonpregnant woman or man can do—maybe better.**

Introductions can put on many faces. Picking the best one for any given essay sometimes depends on your own mood as much as the subject or the circumstance. Sometimes you want to shock, so you dredge up some astounding statistics; at other times you settle for a comical stereotype instead. Use both your imagination and your good sense to make a choice that tailors introduction to essay. But don't strain too hard. If you can't find a quote or a story or a fact, you can always rely on the more convenient funnel paragraph to zero in on your focus. And keep an eye on length. You certainly need more than one or two sentences to get you started, but rarely, for a five-hundred-word essay, will you need more than one well-developed paragraph.

Transitions: connections

Several paragraphs which shift from one idea to another make up the body of an essay. You may be moving from a general discussion to a more specific one; you may be analyzing a situation and illustrating it with examples. Whatever your internal plan, you need transitional connectives to link paragraphs into an essay just as you used transitional markers inside a paragraph to show the relationship between sentences. As a matter of fact, since the tactics are similar, you should reread the pages in Chapter 4 on paragraph coherence as well as follow the advice given here. Simply starting a new paragraph will not guarantee an easing of one thought into the next. Sometimes you need to draw on one of the following devices to bridge the two.

Transitional phrases. You can use simple transitional phrases to connect one body paragraph to the next, just as you use them to connect sentences. Words such as "first, second, third," "however," and "consequently" help paragraphs cohere one to the next.

Overt transition. Sometimes the focus itself will arrange the transition by dividing the content in advance. For instance, a thesis statement might say this:

> Each act of Christopher Marlowe's *Dr. Faustus* progressively contributes to the fall of Faust, the tragic hero.

Each body paragraph could discuss successively one of the five acts and the gradual contribution of each to the destruction of the hero as Faust falls deeper into sin. The transition would be built in and might not need any actual words to announce it. This kind of transition is best since it is the most natural.

Repetition. Sometimes repetition of a word, phrase, or thought between the end of one paragraph and the beginning of another will connect them. If you are discussing your parents' traits, you may write a paragraph detailing your mother's tendency to scrimp and save. The concluding line of the paragraph might be something like this:

> There were times when we thought Mother was downright stingy.

The next paragraph, describing your father, might begin by picking up that theme in a contrasting way:

> But if Mother was stingy, Father was the exact opposite.

Order. Often the natural order of a subject provides the transition. This is true for both paragraph and essay, so you might reread the section in Chapter 4 on paragraph order for a fuller account. In brief, though, in relating an event, the chronological sequence of its parts would separate the paragraph units while simultaneously connecting them. It makes good sense to talk about the beginning, then the middle, and then the end of a battle or a swimming meet or a protest march or a poem. In the same way, if you were giving a detailed description of a place—a theme park such as Six Flags over Georgia, for instance, or a concentration camp such as Dachau—you might well let the spatial order direct the transitions for you. In that way you could talk about one area or one phase of the park or the camp at a time, fully detailing it before going on to the next.

For subjects not descriptive or narrative, you can often rely on the logical order of a topic. Listing reasons why private schools should or should not receive state and federal aid, enumerating the dangers of the present system of atomic waste disposal, analyzing the causes of the Veterans' Bonus March on Washington in the 1930s—all demand a logical approach geared at presenting the most important information either first or last.

Paragraph transition can be achieved in a number of ways. The choice depends upon content, circumstance, style, and, as always, good sense. If transitions are too visible or clatter too loudly, they will distract from the essay rather than quietly further it. If they are missing, the essay could be wooden and stiff. Repetition, order, transitional phrases, and content will all assist subtly in the smooth conveyance of ideas. In a longer paper, there may even be times when a whole paragraph will itself serve as a transitional device. However you ultimately connect the parts, try to achieve the same even flow that you find outlined in the essay on the old Porsche in Chapter 6. Transition there comes both through content and through connecting phrases. The first body paragraph outlines basic repairs. The second paragraph discusses the expense of keeping it running even after repairs have been made. The third ponders future costs. Each new paragraph uses transitional phrases to provide a reference to the subject matter of the previous paragraph:

Paragraph 1: Soon after I bought the car, ...
Paragraph 2: My delight . . . was short lived.
Paragraph 3: . . . experience is . . . not yet over.

Each body paragraph flows smoothly, one into the next, because of the quiet service of its transition.

Endings

Strong endings are as vital and as varied as strong beginnings. They can be mangy and mean, soft-spoken and delicate, comic, satiric, or sad. Their main purpose is to conclude, to end, to tie together all that has gone before—and to do it, if possible, with style. A good concluding paragraph appropriate to the essay you have written will in some way restate or refer to the introductory focus vigorously and concretely. It is far more than a simple repetition of words used before. To illustrate, here are two versions of the conclusion to the essay on advertising mentioned earlier. The original was very flat and straightforward:

> Cigarette ads contain several fallacies. These fallacies are used to prompt the public to buy their products. These fallacies are deceptive. People continue to buy cigarettes, so manufacturers continue to use faulty logic in their ads.

Strictly speaking, this conclusion more or less does what it should. Even without having read the whole essay, you can surmise that this paragraph ties up a discussion of deception in cigarette advertising in a neat package by restating the thesis. But like the original introduction of this essay, the conclusion is too general and uninteresting. Its summary is bland and obvious. In fact, its last sentence simply restates what has already been stated in the first two sentences. There is not one specific image in the whole paragraph. The conclusion falls flat; it is both too dull and too brief.

The revised version of this conclusion duplicates content but pays more attention to language:

> The result of this circus of illogic in the marketplace is a calculated attempt by each of the cigarette manufacturers to cajole, persuade, flatter, threaten, or convince the would-be cigarette smoker to buy its specific product. The beautiful people, the woodland streams, the meadows, and the black eyes are all rigged ways of bribing the smoker into forgetting the potential danger involved in cigarette smoking. To tell the truth would be too risky. After all, there's no harm in a little white lie . . . is there?

With specific detail, more sophisticated phrasing, and the punch of verbs such as *cajole, persuade, flatter, threaten,* and *convince,* this conclusion ends the essay with a bang rather than the proverbial whimper. A richness of language which the first version lacked adds another dimension and elminates the need to resort to a mere restatement of the thesis.

There are almost as many methods for ending an essay as there are for starting one; a few of the more common ones are discussed below. If you keep in mind that concrete language is important in an ending, too, you can conclude a paper in any one of the following ways.

Summary. Summarizing the major thoughts presented in a paper is the most common ending, although sometimes it is the weakest. If handled well, though, the summary can be more than a non-end. It can be a valuable means of recapping a long, complicated argument in need of summation of its several parts. Here is such a conclusion, taken from an essay describing the methodic and ingenious cruelty and dehumanization in German concentration camps:

> Hemmed in by the electric barbed wire and the keen surveillance of the strict Nazis, the prisoners faced an unavoidable death. The process of elimination was comprehensive. It began with the convoy "grave trains"; persisted with starvation, fatigue, and sickness; climaxed with barbaric medical experiments, hangings, and shootings; and ended with mass extermination attempts. The weaker ones died first, but in the end the result was the same. Death was only a question of time. How could the deportees hope to live when there were so many ways to die?

Climactic arrangement. Arranging points climactically throughout the entire paper gives good tension to certain types of argumentative or informative papers. Then, the final point, which is occasionally the most important, can be used as a last or clinching paragraph. Here is the last paragraph of an essay which traced the effects of the carelessness and inconsiderateness of cigarette smokers. The essay discussed several aspects of damage to public and private property, such as burned draperies and upholstery, and concluded with the harmful impact on the general health of others:

> Finally, cigarette smoke can actually harm the health of others. Some nonsmokers suffer an allergic reaction to smoke. It irritates their eyes, making them water and burn. While the dangers of more serious diseases such as lung, throat, and mouth cancer are not as great for those who do not smoke, the nonsmoker who is repeatedly closeted with smokers in unventilated rooms incurs the same health hazards as they do because of the pollution. The most common annoyance that most nonsmokers experience, however, is the general feeling of discomfort when surrounded by a fog of smoke. Certainly, every person has a right to be as concerned or unconcerned about his or her own health as he or she wishes. However, just as they have no right to burn cigarette holes into the draperies and seats of art galleries or concert halls, smokers have no right to disregard the health of others.

Interpretation/evaluation. A valuable method for ending a paper is the interpretation or evaluation of facts, ideas, or arguments which have been presented in the essay. This device gives you an opportunity to refine your position, to explain it further, and to endow it with meaning. Here is a sample conclusion of this sort taken from an essay defending the offer of amnesty to Vietnam draft evaders and deserters:

> These are the questions the American people must ponder in the leisure of peace. We must examine our motives and be sure decisions are not based on vindictiveness or a need to "even the score." President Carter is right. We must try to put the past behind us and understand people of all persuasions so that we can base our decisions on humanitarian compassion. Precedents will be set and the consequences carried down through history. With the seeds of war lying fallow over the earth, does it cause such great harm to make a peace offering to draft dodgers and deserters? This question will be asked again . . . and again . . . and again through successive deadly harvests.

Consequences. Suggesting consequences, causes, solutions, or perhaps even a moral is an approach similar to interpretation. It lets the conclusion act as a kind of springboard into the unknown. However, while assessing consequences or causes, be careful not to introduce new or unrelated material. You want this conclusion to be an end, not another beginning. Here is a sample conclusion taken from a paper discussing the phenomenon begun a few years ago when Burt Reynolds posed for a nude centerfold in *Cosmopolitan* magazine:

> After the shocking first plunge into equality in nudity was taken, men and women alike could catch their breaths and begin to anticipate the further ramifications of this action. Women's Liberation has gained new momentum and, yes, dignity. The death knell was sounded for the male double standard of sex, and women are now recognized for the lusty, sensuous, sex-loving people they are. As more Helen Gurley Browns and Burt Reynoldses are lured from their "respectable" hideouts, the new freedom will flourish and blossom. Indeed, true sexual equality has come upon halcyon days.

A pertinent quotation. A quotation at the beginning of a paper helps set a tone and a context for the essay. At the end, it frequently crystallizes the thought of the essay or adds an interesting comment or frame of reference for it. Here is the conclusion of an essay bemoaning the destruction of the old Metropolitan Opera House in New York City to make way for new office buildings:

> "The queen is dead. Long live the queen." With these words Rudolf Bing closed forever the old Met and ushered in the new. The queen was indeed dead, but her grand majesty will never be duplicated. Our na-

tional heritage as well as our musical heritage was compromised on that day. The Lincoln Center, with all of its glitter and light, can never replace what was lost when the bulldozers leveled the old Metropolitan Opera House.

A personal experience or anecdote. Again, an introductory tactic can work well as a concluding tactic. An anecdote can provide an effective illustration of or comment upon a paper's thesis and can sometimes add life to a more abstract discussion. Here is the conclusion from a paper discussing the advances made in credit availability for women:

> The change wrought by these laws is heartening. Ten years ago, as a working but unmarried woman, I applied for a credit card from a large chain discount department store. I was turned down three times. Then I got married. My husband was an unemployed student. We were given a credit card—in his name—at that same store on our first application. There was no logic to that, but traditional credit policies dictated that he, without a job, was a better credit risk than I was with one. I hope we have left that kind of discrimination behind. But we'll see. The ERA hasn't been ratified yet.

As these examples show, no matter how you decide to wrap up your thoughts, you should strive to maintain the tension or the tone of the essay right up through that last sentence. You want to leave your reader feeling finished and satisfied; a single-sentence conclusion will rarely be adequate. The argument, the descriptions, the discussions should be complete.

Exercises

1. Look back again at the professional essays you had assembled for previous exercises. Be prepared to comment upon the beginnings and endings of those essays. Try to determine also the type of transitions used to give the piece coherence.
2. Look back at the introduction and conclusion of the essay you wrote for the exercise on page 154. Can you improve it by adapting a different beginning or ending tactic? Can you make the introduction or conclusion more concrete or more interesting? Exchange papers with a classmate and make suggestions to each other about what is good and what might be improved on each other's papers.

3. Examine the following introductions and conclusions. Be prepared to discuss the qualities you find present or lacking in each set. What revisions or suggestions would you make?

a. From an automatic peeler/shredder for the kitchen to an electric scrubbing brush to clean our faces, we Americans have more conveniences offered to us than we could ever need, want, or use. To make life easier we have automatic toothbrushes, food bag sealers, blenders, hair dryers, hot doggers, doughnut makers, massagers, pencil sharpeners, and button holers. Where will it all end? We are becoming increasingly dependent on machines and electricity to do our work. The culprit behind this wanton abundance is the fast growth of American technology which has helped create the wastefulness of money, energy, and natural resources.

* * *

We must become more conservative in our use of natural resources; we must teach our children to be. Our money should be spent more wisely in the home and on the national level. Energy suppliers should try cracking down on manufacturers who produce new, wasteful electrical devices. We are a country of opportunity, and we are going in the right direction toward solar energy, but we all have to help by using less energy and thinking of how we can save more.

b. American people should learn to conserve. Wastefulness is a major problem of today, that must be overcome. Our energy and natural resources will be plentiful for only so long, so we must make a goal to save until science has found a substitute for them.

* * *

Whenever you use anything, you should think if you really need it or not. If we do not learn to conserve now, in the time ahead there will be nothing left to conserve.

c. I had heard terrifying stories about the dreaded Mrs. Baumgardner. She was tough. She failed you just for looking at her the wrong way. It was with some concern, then, that on that sunny September morning, I took from my homeroom teacher a white schedule card: Math, Room 202, Mrs. Patton; Science, Room 128, Mr. Clark; English, Room 215—Oh, no!—Mrs. Baumgardner. The excitement of the day vanished; a glum, disheartened feeling took its place. But I say now, six years later, that the best thing that ever happened to me in the study of English was Mrs. Baumgardner. With her old-fashioned methods, she taught me its rules and proper sentence structure so that I never have to struggle with it now.

* * *

Mrs. Baumgardner may have ruined my first day and first month of high school, but she certainly improved the rest of my life. I can now look back and appreciate her. Her course rescued me from the struggle with English that I have seen so many of my fellow students face. In spite of her sternness and her old-fashioned discipline, I deeply regard and respect her for making the students learn English before it became a stumbling block to them.

Developing the Middle

Traditionally, the four major types of essays are description, narration, exposition, and argumentation. Descriptive essays record details; narrative essays tell a story; expository essays give information or explain something; and argumentative essays present or defend a point of view. Much of the writing students do is either expository, requiring the deliverance or evaluation of information, or argumentative. In fact, most essays are essentially argumentative since they reflect the writer's attitude toward a subject whether she is claiming that the District of Columbia should be granted full voting rights or merely expressing a preference for Puma jogging shoes over Adidas. Naturally, the types of essays overlap. Sometimes argumentation contains exposition, narration needs description, and exposition often includes narration.

Working within these four larger modes are the several strategies laid out in Chapter 5. That chapter discussed the different ways in which ideas can be developed into paragraphs. Depending on your intent, you could analyze a situation by giving reasons for it or by tracing the causes and effects that were a part of it. You could make decisions about things by comparing and contrasting them to show their similarities and differences or their pros and cons. You could describe a scene, a person, a process, or an event; you could illustrate a generalization with examples. While details and examples remain the mainstay of most writing, the five tactics presented in Chapter 5, either separately or in combination, give writers different methods for saying what they want to say.

No matter what the writing task, middles of essays are developed in much the same way. You start with a narrowed subject; you frame a working sketch for the body; you translate that sketch into an essay by developing supporting paragraphs. What differs from one essay to the next is the way you flesh out the middle: You can *narrate* a tale of woe, *describe* a special wedding present, *give an account of* the great San Francisco earthquake, or *argue* that oil shale refinery processes should be federally supported. Sometimes you use one dominant strategy; sometimes you mix them together. You could argue that more freeways must be built around Cleveland by giving examples of other cities with large freeway networks. Or you might concentrate on doing a reason analysis of *why* Cleveland needs more highways. Then, too, you might combine reasons and examples if such a coupling would better make the point. In the same way, you could discuss Stephen Crane's naturalism through causal analysis of the influence of environment upon his characters while drawing on examples from his novels *The Red Badge of Courage* and *Maggie.*

Writers need flexibility to adapt methods to thought so they will not be mere slaves to form. Your intent in writing an essay helps determine how you fill in the body. By changing topic sentence focus into thesis statement focus and by building major supports into paragraphs instead of sentences, you can write whole essays of comparison/contrast or causal analysis or exemplification, instead of just a paragraph. The subjects will be larger, the development will be more complete, but the basic pattern will remain the same. However, no matter how you structure the essay, whether you are arguing, explaining, contrasting, or analyzing, details and examples will remain the foundation of most good writing. Whatever method or methods you use will be enriched by selective use of concrete language.

Building an essay with one dominant strategy

As with the paragraph, there will be times when you need one dominant strategy. The essay about the money-eating Porsche does not explain or analyze; the whole paper describes an experience and relies heavily upon examples to do so. In the same way, if your political science teacher asks you to assess the impact of the United States human rights policy on dictatorial governments, you might set up an argumentative essay using causal analysis to show how the Soviet Union responded to human rights pressure while South Africa perhaps did not. Another possibility would be to use a few countries, such as Uganda, Chile, and Boliva, as examples and develop an essay using the examples as major support. Were you to compare a short story by Flannery O'Connor to one by another female southern writer such as Eudora Welty, you might set up an expository essay based upon a comparison/contrast pattern of theme, character, plot, and setting.

These topics could fit either a point-by-point or a subject-by-subject comparison.

Your writing projects will occasionally need similar, single-strategy structuring. If, as president of a citizens' association, you have to write a position paper arguing against the rezoning of a neighborhood, you could write an argumentative essay using reason analysis to reflect, paragraph by paragraph, the group's major points against rezoning. In another instance, you might merely wish to send a friend a description of the way to make fishing flies or a recipe for conjuring up a wicked batch of mint juleps. In other words, in writing any kind of essay—descriptive, narrative, expository, or argumentative—you can, if you need to, use one dominant strategy. While your paragraphs may internally use other devices as well, the basic strategy sketches in Chapter 5 will fit an essay by expanding each major support to fit a paragraph-length discussion rather than a single sentence.

To give you an example of how such expansion can work, here is an essay relying upon comparison/contrast structure. This student wished to talk about the differences between the styles of two contemporary photographers, Helmut Newton and David Hamilton. She focused the paper and made a quick sketch of supports based on the pattern offered in Chapter 5; she then developed these into the body paragraphs of the essay.

Focus: **Helmut Newton and David Hamilton have two very different photographic styles.**

Major Supports

- Use of models
  - Newton
  - Hamilton
- Background
  - Newton
  - Hamilton
- Overall effect
  - Newton
  - Hamilton

The essay itself looked like this.

> **Two European men emerged during the seventies as highly regarded photographers, yet each man's style has a distinct quality and finesse unique to him.** German-born Helmut Newton was raised in Berlin and moved to Paris after he

turned twenty. He has done high-fashion photography for French and American *Vogue* and his photographs have appeared in such diversified publications as *Rolling Stone, Oui, Newsweek, New York, Photo,* and *Playboy.* Newton's style is shocking and blatantly erotic. David Hamilton has lived in Switzerland and Germany and has had his work included in the German publication *Twen,* in *Photo* magazine, and in Nina Ricci advertisements for the company's perfumes Farouche and L'air du Temps. Hamilton's prints depict dreamlike scenes or capture tender moments of innocence in a young girl's adolescence.

The use of models is an important technique employed in achieving the desired photograph. Newton tends to use women from their mid-twenties to their forties. Frequently there are two women together in a picture, sometimes helping each other but more often they appear to be just companions. The outfits his models wear are very provocative and outspoken. Hamilton, on the contrary, uses very young, fragile-looking girls. These models are from ten to eighteen years old. Hamilton, like Newton, uses two girls together but his girls wear billowy nightgowns, antique lace and silk, peasant dresses, and straw hats rimmed with flowers.

The background in a picture is also very important in creating the desired atmosphere and in bearing the artist's message. Ornate hotels, with very high ceilings and enormous gardens heaped with flowers and sculptured hedges, terraces, castles, and swimming pools account for the majority of Newton's backdrops. To Newton, the setting is equally as important as the models because it contributes as much to the total suggestion. David Hamilton's photographs do not use a total scene as much as they use a prop. A rocking chair, a window, or the ballet barre are some of his favorites. He often uses nature to create the tone, frequently shooting at the seashore, in the forest, or in a meadow with willowy trees and flowers. Some of Hamilton's prints don't even have a prop in them as they focus the viewer's total attention on his young girl.

The total impact of each photographer's work is momentous, but Newton provokes certain emotions in the viewer that are quite distinct from the sensations when viewing one of Hamilton's photos. Newton gives the viewer an expensive image, yet his models seem to be arrogant, cold, blasé, and detached, as if they were bored by being pampered. One recurring theme in Newton's work is an older woman scrutinizing herself in the mirror. His pictures also seem to have misplaced characters, such as a woman in an alley wearing nothing more than a full-length silver fox coat and sandals. Newton uses nudity and semi-nudity in an outrageous and unexpected manner. His work leaves one with a hard-gloss, neon-lit after-image. Nebulous and half-perceived, Hamilton's style leads the viewer to believe that he is viewing one of the photographer's dreams on paper. Capturing his young maidens when they are no longer children but not yet adults, Hamilton seems to unveil the nymphish children as languid, fairy-tale creatures. He reveals the innocence and naiveté found in youth but sometimes lost in adulthood.

In this glossy world of high-fashion photography, Newton and Hamilton rise above many others who come and go. While the technical skill of artists such as these can be judged by fixed standards, there is no constant by which to measure the quality of their creative vision. Startlingly different from one another in theme and concept, Helmut Newton and David Hamilton have caught the elusive fancy of the fashion photography world and, for all their diversity, mutually hold it transfixed.

Building an essay from a combination of strategies

Just as paragraphs are sometimes written with a combination of strategies, so are essays. More often than not, in fact, essays are a blend of several strategies that serve the larger purpose of expanding the focus established by the thesis statement. To discuss the impact of the human rights policy on dictatorial governments, you might, instead of a causal analysis, write an essay using a combination of strategies: one paragraph giving examples of countries affected; another paragraph listing reasons why foreign aid might be halted; and still another paragraph analyzing the typical predicament of a country not adhering to the human rights requests of the President. Arguing against rezoning of a neighborhood might include one paragraph of comparison/contrast with another neighborhood which has already been rezoned. It might also include one paragraph of description showing what the neighborhood looks like now as well as a paragraph of causal analysis showing what effects the new zoning may have on the future deterioration of the neighborhood. In other words, ideas flow into paragraphs and essays in various ways, and much of the strategy you might use is dependent upon what you want to say about your subject to best convince your audience that you have a point.

Here is an essay made up of several different internal strategies, illustrating how a combination of tactics can be used to develop a complete unit. Not all of the paragraphs use a special strategy, but those that do are indicated in the margin.

Thesis Statement

In 1975 a small powerboat such as a seventeen-foot Crestliner or Bayliner cost about $5000. An average middle-class family could afford to buy one to enjoy all manner of water sports from water skiing to modified deep-sea fishing. Since that time, however, the price has increased significantly. The same Crestliner or Bayliner now costs over $11,000. Owning a brand-new ski boat is now more prestigious than owning a Cadillac. **It is unfortunate but true that soon small recreational boats may be too expensive for many of the middle-class to buy and operate.**

Paragraph of Exposition

In the past, the value of small boats has always depreciated after purchase. Since 1975, however, prices have escalated, making even used boats worth more than their original price. As prices have gone up, dealers have sold fewer boats. As they attempted to increase their profit margin by raising prices still further, the volume of their sales decreased. What has evolved is a vicious cycle of price increases and sale decreases to the detriment, of course, of the would-be small-boat owner.

Comparison/ Contrast

The expense of the small powerboat may be put in clearer perspective by contrasting it with the cost of operating an automobile. The initial purchase cost of the boat is nearly double that of the Pinto, Camaro, or Toyota which an average family might buy. Gas consumption is another factor. Boats such as the Crestliner or Bayliner, at cruising speed, achieve three to four miles per gallon. Unlike a car, the increased gas consumption of a boat is measured in gallons per hour. Although the gas mileage of these small seventeen footers is economical compared to the one and a half to two miles per gallon of the thirty-foot family cabin cruiser, filling a tank with twenty gallons of marine gas, which is five to ten cents more expensive than regular gas, just to cruise for a few hours cannot compare with filling up at a local gas station. Added into this total expense list are the costs of miscellaneous items such as insurance and dock fees as well as the basic maintenance costs. With respect to miscellaneous items and repairs, the boat is easily equal to the car.

Reason Analysis

Inevitably, we must confront the question of why prices of powerboats have increased so drastically. A combination of labor and material costs seems to produce the net increase in dollar signs. To some extent, small powerboats, made as they are of fiberglass, a petroleum product, may be unlikely victims of the energy crunch. Increased petroleum prices naturally raise the cost of the product so vital to the boat's construction. Then, too, the increased costs of the engineering and the special processes that fit the design of the boat undoubtedly escalate the price. But perhaps more importantly, the increased cost of paying a labor force to hand lay the fiberglass may be the predominant factor in the overall price explosion.

Causal Analysis

At issue then, is what can be done, if anything, to decrease or at least hold stable the price of the small powerboat so that it does not become an anachronism in the front yards of suburbia. One possible solution is for manufacturers to revise construction of the boat itself: to find an alternative for fiberglass. Larger boats are made of ferro cement which is not petroleum based and does not require the extensive hand-laid work which goes into fiberglass molding. In addition, engines should be modified or redesigned to work more efficiently and to effect better fuel economy to make filling up at the gas dock less expensive. With the energy crisis recurring almost yearly, boat manufacturers must begin producing boats that are not so dependent upon petroleum products; this in turn may assist in reducing labor costs to build the boat.

Small weekend ski boats need not become a luxury of the past for thousands of middle-class families who have enjoyed them. Weekend recrea-

> tions such as waterskiing, fishing, or just pleasure cruising are pastimes which encourage families to spend time together. If the high cost of running a boat keeps the ones already bought parked at home or the ones in the showroom unsold, it will be a shame. A small powerboat parked in the driveway or hooked on the bumper of a station wagon is a harmless part of the American dream. Some radical construction and design decisions on the part of the powerboat manufacturers could help keep that little piece of the dream alive.

The student who wrote this essay was obviously a powerboat owner who cared about the problems he was sharing with numerous other small-powerboat owners. He did not adopt a single, dominant strategy to develop his opinions; instead he used several different tactics as they seemed necessary. In paragraph 3, he thought a comparison with an average family automobile would be useful to illustrate his point of boating being an expensive pastime; in paragraph 4 he took time to generalize the reasons for the cost increase; in paragraph 5 he analyzed some of the causes of those increases to try to project some solutions to the problems he had defined. In other words, he used tactics appropriate to the larger argument he was making. Thus it will be with most of the essays you write. The methods you use should flow naturally one into the next to serve the broader issue in need of discussion or expansion.

Exercises

1. Examine the strategies in the essay(s) you have written. Be prepared to identify either the dominant strategy or the combined internal tactics you used within paragraphs and to suggest why you made those choices.
2. Examine a professional essay from a periodical or an essay reader you might be using. Analyze it for the rhetorical tactics it uses, either as an overall strategy or within individual paragraphs.
3. Review the strategies in Chapter 5. Take one (or several) of the paragraphs you wrote for the exercises in that chapter and expand it (or them) into an essay on the same subject. Use roughly the same sketch of development to see how the paragraph can grow into an essay through expansion.
4. Select a subject for an essay which you would develop

through one dominant mode—description, narration, exposition, or argumentation. As you write that essay, highlight in the margin any place where you use internal strategies such as exemplification, causal analysis, comparison/contrast, etc.

Refining the Rough Draft

Chapter 6 and this chapter have a lot of information packed into them. Some of it is mechanical; some of it is theoretical; some of it is even debatable. But much of it is highly practical. The material in these two chapters represents an approach to writing an essay which occasionally may seem too systematic, too programmed. But it offers a solid format, that survival kit for meeting almost any writing need. Perhaps you won't win a Pulitzer Prize by following it, but you should be able to write a drama review for a British literature class or an essay exam for Psychology 101. The plan is simple, yet trustworthy. It provides a practical structure for expressing your ideas so that someone else can read them and understand them.

But in spite of the plan, different people reach the finished essay in different ways. Some make laundry lists; some use scissors and Scotch tape; some even use a tape recorder and then transcribe. However you perform the gyrations of pre-writing and writing, you should have a reasonable draft of an essay when you finish. Then, you can examine it with an eye toward refinement. Look at the shape; look at the language. Polish the transitions; check the misspellings. Do not stop with a first draft. Refine it; hone it; smooth out the edges so that all of the pieces mesh well and make a statement about you which you can be proud of. To make sure the essay is focused, unified, sensible, and complete, refer to the Chapter Checklist.

To illustrate the revision possibilities that lie beyond a first draft, here is a student essay, complete with the instructor's marginal comments which indicated why it was a poor essay receiving a low grade. You can check on the nature of the comments by comparing this essay's structure with the Chapter Checklist for Chapter 6.

In almost every aspect of modern-day life, you are surrounded by advertisements. Watching television, you are fed commercials; listening to the radio, you hear the disc jockey talking about a great place to visit or saying some product is the greatest invention yet. The nation's main highways are flooded with billboards of all sizes and shapes. Everywhere you look, you can't help but see an ad of some sort. No matter how much you ignore them, the advertising agencies are slowly brainwashing you into buying the products they are selling.

Perhaps second person "you" should be replaced by first or third person. Apply throughout essay.

The introduction follows a modified funnel. It works well structurally but could use a few more specifics to illustrate.

Good thesis statement focus.

Television commercials have famous stars endorsing products, saying how they've used certain items all their lives and saying there is nothing better when they probably have what they say is great shoved away in a seldom-opened closet at home.

Taboo—a long winded single sentence as ¶.

A good major support but its expression is too strung out. Development could be built from the matter which follows "products."

Dogs and cats are seen on the television screen rushing to meals, gulping down the food out of their dishes. An actor stands behind the husky animal describing how good the product is and saying your dog will love it, too. What the actor doesn't tell you is that the animal hasn't been fed in three days, or is trained to eat when told.

What is the topic sentence focus?

This is still the television support; shouldn't there be one well developed ¶ about tv ads instead of several splintered ones?

Some commercials have a housewife in a

spacious kitchen saying how nice and soft her hands are after she washes the dishes with Dove. Others show a beautiful model with men chasing after her saying that if you use this certain toothpaste or deodorant soap it will give you sex appeal.

What is the focus of this ¶?

Which?

Again—tv ads What about radio and billboards mentioned in introduction?

Record companies always advertise by stating if you buy this record for $8.94 we will send you two more greatest hits albums free, telling you that you save money on the price of the records, saying to order now because it's a limited time offer, so you won't have a chance to think about the right decision, when really they will be advertising the same dull commercial every day for six months.

who?

Keep in mind that a topic sentence such as this works best when you utilize specific brand names, slogans, etc. Also, each ¶ needs an indentifiable topic sentence focus as well as identifiable major supporting points.

Another of these strung out sentences.

The whole ¶ is one run-on sentence

Tobacco companies have great billboards towering over the highways picturing forty-foot high, crystal clear waterfalls, magnificent green plants and trees surrounding the falls, with the words "Come all the way up to Kool" at the bottom of the billboard, not showing a true to life picture of smoke-filled rooms and saying that cigarettes cause cancer and the fiberglass in the menthol filter makes your lungs bleed.

good image but poor sentence structure

ah, finally a change from tv ads

But again the whole ¶ is one long run-on sentence.

Radio stations, having a commercial after almost every record, try to pound the product into your mind saying how good it is

shift to radio—good

colloquial

several times a day. They say how elegant a condominium is, using words such as "spacious living quarters and plenty of parking space." Large shopping centers and buses are supposedly close by and downtown Washington a few minutes' ride away. The apartments turn out to be just like any others when you see them.

good to use actual words and brand names such as this

Getting a product into interesting and exciting backgrounds, the advertising agencies seek to mislead and fool the American consumers into buying a certain item at any cost. Many times the product doesn't seem to look, taste or do the wonderful things they say or you see done on television, when you bring it home to your household. Much to your grief and expense, it is too late to do anything about it.

meaning?

Good concluding tactic — Beef it up a little

John,

There is a good plan and idea hidden within this paper, but you have to make some structural changes to bring it out. The introduction speaks of television, radio, and billboard ads, a logical threefold division for the body of the paper. Using four undernourished ¶'s about tv ads followed by one quick example of a billboard ad and one of a radio ad does not do justice to your idea. If you want the generalization to be valid, then you really need several specific supports for each one; one developed (i.e. amply illustrated and explained) ¶ about tv ads, one about radio, and one about billboards. A second important problem lies in the sentence structure. You would be winded long before you finished reading some of these sentences aloud. Please revise and resubmit.

As you can easily see, this essay had structural problems as well as grammatical and mechanical problems. It does have a thesis statement focus—advertising agencies are brainwashing the consumer—but the development is so erratic that the paper is hard to follow. This student rewrote the essay to try to correct some of the problems which the instructor had indicated in the margin. Many of the corrections he made in the second version would have been unnecessary if he had used the checklist before he handed in the original essay. Having the benefit of the commentary and the opportunity to resubmit the paper, the student rewrote it and turned in the following paper. While there still are some problems with development, this revision is greatly superior to the first copy. Notice that most of the original focusing and development problems are now gone.

In almost every aspect of modern-day life, you are surrounded by many different types of advertisements that are quite deceiving. Watching television, you are fed commercials; listening to the radio, you hear the disc jockey talking about a great place to visit or saying a new product on the market is the greatest invention yet. The nation's main highways are flooded with billboards of all sizes and shapes. Everywhere you look, you can't help but see an ad of some sort. No matter how much you try to ignore them, the advertising agencies are slowly brainwashing you into buying the products they are selling.

The television media is a major selling power for many companies which use hundreds of different approaches and angles to catch the viewer's attention. Many commercials have famous stars endorsing products, saying how they've used certain items all their lives and that there is nothing better. They probably have what they say is great shoved away in a seldom-opened closet at home. Well-known sports figures are always slapping on a certain type of after shave and saying it smells and feels great. Dogs and cats are seen on the television screen rushing to meals, gulping down the food out of their dishes. An actor stands behind the healthy animal describing how good the product is and saying your dog will love it, too. What the actor doesn't tell you is that the animal is hungry enough to eat almost anything, or is trained to eat when told. Some TV commercials show a housewife in a spacious kitchen saying how nice and soft her hands are after she washes the dishes with Dove. Others show a beautiful model with men chasing after her saying that if you use this certain toothpaste or deodorant soap it will give you sex appeal. The consumer is not told why this product is better than the others. Certain record companies always advertise by stating if you buy this record for $8.94

along with it will be sent two more greatest hits albums free. They tell you that you save money on the price of the records if you order now because the offer is for only a limited time. But really they will be advertising the same dull commercial every day for six months.

Roads from California to Maine are covered with thousands of different types of signs. The American Tobacco Company has great billboards towering over the highways picturing forty-foot high, crystal clear waterfalls, magnificent green plants and trees surrounding the falls, with the words "Come all the way up to Kool" at the bottom of the billboard. The ads do not show a true to life picture of smoke-filled rooms or say that cigarettes cause cancer and the fiberglass in the menthol filter makes your lungs bleed. Winston has a picture of a person holding up their cigarettes saying, "If it weren't for Winston I wouldn't smoke" written on the billboards across the nation. The ad tries to give the impression that the taste of the cigarette is superior to others because of a special blend of tobacco. Traveling to another state on a vacation, you are reminded of the refreshing taste of Coke to quench your thirst.

Radio stations having a commercial after almost every record try to pound the product into your mind saying how good it is several times a day. They say how elegant a condominium is, using words such as "spacious living quarters" and "plenty of parking space." Large shopping centers and buses are supposedly close by and downtown Washington a few minutes' ride away. The apartments turn out to be just like any others when you see them. One real estate commercial is a humorous satire of the Waltons sitting around the dinner table eating their evening meal. A family talks about the luxuries of a certain apartment project, then you hear them start to pack their belongings and move to the apartments they were just discussing over their evening meal.

By setting the product into an interesting and exciting background, the advertising agencies seek to mislead and fool the American consumers into buying a certain item at any cost. Many times the product you bring home to your household

```
doesn't seem to look, taste, or be as
wonderful as seen on television. Much to
your grief and expense, it is too late to do
anything about it.
```

The problems that remain in this essay are more matters of refinement than of basic structure; the student corrected most of the glaring focus and development problems. He added lots of specific support for the generalizations about television, radio stations, and billboards. The problems now are more on the level of reworking the introduction and conclusion to make them more lively or more interesting; working more on concrete language throughout the essay to enhance this discussion of strategy; tightening and shortening some sentences; and smoothing the connections between the paragraphs. The point to be learned from this may well be, however, that had the student done the basic structure check before submitting the paper, he would probably have caught most of the structural errors himself and then had more time to concentrate on refinement.

Chapter Exercises

1. Cast yourself in the role of teacher/grader and analyze the effectiveness of the short papers presented here. Base your judgment of the way each paper matches the list of elements for a good essay in the Chapter Checklist. If you can, make suggestions for revision.
   a. Interest in backpacking has been rising at a fast rate over the past few years. This can be gathered from the sharp increase in sales of backpacking equipment such as hiking boots, lightweight tents, sleeping bags, and backpacks. National park records show that more people are applying for back country permits now than ever before. These people hike back country trails for a variety of reasons. Some go to

get back to a natural way of living. Others go for the peace and quiet which they don't find in the city. Everyone who goes enjoys the restful feeling and adventure of life in the wilderness.

Backpacking gives a person a chance to experience the freedom of nomadic life. You can go where you want to, when you want to, or stay where you are. On your back you have everything needed for survival: food and shelter. The food is freeze-dried to be lightweight. To prepare it, add boiling water and wait five minutes. Shelter is provided by a pup tent that can be folded to the size of a loaf of bread. Water is easy to find along most trails, so you only carry enough to drink during the day. Your home is wherever you can put your tent. Living this way is a quiet adventure and going back to the pressures of life in suburbia or the city is always a letdown.

There are many fun and interesting things to do in the back country. Sitting on the bank of a cool mountain stream dangling your feet in the rushing water. Listening to the water splash and gurgle as you bask in the warm sunlight seems to relax the mind and make time stand still. Hours can be spent watching the constantly changing clouds. As they drift through the tranquil sky, you can imagine familiar objects and animals. While sitting quietly in a clearing, you can take pictures of passing animals in the morning.

The sun rises over the mountains. The sunset is even more spectacular. At night there are billions of stars, bright and dim. A hundred times more stars than can be seen from a city. The sights and sounds of nature are all around and being a part of it makes life worth living to the fullest.

There are physical strains that go along with backpacking. Carrying a fifty pound pack often leaves you with sore legs and shoulders. Camp has to be set up each afternoon, the set-up takes at least an hour. Wood gathering takes another hour of scrounging through the woods. By the time you finish dinner, the sun is going down and you're ready to sleep forever. In the morning you wake up with the birds fresh and strong. After gathering more wood, eating, and breaking down camp, you're ready for another day on the trail.

The rejuvenated feeling you have in the morning comes from a combination of things. The walking of the day before has strengthened your body, cleaned out your lungs, and unclogged your arteries. The fresh mountain air is clean, free from city smog. It's refreshing to breathe it in and smell the pine trees and wild things. Living in the sunshine, though, I don't know why, makes a person feel better. The peaceful feeling of being one with the environment can be carried back to civilization for a time. Memories of the back country are strong and make hard days at work and long waits in rush hour traffic more bearable because you know that if you want to give up the city life you have somewhere to go, the wilderness.

b. Traveling across country with my vabagond mother via Greyhound bus lines enriched my values and senses greatly at an early age. "California Fever" struck my mother when my sister and I were just kids, so most of our summers were spent on the road. We were at a rambunctious, impressionable age, and though we sometimes balked at the thought of four days on a bus, we always ended up enjoying the trips. My mother, though fever stricken, seemed to have a hidden motive for our adventures. In her own special way, she knew we were growing and learning with each journey. My mother and these trips helped my sister and me develop a special sense of of appreciation for the simple things in life.

Psychologists say that children do not start to develop an aesthetic sense of values until ages eight and nine. If this is true my sister and I were far advanced for our ages. We spent countless hours gazing out of windows at towering skyscrapers and humble farmhouses. We were captivated by the oceanlike effect of Kansas wheat fields and hypnotized by the barren, monotonous wasteland of Wyoming. My mother taught us to appreciate these things for what they were worth, to realize that all objects hold some sort of value and beauty. She would leave the smoking section in the back of the bus to point out antelopes and other such animals that were foreign to our city children's eyes. Our sense of appreciation grew and was enhanced with each motion of Mom's finger out the smoked glass window.

Since Bonnie and I come from a rather small family, it was rewarding to get out and meet people. On the bus, we had a wide range of different acquaintances. Cowboys and Indians, mental patients and grandmothers, we met them all. With each acquaintance came a quick rundown of their life history. How and why they came to be on this bus, the place they left, and their destinations were just a few of the subjects they related to us. Some people even opened up their suitcases to share their dog-eared magazines and week-old candy with us. We learned that long travelers could seldom resist eagerly interested youngsters. Their stories broadened our concepts of how people outside of Columbus, Ohio, really live.

At times when the bus was sparsely filled, and the rolling scenery faded into night, the feeling of adventure still kept us awake. We were traveling through new and different places and would be stopping in towns and cities we never even heard of. The excitement of being somewhere else other than our own neighborhood had my sister and I talking and giggling late into the night. We were vabagond kids enjoying the thrill of it all. In my opinion it was a healthy feeling to experience; the state of being unbound and free. At our young ages we were lucky enough to enjoy something that most people can only dream about.

It's been four years since we last saw California, but memories still continue to call us back. My mother has made a thorough recovery from her fever, and I am almost sorry she did. I think I've developed a fever of my own. At any rate, I still have that special sense of appreciation. I still love to watch sunsets and meet new acquaintances. I believe every child should be as lucky as my sister and I were, lucky enough to get out in the world and truly enjoy simple things in life.

c. In order for a professional basketball team to achieve any level of success, each position must be filled by a capable player. These players must be molded into one coherent unit. Of the teams in the National Basketball Association, the Philadelphia 76'ers combine talent at each position with great individual stars to become the most balanced ballclub.

The center position requires a man of great strength, superior height, and mental alertness. Philadelphia does not have a great center but compensates with two better than average players. The starting center is Caldwell Jones, a lanky man of six feet, eleven inches. Jones's greatest attribute is his ability to play defense. While he does get into foul trouble quite often, Caldwell is a smart player who adjusts quickly to situations on the court. His replacement is a smart youngster, Darrell Dawkins. Dawkins, in his first year as a professional, proved he had the potential to be a quality center in the NBA. He made mistakes but also gained valuable experience for a player of such a tender age. Once he learns to channel his emotions in a positive direction, he should become an outstanding starting center.

The guards on a team must have above average ball handling abilities, quickness to rival a cat, and the ability to score points when called upon. The six-foot, six-inch Doug Collins combines all of these qualities, plus an uncanny ability to position himself for unmolested shots to become one of the finer guards in the league. Collins's height enables him to take opposing guards under the basket where he either is fouled or scores an easy field goal. Henry Bibby starts opposite Collins at the other guard. He is a smart, scrappy player who plays solid defense, handles the ball well, and can score. The first substitute at guard is Lloyd Free. Free is never bashful about shooting the ball and can be a prolific scorer at times. He is also one of the quicker guards with tremendous leaping ability.

The 76'ers start George McGinnis at the strong forward position. McGinnis is a bull of a man, standing six feet, eight inches tall and tipping the scales at two hundred forty pounds. He is usually too quick or too strong for most opponents. At the other forward position is the legendary Julius Erving, or Doctor J. as he is most commonly called. Erving is perhaps the most exciting player in the game today. His acrobatic swirls and twirls in midair often defy human description. Erving, known mostly for his offensive skills, is a very competent defensive player. Along with McGinnis, he forms one of the strongest pair of forwards in professional basketball.

Position by position Philadelphia has meshed its players into a machinelike unit. Each component is balanced with the next. Individuals have become one in striving for a common goal—the NBA championship.

d. Tears began to roll down the face of the small child as she watched her mother walk away. The small child soon began to look around the large, unfamiliar surroundings. Upon one of the walls were the letters of the alphabet. Proudly, the child recalled how her mother had taught her to recite these letters. On another wall, the numbers from one to ten were displayed. Again, the child remembered her earlier teachings and realized her ability to count far beyond the number ten. Her fears soon began to vanish. Her first day in school started to become a delightful experience. Nearly all children anticipate their first day of school with some degree of apprehension. As universal as this emotion may be, school systems within Western countries differ immensely. Two school systems which may appear similar, but in reality are very different, are those of England and America.

England and America have always been bound together by their mutual use of the English language. However, the sounds heard within the classrooms of these two nations are comparatively different. On first entering an English classroom, the sound level becomes comparable to that of a library. An occasional sneeze is about the only sound that is released from the mouths of these small children. Only the authoritative voice of the school mistress can be heard. A child requiring attention must wait until the teacher acknowledges his individual plea. Upon entering the classroom of an American school, one can hear the constant chit-chat of small voices. In the background, the clatter of children's toys can be heard. Request for assistance from the teacher comes from all corners of the room. Group discussions seem to be a major part of the learning process. The entire atmosphere within an American school appears relaxed, with less emphasis placed on stringent rules and regulations.

One of the more noticeable regulation differences between the two school systems is that of dress. The majority of English children leave home each morning wearing their official school uniform. Both males and females are often required to wear ties. No female student would dare consider attending school with polish painted on her nails. Even the bravest of the female sex would never show up for school with make-up on. The consequence for such misconduct could be expulsion. With the start of a new school day in America, one's eyes can feast upon every conceivable design that denim has ever been used for. There is no doubt that blue jeans and tee shirts are the official uniform of the American student. Total "freedom of dress" is openly expressed and accepted.

Freedom to express individual feelings has always been part of the American life-style. This is also apparent in the American school system. At the beginning of a school day, American students will pledge allegiance to their flag. There is no mention of prayer or religious instruction throughout the school day. Students within the same school are often of different religions, races, and cultural backgrounds. Teaching or displaying religious tendencies would only result in a biased situation. Therefore, religious activities are left to the individual student to perform out of school. Unlike America, the majority of English students are of the same faith. Each morning, students must assemble in the main hall to pay their respects to God. Also at this time the Headmaster reports any new activities or items of interest to the students.

Out-of-school activities are limited for English students. In high school, boys sometimes participate in after school rugby or cricket teams. Girls often become members of the netball or hockey teams. Students of neither sex are allowed to participate unless their grades are of an outstanding nature. During the last two years of high school, students normally join the school teen club. Unfortunately, this doesn't result in an overwhelming amount of excitement. Teen club activities are required to be over by ten o'clock. Upon graduation there are no ceremonial activities. In contrast, American schools put great emphasis on after school activities. Most boys join every team possible in order to please everyone from their school gym instructor and parents to their girl friends. Girls spend many hours learning correct chants to accompany their acrobatic feats. This art called cheerleading is then used to encourage their school's team. Great emphasis is placed upon the team spirit. After school dances are very common, and many different awards are given to the more popular students. Graduation is celebrated by both family and friends. Tremendous emphasis is placed upon this very special event in an American student's life.

Both England and America offer their young citizens a good wholesome education. While both systems have their differences, they also have a common goal. From the moment the small child enters the classroom, the school system tries to educate and prepare this little human for the many years ahead.

2. As a class or as a small group, select a topic suitable for a five-hundred-word essay. Together, devise a focus for it and sketch a possible body to develop the paper.
3. Each member of the group should now write a separate introduction for the topic you outlined together. Try to use several introductory techniques, with each of you taking a different method. You may be interested in seeing how many different approaches there can be to one subject. Compare the finished paragraphs and decide which one might be most appropriate.
4. Each of you should now write a conclusion for this essay you are collaborating upon. Follow the same plan as with the introduction. Divide the techniques, criticize the effectiveness of each, and then choose the one which seems most successful.
5. Independent of one another, develop the topic you have been working on into a complete essay following the agreed-upon body content.

Chapter Checklist

1. In a well-developed introduction, clearly spell out the thesis statement. Attempt to interest the reader by using one of the introductory tactics: inverted paragraph, interesting fact, quotation, anecdote, or stereotype.
2. Connect body paragraphs to one another in a logical, coherent way.
3. Round out the development of the thesis statement, without introducing any new ideas, using one of several tactics: summary, climax, interpretation/evaluation, consequence, quotation, or anecdote.
4. Structure supports either with one dominant strategy or with a combination of strategies.
5. Consider revision a regular part of the writing process. In addition to overall structural matters of focus and development, revise for concrete language, good mechanics (grammar, punctuation, spelling), good sentence structure, and good paragraph structure.

Thinking Clearly

"Politicians are crooks." "McDonald's hamburgers are lousy." "Classical music is boring." "To get a decent job these days you have to be black or female." Pronouncements such as these echo through our days. We utter them or listen to them without flinching. However, are there not at least a few politicians who have refused a bribe or hired an aide on merit? Have you never had a McDonald's hamburger that was warm and juicy and done just right? Aren't there at least a few Tchaikovsky symphonies or Beethoven concertos that are exhilarating? And have no white males become law partners or stockbrokers or accountants recently?

Taken in isolation, the illogic of those initial statements is easy to see. Yet such generalizations are often so much a part of our thinking that we no longer glance behind them to see the exceptions. We just accept them as truths. And if we think that way, we will speak that way; if we speak that way, we will write that way. While many generalizations are more or less accurate—war is painful, radiators are hot in the winter, and ants like picnics—they have to be scrutinized to avoid the oversimplifications, distortions, and exaggerations which make our writing vulnerable to criticism which finds it illogical.

Thinking is a vital part of writing any paper—not only those labeled "argument." Almost every essay we write has an argumentative base to it, simply because it is expressing our opinions. The thinking behind an idea—from the pondering of a water lily to a debate about the merits of vitamin C—influences the twofold process of giving that idea shape and meaning. Chapters 6 and 7 talked about ways to structure an essay; this chapter probes the thought processes that underlie its content.

If the structure is good but an essay is still weak, that usually means content trouble. Sometimes that weakness comes from a thesis that is too broad to be of much value. No matter how well-written, an essay asserting that ex-astronauts usually become politicians has to be weak because the generalization is not entirely true. Although some astronauts have become senators or congressmen, others have become business executives, remained in the military, or become educators.

On the other hand, sometimes the thesis statement is fine, but the supports are too flimsy to hold the paper together. While you should be able to write a paper claiming that California wines are as good as many French wines, you can't prove your point if you use Almaden as your only support. Almaden may be a good wine, but it is just one of many wines from California.

People will disagree as well as agree with what you have written. Likes and differences, preferences and prejudices—both yours and the reader's—will enter into your discussions. Your essays need to be logical and well-supported so that your position is firm whether or not you and your reader agree. That means not only making sure that your paragraphs and essays have focus and support, but paying some attention to the quality of that focus and support as well. The natural thought processes of inductive and deductive reasoning form the underpinnings of our thinking, and understanding them should help ensure content quality.

Induction and Deduction

If you stop to think about how you know what you know or why you believe what you believe, you might, at the risk of oversimplification, come up with two general answers. One is that you learn many specific things from your own experience: You look good in blue; your math teacher likes redheads; you like hot dogs with horseradish. The second is that you learn beliefs, opinions, and prejudices in a general way as you absorb them from your culture—parents, media, teachers, peers: Christmas is nice; Saks Fifth Avenue is a high-quality store; a college degree is useful. In other words, while you form rules of your own by observing the specific things that happen around you, you also have a collection of general principles to guide you in your individual actions and pursuits. These two processes are what induction and deduction are all about. They are the processes we use to arrive at the conclusions or judgments which find their way into our topic sentences and thesis statements.

Induction

Induction helps you reach a general conclusion by observing the specifics behind it. If you go to the same singles club several nights in a row and really enjoy yourself each time, you begin to tell your friends that this club is a "swinging place." The *several* enjoyable visits led you to a logical inductive conclusion, a conclusion which would not be as valid if you had gone to the club only once. If you attend a certain school and consistently find that the courses are challenging yet enjoyable, you reason inductively—from these several experiences—that this is a good school. If you are doing research for a paper on Eleanor Roosevelt and read that she resigned from the DAR to protest its refusal to allow Marian Anderson to sing in Constitution Hall, that she sat in the black rather than the white section at an Alabama rally, and that she encouraged the appointment of women to high government offices, you begin to understand inductively that she had a great commitment to minority causes. Induction, then, is the process by which you move from the specific situation to a general application.

We reason inductively every day—when we select toothpaste, when we read a book, when we buy a vacuum cleaner. If you try Colgate, Crest, Aim, and Sensodyne toothpastes and decide you like one more than the others, you have made an inductive decision which is valid for you. Inductive reasoning can stand firm as long as the specifics which feed it are solid and ample. Receiving poor service at a department store on four different occasions might justify a generalization about the poor quality service you have received there. On the other hand, discussing college tuition costs in this country would require more than just a study of tuition costs at one school or even at the schools in one state or section of the country. To make a reliable inductive generalization, you need a sampling of tuition costs from several different types of schools in several different places. The cost of a state university in Nebraska might be much different from the cost of a private university in New York City.

Deduction

Deduction is the other side of induction. Induction uses specifics to reach a generalization; deduction applies that generalization to yet another specific. The following chart illustrates this principle:

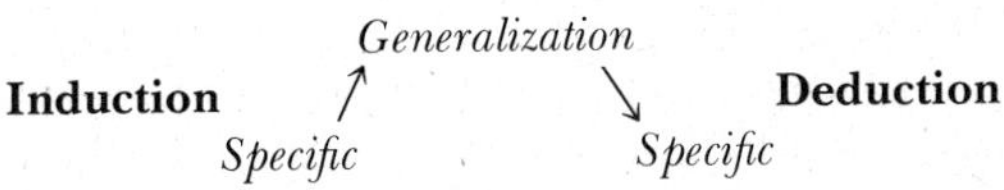

We apply a general idea that we believe to be true or valid to specific people, places, experiences, or things. We come to a conclusion about them on the basis of what we know about the general class to which they belong. For example, if, from long familiarity with a certain chain store such as Sears, Roebuck, you feel you get good merchandise at a fair price, then you would probably not hesitate to go to a Sears store should you be in a strange town and need a battery for your car or a wedding present for a friend. If you know that many graduates of a certain high school do well on the National Merit Scholarship exams, you might choose to go there if you are of high-school age or to send your child there if you are a parent. In other words, deduction helps us make a decision in a specific instance because of what we know about the matter in a general way.

Sometimes these conclusions are accurate; sometimes they are distorted. Their quality depends upon the soundness of the parts that make up the conclusion. If you were in a formal philosophy class, you would learn to test the validity of these conclusions by setting them in a *syllogism.* A syllogism is a way of outlining an idea, a way of probing what lies behind an opinion or conclusion. Its three parts are a *major premise* (a generalization), a *minor premise* (a specific application), and a *conclusion* (the thought drawn from the other two). In practice a syllogism works this way:

major premise (generalization):	All men are mortal.
minor premise (application):	John is a man.
conclusion:	Therefore, John is mortal.

In other words, if all men eventually die . . . and they do; and if John is a man . . . and he is; then we know that someday John will die. What we know about John is based upon sound logic. This is the same logic by which we know that if all liver is rich in vitamin B, the piece of liver eaten on Monday will be as rich in vitamin B as the piece eaten on Friday. If all raisins have a high iron content, then you can be reasonably sure that the handful of raisins you grab on your way out the door in the morning will also have a high iron content. If corduroy gets shiny as it gets older, then you can be sure that your new corduroy pants will get shiny after a year or two of wearing. This kind of deductive reasoning is based on sound logic.

Induction and deduction together

Induction reasons from the specific to the general; deduction reasons in reverse. They go together. Our thinking moves from inductive to deductive effortlessly and continually. Induction leads to a generalization; deduction applies that generalization to specific cases. If you see several James Bond films and enjoy them, you conclude inductively that you like James Bond films. The induction would look like this:

> I enjoyed *Goldfinger.*
> I enjoyed *From Russia with Love.*
> I enjoyed *On Her Majesty's Secret Service.*
> Therefore, I enjoy James Bond films.

Then, when you see that *Thunderball* will be the feature on the Saturday night late movie, that conclusion may spur your deductive decision to make plans to see it. The deduction would look like this:

> James Bond films are enjoyable.
> *Thunderball* is a James Bond film.
> Therefore, *Thunderball* will be enjoyable.

There is enough history to suggest that this logic is appropriate, although you can not be too certain in your statement until actual fact proves your assumption to be true. It can, however, be a rational guide for action.

Almost every time you write a focusing topic sentence or thesis statement, you are using induction and deduction, although the two processes need not occur simultaneously. In Chapter 7, for instance, the student who wrote the essay on the photographers Helmut Newton and David Hamilton was familiar enough with the work of the two to have an opinion about their styles. She felt they were both excellent photographers but for very different reasons. To write the essay, she consciously sat down to draw up a list of specifics to support her idea. In doing so, she came up with ample proof of both their excellence and their striking differences. Had she shown that the two men differed in only one respect—portrayal of models, for instance—the focusing generalization would not have been strong enough. Her thought process, then, looked like this:

> Newton and Hamilton make excellent use of different types of models.
>
> Newton and Hamilton rely on different backgrounds to convey their subtle and original themes.
>
> Newton and Hamilton work toward different overall effects.
>
> Therefore, their photographic styles, although equally effective, are strikingly different.

Within each paragraph in the essay, the induction works the same way. If Newton uses mature women and Hamilton favors fragile adolescents, then their choice of models is different, although effective. The same would be true of backdrops or the general effects of the two photographers—differing strokes toward excellence. When this student actually wrote the essay, she turned these conclusions around and wrote about them deductively: In each paragraph, she started with the generalizations and then provided the specifics to prove them.

Unless we study formal logic, we rarely analyze the thinking lying hidden behind our written or spoken statements. But sound logic is vital to a writer. Sloppy or flabby thinking, more suggestive of prejudice or emotional reaction than of common sense, destroys the content of even a well-written essay. Most important, the focus must be clear and the supports must be ample. If the quality of focus and support is assured, the content is well on its way to being strong. A simple examination of your thoughts can help expose any problems so you can write precise, careful prose.

Exercises

1. Give an example of an accurate inductive conclusion and application.
2. Give an example of an accurate deductive conclusion and application.
3. Look over one of the essays you wrote earlier, before you were concerned with quality of thinking. Analyze the induction and deduction which form the essay's base. Work out a syllogistic format for the ideas found there, if such is possible.
4. Exchange one of these essays with a classmate. Examine the quality of the induction and deduction in each other's papers. Point out both strengths and weaknesses and discuss any possible improvement.

Some Problems with Induction and Deduction

Obviously, not all induction and deduction work as smoothly as the examples given above. In fact, one of the reasons why we must talk about thinking clearly is that many of our inductive and deductive conclusions are incorrect. We often do say things like "Politicians are crooks" and "McDonald's hamburgers are lousy," or think that all truck drivers are virile men or librarians are crotchety old spinsters with their hair tied back in a bun. Such broad generalizations cannot always be true, so it is worth looking at some of the problems which can cause our reasoning to go awry. These problems are called *fallacies,* or mistaken ideas; they can take any of the numerous forms discussed below.

Hasty generalization

Problems with induction are largely a matter of generalizing too quickly from inadequate support. Problems with deduction grow mainly from generalizations which are too broad, or too hastily applied, to work properly in a specific instance. Either inductive or deductive thinking, then, is hampered by the *hasty generalization.*

Inductively, the hasty generalization occurs when you conclude that what is true for one individual or place or incident is true for all others in the same group. To decide that all political appointees are incompetent because you work for an inefficient one is a dangerous kind of thought. To determine that Kelvinator washing machines are the best because the Kelvinator you own has been functioning for years is a complimentary but nonetheless hasty generalization.

Deductively, the hasty generalization starts with a generalization that is too broad. The "man is mortal" syllogism works because all of its parts are valid. The generalization is true; the application is true. But if the syllogism began with "All men are poker players" or "All men are fathers," it would not work. Some men play poker and some men are fathers, but John can be a man and be neither a poker player nor a father. The same point can be made about many of the generalizations we make. If we assume that people are either rich or poor on the basis of the car they drive, the house in which they live, or the clothes they wear, we are operating on hasty generalizations which may not necessarily be accurate, either in themselves or when eventually applied to a specific case. Think, though, of some of the assumptions you make about a person who drives a Ferrari, a Volkswagen, or a Dodge station wagon. A sample syllogism might look like this:

major premise: People who drive Ferraris are wealthy.
minor premise: This person drives a Ferrari.
conclusion: This person is wealthy.

And so the syllogisms might work for the other two generalizations as well. If you assume that the Volkswagen driver is an unemployed student or that the Dodge station wagon is driven by the typical suburbanite because of some generalized idea of the kind of drivers of those vehicles, then the deduction may very well be faulty. While it is true that the Ferrari driver may also have a Rolls Royce sitting at home in the garage, it is also true that he or she may have borrowed the car from a brother, an employer, or a girlfriend or may even be two months behind in car payments. The car *alone* is no more proof of wealth than the Volkswagen is of a shoestring budget or the Dodge station wagon of suburban mediocrity.

Stereotype. The stereotype is a special kind of hasty generalization that affects both inductive and deductive conclusions. If on the basis of the actions of one person you condemn or applaud a whole class of people, you are guilty of stereotyping. Suppose you go to a fraternity party where the evening's entertainment is provided by a two-hundred-eighty-pound fullback who tears apart a live chicken with his hands and then eats the pieces, feathers and all. On the strength of this event, you might decide you should stay away from this particular athlete. You would be making a faulty inductive decision, though, if you concluded that all other athletes are like this one, so you should stay away from them all. All landlords are not misers just because yours is. All scientists are not bald and bespectacled, although your biology teacher might be. And not all artists live in garrets and wear grimy turtleneck sweaters just because your boyfriend the art student does.

The problem extends from there into deductive stereotype. If from meeting one athlete who seems barbaric you induce that all athletes are barbaric, then the next time you meet an athlete you may well put him or her in that same category. Deductively, the stereotype is a standardized image of a person or a thing that neglects individual differences and concludes that anyone or anything with similar qualities must be like all of the others. If we assume that men with long hair are radicals, Germans drink a lot of beer, and bankers wear pin-striped suits, we may reach some incorrect assumptions about the individual banker, German, or man with long hair we wish to write about. Not everyone who goes to Harvard is a WASP; not everyone who wears an Afro is a Black Nationalist; not everyone who teaches at a university is a liberal; and not everyone who belongs to the carpenter's union is a conservative. Unless we are careful about our thinking, we may subscribe all too often to this kind of hasty generalization, assuming that a person fits a stereotype we have.

Status. Another variation of the hasty generalization is the conclusion influenced by the status of a famous or important person's recommendation or attack. To have voted for Richard Nixon because John Wayne endorsed him or to buy Gilette razor blades or Chanel

No. 5 because Johnny Bench or Catherine Deneuve tells us to do so does not make much sense. If you write an essay about some contemporary event or analyze a short story, a poem, or a novel, you should not base your analysis upon that of one critic or one politician or one presidential aide. Certainly you should value the opinions of someone who is an expert in his or her field. However, just because Marie Bonaparte, for instance, is reputed to be a niece of Napoleon as well as an Edgar Allan Poe scholar does not make her Freudian interpretation of "The Fall of the House of Usher" the definitive one. Her relationship to her illustrious uncle would not give her comments more value or make them more correct than those of other Poe scholars. One critic's interpretation is part of a larger interpretation, and it must be sifted and weighed, rather than accepted as the only one or the right one. Caution would be especially wise if you were tempted to use the testimonial of someone quite outside the field of expertise. Just as Don Meredith may not know a lot about the Lipton tea he praises, one might have as little cause to quote Bette Midler making a foreign policy statement as Walter Cronkite making a pronouncement about music.

Appearance. Another variation of the hasty generalization is a conclustion based on the appearance of something. Presumably, you would not buy a new house just because of its new coat of paint or its freshly mowed lawn. To do so might leave you with leaky roofs and ancient plumbing. The $300 spent to buy an Yves St. Laurent original advertised in *Vogue* may be wasted if you are too plump or too short or too thin or too tall to make the dress fit you the way it fits the model. Your reasoning would be faulty if you decided to write an indictment of a neighborhood or a town based only on its appearance. To come to a negative conclusion about the people of a slum, for instance, because of the trash in the streets, broken windowpanes, or dirty children, would be unjust. So, too, would a conclusion about the wealth of a suburban neighborhood concealed behind well-kept, air-conditioned walls be unjust.

Perhaps one of the easiest ways of lessening problems with hasty generalizations is to qualify continually. Instead of devising a thesis statement which announces that *all* or even *many* third-world nations are beset by internal problems because Guinea, Uganda, and South Africa have been, qualify the generalization with words such as *some, several, many* (if you have sufficient support for *many*), or *sometimes*. These language markers can lessen the finality of a generalization and save you from making statements that are too broad to be justified by experience or fact. Statements which begin with *all* or *every* (or even *many* when the incidence is small) often lead to trouble because invariably someone will think of an exception to whatever you are saying. If you are careful to qualify, your assertions will often be workable.

Essentially, if you begin with a valid generalization through deduction or reach a valid generalization through induction, you should reach a valid conclusion. If you start or end with a faulty generalization, you will end up with an invalid conclusion. However the error is committed, the result is that careless thinking will be reflected in your writing. If you have an innate disrespect for intellectuals, it may show up in an essay about Henry Kissinger or Albert Einstein unless you carefully examine that generalized prejudice as you write. If you are too strongly influenced by someone you know who you think lives as a parasite on welfare, you may have difficulty writing a good paper about welfare problems. You must be able to adjust your ideas to a broader, more realistic assessment of welfare recipients. Unless you show the proud but helpless poor along with the frauds, your discussion may well miss its mark. Showing both sides would keep the generalizations workable.

To illustrate how crucial sound generalizations are to good writing, here is a short student essay which contains some serious problems with induction and deduction. The student was very serious about his beliefs, but the series of hasty generalizations he presented sadly diluted the effect he otherwise might have achieved.

> For some odd reason, the American economy is slipping away from us a little more each day. Prices are going sky high and consumers just do not have the money to cope with this kind of situation. Farmers are parading around the White House complaining about various inconveniences they experience each day. People cannot afford the prices, so they are stealing more each day. Yet we can go out and spend millions of dollars on space programs, movie stars, and athletes while there are thousands of little children in the slums starving to death.
>
> Let's face it! The United States has many problems to deal with and our slums is one of them. It is really embarrassing to this fabulous country of ours to go down the streets of Harlem and view some of the trashy scenes. Detroit is another city that is uncleanable and unlivable. Our government should make a point of straightening out the slum areas in our world to make our cities inhabitable again, for they sure aren't now.
>
> Farmers are not being treated fairly by our government either. They plead their cases constantly to Mr. Carter. But to no avail, they are rejected time and time again. They complain about prices being so high and then getting nothing out of it. The farmers plant the crops, but they never get their due.

Prices in our economy are becoming very ridiculous to say the least. For instance, I went into a restaurant and it cost me 80¢ to buy a small cup of orange juice. I asked the lady what the meaning was for this. She replied, "It costs us 60¢ to buy it and we need a 20¢ profit." That means to hell with the consumer. Once again, it is time for the government to step in and put some kind of control on prices in our economy.

President Carter made many promises at his inaugural speech, but he is not living up to them. When he walked down Pennsylvania Avenue that day several years ago, I was sure there was a great president for our country. He looked ambitious and willing to lead our economy minded nation to a common goal. But our economy is no better and in fact worse. Inflation is eating at all the American people's wallets. Our economy is suffering bad and there has to be some way to stop it. We as a total American family must find ways to head our economy into a respectable position so we can hurdle to the top as the number one nation.

From first paragraph to last, this essay makes generalizations which are unsupported and unsupportable. While inflation is certainly a fact of American life, some of this student's statements about the problem hover more in the realm of hasty generalization than in fact. A few of the more outrageous generalizations assert:

People cannot afford the prices, so they are stealing more each day.

. . . there are thousands of little children in the slums starving to death.

Detroit is another city that is uncleanable and unlivable.

. . . to make our cities inhabitable again, for they sure aren't now.

The farmers plant their crops, but they never get their due.

These are only a few of the generalizations which are offered in the essay as support for the state of the American economy. The problem of inflation may be real, but the extremes suggested by these statements are not supported in the essay. Most people do not steal; thousands of children actually starving to death in the slums may be an exaggeration; there are some parts of Detroit that are lovely; if our cities are not habitable now, where does our very large urban population live? And are there no farmers in America who make a profit and live comfortably? Obviously, these and other broad, hasty generalizations reduce the effectiveness of the argument this student wished to make.

Faulty causality

Chapter 5 discussed causal analysis to some extent. Such analysis reappears here because establishing causal relationships is actually a complex kind of induction, even if the best we can do is arrive at probable causes. Causal analysis is a daily routine for most of us. If the car refuses to start, we use inductive reasoning to try to find out *why*. We might check the gas gauge; we might jiggle the key in the ignition to see if the battery is dead; we might consider mechanical problems with the starter, carburetor, or fuel pump. Either we or our mechanics go through a logical process of elimination to determine why the car won't start.

This kind of induction can lead to false causes, however. Sometimes the cause is *oversimplified.* To say, "I failed the course because the teacher didn't like me" may well be oversimplifying the matter if you have completed few assignments and missed many of the classes. To say, "The slump in the airline industry is caused by inept management" may touch on one of the causes but there may be others—both immediate and long range—which you need to think about.

Another causal fallacy, *non sequitur,* assumes that one event is caused by another simply because they follow each other chronologically. *Non sequitur* means *it does not follow.* Few of us would say that the rooster's crowing causes the sun to rise. So, too, the off-brand of gasoline you used is not necessarily the cause of your car's breaking down two days later. The tuna fish you ate at lunch is not necessarily the cause of your stomach ailment that evening. The off-brand gas or the tuna fish could be responsible for your problems, but not just because they came first. In the same way, just because Bob Cousey was a good basketball player does not *necessarily* mean that he will be a good basketball coach. Just because Norman Mailer was a noted author does not mean that he would *necessarily* have made a good mayor of New York. Causes do come before their effects, but many events or incidents come before others which have no bearing on them whatever.

Another type of incorrect causal analysis occurs when someone offers only two alternatives to a given situation. Such a limitation presents an *either/or* fallacy. Sometimes blind to the complex elements which combine to form any situation, we conclude that there can be only two: Either we do this *or* we do that. Sometimes this stifles other possibilities. How many times, for instance, in the sixties and early seventies did we hear, "Either we get out of Vietnam or we go in there and bomb the hell out of them"? Then there was the bumper sticker which said, "America, love it or leave it." Even though Patrick Henry is immortalized for grandly proclaiming "Give me liberty or give me death," such thinking sometimes admits of no compromise or middle ground or additional options. The father who says to his son, "Either you get a haircut or pack your belongings and get out of here," is just as guilty of nearsighted thinking as the son who says, "Buy me my own car or I'll run away from home." While there must be some situations for which there are only two alternatives, most are more complicated than such limited thinking acknowledges. The either/or syndrome short-circuits logical investigation of other options.

Trivial analogy

A metaphor is a device to show a comparison without *like* or *as*. An *analogy* is really an extended metaphor which lets you explain a complex phenomenon by comparing it to one more easily understood. It is yet another type of inductive thought process which offers good support if handled correctly. An essay by Sydney J. Harris developed the thought that war is the cancer of mankind. Throughout the essay, Harris showed how the growth and habits of cancer cells could be likened to those forces in the world which culminate in the ugliness of war. He concludes the essay with:

> The cancer cells cannot exist without the body to inhabit, and they must be exterminated if they cannot be re-educated to behave like normal cells. At present, their very success dooms them to failure—*just as a* victorious war in the atomic age would be an unqualified disaster for the dying winner.

Analogies can be very effective if they are not strained too much, if there are real similarities to be explored, or if the comparison is not farfetched. An analogy is never proof in itself but it can work as a strong inductive support if it is not stretched. However, the analogy will fall flat if there is not enough similarity between the two parts or if that similarity is exaggerated. It then becomes a *trivial analogy*. For example, in one of the NFL player strikes, Roger Staubach, one-time quarterback for the Naval Academy and then quarterback for the Dallas Cowboys, went back to camp after only a few weeks of striking. Ed Garvey, Executive Director of the NFL Players' Association, commented in disgust on Staubach's action: "I sure as hell would hate to have been at Pearl Harbor with him." The difference between abandoning your colleagues under a destructive attack and going back to work during a strike is too broad to make this comment a workable analogy.

Exercises

1. Devise two examples of hasty generalization.
2. Devise two examples of each of the types of hasty generalization highlighted in this chapter: stereotype, status, appearance.

3. Create two examples of each of the types of faulty causality: oversimplified cause, non sequitur, and the either/or syndrome.
4. Try to think of two instances in which comparisons might become trivial analogies.

Some Other Fallacies and Pitfalls

Up to this point we have talked about fallacies which oversimplify or exaggerate generalizations. Some other fallacies openly distort a position—sometimes by attacking a person rather than the argument, sometimes by altering content, and sometimes by misusing language. Although we slip into these fallacies quite easily and innocently at times, there are other times when we use them, or they are used against us, quite calculatedly. Deliberate use does not make them any more logical, however, so we need to be aware of them also.

Distorting by attacking the opponent

One device often used by those who cannot successfully refute a clear, logical argument is *argumentum ad hominem,* or "Attack on the person." A bad habit, a way of dressing or speaking, or a belief is easier to attack than a strong argument. History has shown this device to be a much used and often successful political ploy despite its flimsy logic. Both Al Smith and John F. Kennedy, for example, were attacked by their political enemies for being Catholic, with the implication that they would thus be pawns of Rome. And of course *argumentum ad hominem* occurs in other arenas as well. Waslaw Nijinsky, for instance, was a brilliant ballet dancer whose reputation was often overshadowed by his homosexuality. Catholicism or homosexuality has nothing to do with a person's ability. *Argumentum ad hominem* aims a low blow and should be quickly exposed for the weak tactic that it is. In a debate of your own, you may find yourself threatened by someone who persists in bringing up your dating habits, your morals, your poverty, your wealth. Someone may tell you that you have no right to speak about the plight of the poor because of your middle-class background.

Distortions of content

Another approach to guard against is one which in some way distorts or alters the content of someone's ideas. Rather than honestly representing a position, occasionally people tend to twist, change, or otherwise misrepresent meaning in one of several different ways.

Attacking a straw man. There are times when we distort or exaggerate the content of someone's statements to try to destroy their logic through misrepresentation. This tactic is known as "attacking a straw man." Just as it is difficult to knock over a real man, it is difficult to attack a sound argument. But since it is easy to knock over a man made of straw, it is also easy to attack someone's position after you have distorted it to suit your purpose. *Argumentum ad hominem* diverts attention from a strong argument by dragging in personal traits; attacking a straw man distorts a strong argument by replacing it with a weaker one which can be assailed more easily. The weaker one can be an exaggerated version, a distortion, or sometimes an outright lie. Such a device is common in discussions of controversial subjects such as abortion, capital punishment, or rape. If someone says she does not believe that capital punishment is effective in discouraging murder, you would be attacking a straw man if you reduced the seriousness of her statement with "I bet you think we should just send killers back onto the streets with a little slap on the wrist." Belittling someone's idea is, unfortunately, quite a common way to try to destroy someone's credibility.

Red herring. To divert attention from a real issue, you may sometimes introduce a false, often emotional, yet irrelevant, issue to lure discussion away from the real point. For instance, a store owner, trying to soothe a customer whose order had been delayed, attempted to excuse his own neglect by saying, "You know, you can't depend on the long-haired, freaky help you get these days." He attempted to evade responsibility for the delay by using a red herring, the customer's own possibly negative attitude toward young people.

Distortions of language and numbers

Some other types of problems with logic rely upon actual words and numbers to create distortions.

Name-calling. Name-calling is not the standard tossing back and forth of naughty names that a group of children might do. Instead, it is the presentation of an issue in emotionally "loaded" language, often insulting racial, religious, or political slurs, which interferes with an objective, logical view of the subject. An example arises from the label "Irish Mafia" which is sometimes pasted on the Kennedy clan. And here is a passage of a "White Power" newsletter written in very loaded language:

> SLIMY SEX SITE
> Rodney Bingenheimer running latest youth sensation in L.A.: Rodney's Discotheque on Sunset Strip. . . . Many dressed as girls are really boys and vice-perverse-a.

"Many dressed as girls are really boys" and "vice-perverse-a": The language of this short piece is too loaded not to miss the distortions created to reflect the author's prejudices.

Slogans. Because of its familiarity, a well-known phrase or proverb can sometimes be seen as obvious "proof" to suggest a certain reaction or belief or to stop discussion. To make people feel they must buy Hallmark greeting cards to maintain status, that company devised the slogan, "When you care enough to send the very best." A young couple about to purchase appliances may really believe "You can be sure if it is Westinghouse." In another situation, if you overhear two people discussing an attractive third person, you might also hear one of them jealously say, "Ah, but beauty is only skin deep." We often use these slogans and proverbs as a stopgap, a way of proving something without actually offering any real proof.

Technical jargon: Sometimes we use unfamiliar words or technical terms to impress a reader or to cloud the real issue. On a simple, day-to-day level, if you are told that Sears Radial 36S tires have "one steel belt, four rayon cord belts and two polyester radial plies," you might feel that you should be impressed with the sturdiness of the tire. You may, however, have no idea of what any of those terms mean. On another level, you might find a phrase such as *terminate with extreme prejudice* intended as the military jargon for *kill.* Technical jargon can be perfectly harmless, but it can also create a web of confusion and misinterpretation.

Ignoring the context. Another way to distort an argument is to ignore part of it. If you quote from someone else's ideas, but omit meaningful sentences, words, or phrases, you are guilty of ignoring the context. In this way, either to support a position of your own or to praise or criticize someone else's by selective omission, you can slightly distort or misrepresent the original meaning and intent. Here is a simple example: You may have said to a friend, "You know I really like Mary, but when she gets in a bad mood, she really gets on my nerves." Then, your friend may have gone back to Mary and said, "Mary, she said you get on her nerves." Frequently, this kind of problem occurs when students do research. If the information does not quite support the point they wish to make, they sometimes bend it a bit. For example, a student doing research to prove that artificial sweeteners such as saccharin are dangerous might read the following item:

> Dr. Ernest Wynder, president of the American Health Foundation, cited an unpublished work of Sir Richard Doll and Bruce Armstrong that failed to reveal any impact of saccharin on the incidence of bladder cancer among thousands of diabetics who consumed larger quantities of the artificial sweetener than the general population over a twenty-year period. Dr. Wynder did not say whether the ingestion of large amounts of saccharin increased the incidence of other tumors in the diabetics.

The student would be ignoring the context if, to prove his point, he lifted the last part of the item:

> . . . the ingestion of large amounts of saccharin increased the incidence of other tumors in the diabetics.

Numbers and statistics: We tend to trust numbers, especially statistics, because they seem to be so objective. But they can be manipulated in a variety of ways to convey impressions that are false even though the underlying figures may be genuine. A common example of this kind of manipulation can be found in the numerous ads for devices for body building, chest stretching, and reducing. Typically such ads will say:

> I lost 6-½″ off my waist, 15 pounds of excess weight, 2-½″ off my hips . . . . I shaped up in just 14 days.

The numbers sound appealing, but of course they are deceptive. Ultimately other conditions, such as diet and exercise, are usually part of the hidden background of the satisfied customer appearing in the before and after pictures that accompany them.

Often numbers are distorted when they are offered as statistics, especially when the source of the statistics is not identified. Here is a typical passage taken, from a student's paper, showing how that abuse occurs:

> It is common knowledge that America has a severe case of the lazies. There are hundreds of thousands of jobs in the United States that constantly remain open. These positions stay unfilled and yet seven percent would rather sit back and collect unemployment insurance. This is a pure waste of manpower, usually at the taxpayer's expense.

Unless you qualify the source of those statistics, they are very suspicious and carry little weight. With the right kind of back-up, however, statistics could help you make a point:

> According to a 1975 University of Michigan survey on America's use of time, women workers waste less time on the job than men do. The average woman wastes thirty-five minutes in a typical day compared to fifty-two minutes for the average man.

But in all cases, statistics must be used carefully so that they are not deceptive. An article in *Reader's Digest* showed that in 1971 the percentage increase of unemployed in Switzerland was the highest in the world. Such a statement in itself would be rather startling to anyone who knows of the soundness of Switzerland's economy. The truth behind the statistic is that in 1970 there were 34 jobless persons in Switzerland; in 1971 the unemployment figure rose to a grand total of 51 – a devastating fifty percent increase.

Exercises

1. Try to create two examples of the fallacy which distorts content by attacking the opponent (argumentum ad hominem).
2. Create two instances in which content is distorted through attacking a straw man and then through red herring.
3. Find or devise some examples which illustrate how content can be distorted by the abuse of language or numbers. Give two for each of the following fallacies: name-calling, slogans, technical jargon, ignoring the context, and numbers/ statistics.

The Illogical Essay

Throughout this chapter we have talked about some errors in thinking and have given them labels to help identify them. Sometimes you can pinpoint a single problem; sometimes several problems work together to create a larger problem. To help you see these fallacies in a larger written context, here is a student essay which has a number of logic errors within it.

America's high rate of unemployment seems to rest within the fact that this country has become too highly automated and technical to hire the average unskilled laborer. *[Hasty generalization]* Even our government has proven that our society has become too technical for the average unskilled laborer. *[Hasty generalization]* They have issued statistics showing that the average unemployed man has only high-school education without a vocation of any kind. *[Questionable statistics]*

America's farming industry has become incredibly complex as compared to what it once was. Take dairy farming for example. That used to be just a matter of getting up early in the morning with a milk pail and going to the barn to milk the cows. *[Stereotype]* Anybody who thinks it is still that way is crazy. *[Argumentum ad hominem]* Dairy farmers have now all become computerized for maximum milking production. *[Hasty generalization]* This occupation, which at one time needed only unskilled labor, today is a highly specialized field.

The new architecture of today has made an increase in demand for specialized construction workers. In the recent past the construction of a building only needed to be supervised by a few skilled men. *[Hasty generalization]* It was the unskilled man who accomplished the task of the actual building. Today it is very rare to find unskilled laborers on a construction site: *[Hasty generalization]* Each man is required to perform a specialized skill which he must have some sort of formal training to accomplish.

At the present rate at which this country is growing technically, it's evident that growth will have the effect of leaving more and more people out of work. *[Faulty causality]* I don't believe America is going to become unautomated or untechnical so that all unskilled labor can work again. It's obvious that in order to get the unemployment rate down, America must devise some way to educate these unemployed people beyond high school. *[Non sequitur]* It might be argued that these unemployed individuals haven't the financial means to further their education beyond that of high school. Our good President Carter, however, has made provisions for the financially underprivileged to obtain funds for furthering their educations. These unskilled people should make use of this opportunity. Then, the unemployment rate will indeed eventually decrease to a more normal rate. *[Faulty causality]*

An essay such as this one is a common product of a freshman composition class. Its message and its impact are short-circuited by its series of hasty generalizations and stretched logic. We have to recognize that politicians and advertising copywriters who use fallacies frequently to sway public opinion are not alone in their deceptions. Most of us are also guilty of bending reason a little when we want to convince our children that they should be in bed by eight or to persuade our mothers that sixteen-year-olds are indeed old enough to drink beer. The labels are artificial; the problems are not. Sound inductive and deductive thinking is not native to all of us. It takes a little work but it is worth it.

The Essence of Argument

Non sequitur, argumentum ad hominem, induction, deduction, red herring, and other fallacies are traditionally included in a segment or chapter labeled *Argumentation.* Argumentation does not mean picking a fight; it means instead presenting and defending a position in a reasonable, logical way. That definition of argumentation has been an underlying thesis of this book from its beginning. In a sense all of the writing that you do is a kind of argumentation since the essence of a topic sentence or a thesis statement lies in your vision, attitude, opinion, or interpretation. Clear, logical thinking is at the base of all good writing, not just of argument. You can be just as illogical in making a hasty generalization in a description of how cute your child is as you can in an argumentative statement like, "The European Common Market is useless."

Description, narration, exposition, and argumentation are official labels for writing types, but in reality these types often meld into a functional combination aimed at convincing a reader of a point. While we may pass on information or describe or narrate, we are still usually attempting to make a point as well, and to persuade a reader that the point is valid. Even when you think you are passing on foolproof information, such as how to give first aid for a bee sting, there will be someone who will disagree either with your remedy or your process. Therein lies the essence of argument, the point of view which is the underlying substance of the thesis statement.

Just as witnesses to a robbery will have differing descriptions of getaway cars and villains, or varying tales about how the holdup took place, writers have different impressions and interpretations even when they are writing about the same subject. One person says, "Painting a house is a lot like creating a work of art"; another person says, "Painting a house is the epitome of coolie labor." Colored by point of view, the information each one passes on will differ, despite their common subject. Each house painter has as valid an argument as can be found in a more traditional argumentative statement, such as "The United States needs socialized medicine" or "Abortion is wrong."

Argument does not start or stop with heated discussion and pounding fists. It occurs whenever you are attempting to persuade a reader, even in a gentle way, that you have a point . . . and that means almost every time you pick up your pen or tap out something on your typewriter.

This chapter, then, should be an encapsulation of almost everything that has gone before. You need reliable support for a reliable focus. The quality of induction and deduction that goes into forming a thesis statement is as crucial to the success of any essay as is the quality of the supporting facts, statistics, examples, and reasons which flesh out its body. If you want to prove that Pan American Airlines is inefficient, you will not do so if you have only one incident of lost luggage or late takeoff. An airline of that size is not inefficient just because of one or even several such offenses. The support must be sensible and meaningfully arranged, making the best use of the gamut of rhetorical strategies and types available. You can prove that one department store is better than another by comparing and contrasting the two. You can take exception to a music critic's negative review of the Cleveland Symphony's All Brahms Festival Concert by mustering specific reasons. You can address the ill effects of gas rationing by making a causal analysis.

The material about muddy thinking on the preceding pages is important to all of the writing that any of us wish to do. Talking about errors in logical thinking is not just a futile or theoretical exercise. The traps are there. Although the labels may seem contrived, they help identify real problems. They should also help you think seriously about the assertions you make as you write. In this way, you may become sensitive to illogic in your own writing and in the writing of others, either by pinpointing single problems or several problems together.

Chapter Exercises

1. Examine the individual items given below and try to identify some of the distortions which each illustrates. Use the specific labels (i.e., stereotype, non sequitur, etc.). A single item may contain several types of errors.

a. Montgomery Ward ran an ad for a sale on a corrugated file on which the buyer could save a "big 22%." The original cost of the file was $3.00; the twenty-two percent savings amounted to sixty-six cents.

b. I really got cheated on that research paper I did. I put in so many hours on that thing that I should have gotten an *A*. And look what she gives me—a *D*.

c. After a last-period study hall in the cafeteria, the teacher shouts, "All right, I need a couple of volunteers to put the chairs up on the tables before we leave."

A student, a bit put off by this chore and brave enough to speak up, says, "I don't really think it's necessary for the kids to have to stay after school to pick up the chairs; after all, we have a maintenance crew that gets paid to do this job."

The teacher growls back at her, "Listen, you lazy, smart aleck! Do you think someone else should have to pick up after you like a baby? Or maybe you think they should pay you for coming to school!"

d. New Cold Power has enzymes to get out the worst kind of dirt in cold water.

e. You are a high-school senior trying to decide where you will go to college in the fall. You check the list of faculty in the state university catalog and find columns and columns of PhDs. You conclude that you must go to the state university to get a quality education.

f. Two women are arguing about abortion. One says "Abortion is wrong; it is against my religion and ethics." The other says, "I bet you'd change your tune if your thirteen-year-old daughter came home pregnant."

g. She should live to be one hundred years old. Look how healthy she is.

h. Johnny Carson said *Tinsel* was a good book. I'm going to get a copy.

i. McDonald's arches proudly proclaim "Over two billion sold."

j. Oh, he must be an excellent surgeon. Look at all the degrees he's got.

k. If you don't like the police, next time you're in trouble, call a hippie.

l. An ad for Lincoln Continental or Cadillac will often show the car parked on a wide green lawn in front of a pillared white mansion. A long-haired blond in a riding habit will be standing next to a sleek horse, and a tanned, mustached man in a plaid jacket with leather patches on the sleeves will hover nearby.

2. Here is a student essay based upon fairly respectable logic. Examine it to see if you can identify some of the strengths of its induction and deduction.

The viewer sits on the edge of his chair, eyes glued to the television set, oblivious to background noises. The stripper wiggles seductively, causing her bikini bottom to inch slowly downward. The girl, hanging desperately onto the edge of the cliff, screams in terror as the man with the scarred face begins prying her fingers loose, one by one. The world famous detective glares at the courtroom and prepares to announce the real identity of the murderer. Suddenly, the images vanish, and the bane of the television viewer's existence occurs: the commercial break. Despite their unwelcome intrusion, commercials can sometimes be as entertaining as the programs they interrupt.

If you stop to think about it, commercials introduce us to a conglomeration of truly unusual characters. An eccentric, four-inch-high man lives in and rows around the insides of toilet tanks while keeping them clean. Noses, varying in size and sex, hold meetings to discuss what is new in nasal sprays. Two confused containers of margarine, undoubtedly related, take turns claiming that they're butter. The infamous Fruits of the Loom are known for their ability to grow and shrink at will while a troupe of grinning, mustached scrub brushes shine bathtubs while chanting "scrubbing bubbles, scrubbing bubbles . . . scrubbing bubbles."

Not to omit the element of drama, psychotics and sadists, disguised as visiting neighbors, relatives, and friends, run rampant through commercials. A merciless visitor, ostentatiously sniffing, announces to the surrounding company that their hosts have obviously acquired a kitten. Another guest smirks as her white-gloved finger leaves a glaring path through the dust on the furniture. Relatives carefully smell sheets and pillowcases and leave reassured that their own have a more pleasant aroma. Even toilet paper is tenderly stroked by visitors and always found lacking in softness. A bridge team interrupts the card game to hunt for the air freshener. One unbalanced neighbor unable to find anything amiss next door becomes so desperate that she grinds a crayon into a table and then demonstrates that her furniture polish can remove even crayon smears.

Commercials also set up some ridiculous situations. Women need not curl their hair, when they can go from flat to fluffy just by shampooing. Afterwards, assured that their families don't want delicious fried chicken and hot, freshly baked potatoes, they can serve packaged stuffing with chicken they have just "shaked'n'baked." Before leaving for a night out, husbands can paint a few rooms in their tuxedos while their wives clean carpets wearing evening gowns. The night's entertainment might include a fast-food restaurant where never tired workers sing and dance while serving or a soda shop where the waiter imagines he is Gene Kelly the moment the magic words "Doctor Pepper" are spoken.

Finally, we have commercials to thank for giving us tantalizing glimpses of the exciting part-time activities stars pursue. Ex-Starship captain, William Shatner, is a cholesterol expert and explains various charts and graphs on lowering cholesterol. Juliet Mills runs a boutique for babies and is always on the lookout for a more absorbent diaper. When Farrah Fawcett-Majors and Jaclyn Smith are not occupied with selecting their crook-chasing outfits, they test hair conditioners and cream rinses. Bill Cosby spends his free time consuming Jello Pudding and Del Monte Green Beans by the case. And kindly Eve Arden prepares snacks of crackers spread with butter or margarine for hungry supermarket shoppers.

But all great entertainment must come to a finish. The commercials end, and the screen is blank for a second. Sadistic neighbors and unbalanced relatives return to their own homes. Farrah slips into a low-cut evening gown. The Tidy Bowl Man and the Fruits of the Loom leave to have a Doctor Pepper at the soda shop, and the viewer reglues his eyes to the television set as the picture reappears.

3. Examine some letters to the editor from your college newspaper and from your local newspaper. Analyze the logic and the quality of the thought you find in them. Identify the weak arguments as well as the strong ones and try to identify the techniques which the writers have used.
4. Pick at random one of the essays you wrote earlier in the course. Scrutinize it for the broad range of fallacies covered in this chapter. Identify each fallacy in the margin and suggest how it might have been avoided.
5. Choose a controversial subject, such as abortion, Salt II, use of life-support machines, etc., and write a short passage (one paragraph) in which you consciously distort the issue in some way by using one or several of the fallacies. Exchange papers with a classmate. Discuss together the fallacious elements that you find in each other's papers.
6. Cite by name the fallacies you find in the quotations given below. Again, you may find that more than one applies.

a. In a discussion of America's ecology problems at a national conference unsympathetic to the ecology movement, one delegate said, "My husband is a scientist . . . I wish he were here to tell you about the problems of our environment. It is a very serious matter." Her objections were overruled by comments such as, "Oh, scientists are a dime a dozen."
b. An item taken from an editorial in a local newspaper lamenting the state of affairs in America: "If we are to fight communism at any distant point where an incident is kicked up we will never find peace. And we will never find the cure for dread diseases due to lack of funds for needed research, and our personal conveniences will be held to a minimum."
c. A criticism of the Equal Rights Amendment: "The good Lord made us male and female and no constitutional amendment can do anything about that."
d. In a heated debate and mild scandal, the chairperson of a county Board of Directors was accused of "misappropriating county funds" and was asked to resign. Investigation showed that the man was indeed guilty of "misappropriating county funds"—$8.35 worth used to print and mail forty-five copies of a press release.
e. A statement by the Marijuana and Drug Abuse Commission: "There are very few heroin addicts . . . who did not begin by smoking marijuana."
f. A quotation from a noted presidential candidate: "The streets of our country are in turmoil. Communists are seeking to destroy our country. Russia is destroying us with her might. And the republic is in danger. Yes, danger from within and without. We need law and order! Without law and order our nation cannot survive."

7. Write an essay in which you discuss the presence of logical fallacies in one of the following areas:
a. advertising (you may need to narrow this discussion just to television ads or just to magazine ads or perhaps just to ads geared to sell a certain product such as cigarettes, automobiles, or shampoo).
b. politics (again, narrowing is in order; you might deal with a particular speech, a particular politician, a particular situation such as a convention, etc.).
c. a particular controversy (you may choose to deal with the arguments that line up evidence on just one side of a debate concerning something like federal financing of abortions, prosecution for political corruption, regulation of gasoline prices, or higher energy prices to enforce conservation, for example).

In your discussion, try to track down the errors in thought, whether they are due to simple distortions or to oversimplification or exaggeration. Use concrete references if you can. Cite actual quotes, clichés, jingles, slogans, statistics, etc., which are generally a part of the argument for one side or the other and which are generally guilty of some bending of reason. If the ad agent sets up a trivial analogy to sell a product or the candidate for mayor stoops to mention that an opponent had once been suspended from junior high school for smoking in the lavatory or the opponent of federally funded abortions begs the question by saying that poor women keep getting pregnant because they are naturally promiscuous, your essay should point out these and other errors which surround the subject. Be as specific as you can and beware of slipping into some of these fallacies yourself.

Chapter Checklist

1. Think through ideas to be sure they are clear and logical.
2. Arrive at the conclusions and judgments that become thesis statements and topic sentences by inductive reasoning (moving from specifics to a generalization) or deductive reasoning (moving from a generalization to specific applications).
3. Avoid common problems with inductive and deductive reasoning: hasty generalization (stereotype, status, appearance), faulty causality (oversimplified cause, non sequitur, either/or), and trivial analogy.
4. Try to control generalizations by using words such as *most, sometimes, several, some,* etc.
5. Avoid logical fallacies that attack the opponent (argumentum ad hominem), distort the content of an opponent's position (straw man, red herring), or distort the content of an essay by abusing language and numbers (name-calling, slogans, technical jargon, ignoring the context, statistics).
6. Make the thesis statement the essence of the argument, the attitude or opinion you express about the subject.

Researching and Writing

Tacked up on college bulletin boards across the land is a legion of note cards, scraps of paper, photocopied sheets, printed cards, or formal signs scrawled in longhand, neatly typed, or elegantly hand lettered. They all bear some variation of this message:

> Book Reports
>
> Term Papers
>
> Etc.
>
> Written for You Cheap
>
> Call John
>
> 829-6186

From actual companies with catchy names like Term Papers Unlimited to clever students peddling the fruits of their own last semester's labor, there is a crowd of ghostwriters waiting in the wings to offer their services for a price. Unfortunately, there are also some eager souls who out of fear or desperation are ready to accept. Needless to say, Term Papers Unlimited should be off limits . . . and your benign friend who is ready to sell a *B* paper for a lower price since it did not get an *A* should be avoided. Few composition instructors exist who can not recognize their own students' styles by the time the research paper assignment comes around.

The nervousness, the dread, the anticipation that many students bring to the task of producing a research project of some kind should not drive them into the arms (or the typewriters) of the enemy. Just as writing an essay is an extension of the skills used to write a paragraph, writing a research paper is an extension of the skills needed to write an essay. The paragraph structure will be similar; the focusing thesis statement will be the same; the introduction, body, and conclusion formats still hold. The main difference will be that the support for a research paper thesis will come at least in part from the ideas of others. The mechanical skills of note taking, footnoting, and bibliography compiling will be useful overlays on the basic skills you already have.

The Nature of the Research Paper

Research involves two sets of skills—handling your own written thoughts and handling those of others. High-school efforts at research often consist of copying carefully from encyclopedias, but that is not really research. Doing research is a process in which you integrate the thoughts, statistics, and details of other writers into your own work.

In a sense, as you research a subject, you become something of an expert in it. You soon know more than most people about the production of soap operas, the habits of beavers, the last ten days of Hitler, or sickle-cell anemia. But research is not just an academic exercise. These same research skills may serve you well later in your career when you must prepare a report for your company on which computer it should lease or on which stocks and bonds it should buy. The Congressional liaison, the real-estate agent, the insurance sales agent, the doctor, the biologist, any number of people besides English teachers and their students need some skill—a little or a lot—in doing some type of research. Their needs may not be quite as literary as those of the student researching the classical analogies in Milton's *Samson Agonistes,* but they are just as real. In part, this chapter is geared to information gathering no matter what the field; it should help you find what you want when you need to know it.

Preparing a research paper, then, is an extended exercise in finding, compiling, and assessing information. This information usually serves one of two purposes. It may act as support for an argument presented in essay form, To argue in support of or in opposition to the Equal Rights Amendment, for instance, you might need some supporting research to come up with facts and statistics to prove your point. But research may provide instead an overview or an explanation of a subject, a problem, or a question, such as the pollution of Lake Erie or the role of viruses in causing cancer. These are times when your thesis will hinge heavily on straight exposition.

The nature of the research paper demands that you find and examine the available oral, visual, and written materials relating to your subject and then integrate and interpret them to produce a new presentation of the topic. Whatever the nature of the research, it should give you some skill in all these areas: locating sources of information; sifting through and judging the value of the information you gather; integrating researched facts and opinions into the mainstream of your own work; and communicating ideas—your own and those of your sources—effectively. Good research is more than a long summary taken from one or two books; it is more than a string of quotes linked together with an original sentence or two; and it is certainly more than wholesale borrowing of other people's work. Good research involves a careful organization and presentation of information borrowed from others, but always as support for or explanation of *your* work.

A Sample Research Paper

On the following pages, you will find a sample research paper prepared by a freshman composition student. Read it to get an idea of what a research paper is and what it does. Do not be too concerned about the format. You will soon learn how to deal with footnotes and bibliographic items.

Generating a Topic

The first step in writing a research paper parallels the first step in writing an essay—selecting a topic of workable size. The subject of a fifty-page paper will differ from the one for a ten-page paper. Often your instructor will give you a topic or a list of topics. But if you are allowed to choose your own, you can do so easily if you keep in mind the principles for narrowing down an essay topic: Pick a subject—say, problems in prisons—and narrow that down to a smaller, more usable one—educational opportunities—in other words, one specific problem. Narrow that down even further to the problem as it relates to men, women, or juveniles.

The best topic is one about which you have some natural curiosity. Researching ten or fifteen pages about the habits of field mice can be awfully boring if you care little about the subject. A feminist might investigate the ideas and writings of Germaine Greer or Gloria Steinem. Someone involved in consumer affairs might wish to know more

While title page formats may differ according to instructor preference, this one is both standard and serviceable. It displays the basic information about subject and author.

About one third from the top of the page, type the title of the paper and your own name.

About one third from the bottom of the page, put the course, teacher, and date.

PASSIVE USE OF SOLAR ENERGY

IN HOUSING

by

Delia D. Gerace

English 101, Section 062

Ms. Sandra Kurtinitis

December 11, 1978

One well-developed paragraph of introduction is sufficient for most research papers.

This introduction uses a type of funnel to work down to the thesis. It begins with a broad reference to energy concerns, works down to the issue of solar energy, and descends further to one specific way in which individuals can take advantage of the sun's energy—through passive solar heating in their houses.

Passive Use of Solar Energy in Housing

During the last ten years, the United States has become acutely aware of the shortage of fuels for energy. While we have oil, gas, and coal within our own boundaries as well as geothermal energy, wind, and sun, we have allowed ourselves to become dependent on the Arab nations since oil is our main source of energy. We do have the other options, however. The Alaskan pipeline already furnishes adequate oil supplies to the West Coast, and if the present project in the Baltimore Canyon in the Atlantic Ocean bordering New Jersey is successful, we will have enough oil for all our needs for many years to come. The central states such as Kansas and Oklahoma are subject to strong, recurring winds which could be harnessed to supply energy. In the West, studies are in progress to help us make better use of the geothermal energy of geysers. In the East to a larger extent and in the West on a smaller scale, there is still coal to be mined. The greatest source of energy, however, is the sun, which is available to all states and all nations practically all of the time. As

Pages are numbered with Arabic numerals in the upper right-hand corner. Any page that has a heading on it is not numbered but is counted into the numbering.

Quotations should be used as supporting evidence. To help the reader evaluate their significance, the text introducing them may, as here, indicate the nature of the source. Short quotations should be included in the text as shown here. Quotations longer than three lines are set off with indentation on each side and single-spacing; quotation marks are omitted.

The actual thesis statement of the research paper works exactly as the thesis statement of an essay.

As in an essay, each paragraph has a focusing topic sentence. In this instance, it is the first sentence in the paragraph. Each paragraph is then developed by specific support, some of it research, some of it general information.

Footnote documentation covers quotations, paraphrases, and summaries. Number footnotes sequentially from 1 to 30, 40, etc., throughout the paper. Place the number after the material to be documented and elevate it one half space. (See page 271 for information on footnoting.)

Footnote documentation can come either at the bottom of the appropriate page or it can be compiled as endnotes at the end of the paper. The basic format varies for each entry according to the type of source. This first entry is a footnote for a magazine article. (See pages 274–76 for specific directions on how to do each type of footnote/endnote.)

The Sierra Club Bulletin of May 1974 says, "It is somebody's oil, but everybody's sun."[1] While we wait for the scientists, the technicians, the federal government, and the business community to develop and make available to us the various sources of energy, it would be to our advantage, as individuals, to make use of the sun. While we can choose either active or passive solar design systems, applying simple, passive designs to our houses would allow us to employ solar energy without costly outlay or extensive equipment.

An active solar energy system combines technology and engineering to produce a functioning system of solar collectors and reactors to both heat and cool a structure. Such systems are not just dreams of the future. As early as 1913, the Shuman-Boys solar power plant in Meadi, Egypt, was successfully powered by solar steam on the banks of the Nile.[2] But fossil fuels were plentiful and inexpensive in the first three-fifths of this century, so no incentive propelled the development of solar energy. Now, when the cost of a gallon of

[1]"Solar Energy," The Sierra Club Bulletin, 4 May 1974, p. 16.

[2]U.S. Department of Energy, Solar Energy (Washington, D.C.: U.S. Government Printing Office, 1978), p. 21.

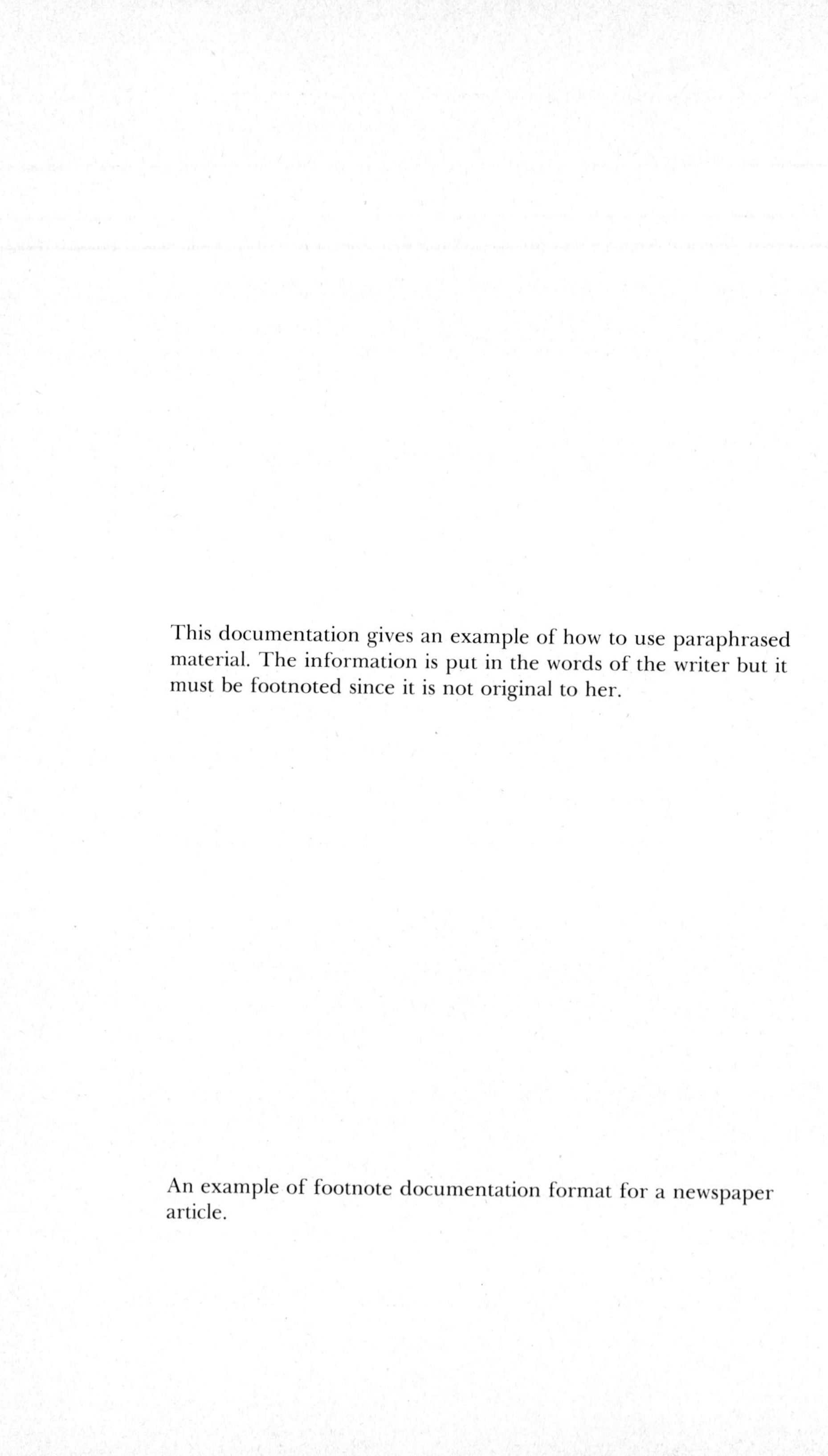

This documentation gives an example of how to use paraphrased material. The information is put in the words of the writer but it must be footnoted since it is not original to her.

An example of footnote documentation format for a newspaper article.

heating oil exceeds a dollar, the concerns are very different. An elementary school in Fairfax,, Virginia, a library in Silver Spring, Maryland, and a home in Forestville, Maryland, are some of the few buildings which have been designed and erected in the past decade as consumers and builders attempt to grasp the energy from the sun. But active solar energy systems are expensive and cumbersome. A solar system that would save one hundred gallons of fuel per heating season might cost $5,000 to $6,000 to build. It would also require costly maintenance throughout its lifetime.[3]

A passive solar energy system is a very different concept. Rather than existing as a workable machine with components, passive solar energy exists as a concept with many manifestations. These are several architectural and landscape designs, many of which can be employed in an existing structure with almost no expense. The way a house is built, the manner in which it is sited, the way in which it is furnished can all help a consumer curtail the heating costs of a home to some degree.

One of the main features in passive design is the

[3]Thomas Grubisich, "Fuel Costs Cut Sharply in Six New Virginia Homes," <u>The Washington Post,</u> December 9, 1978, Sec. E. p. 1. col. 1.

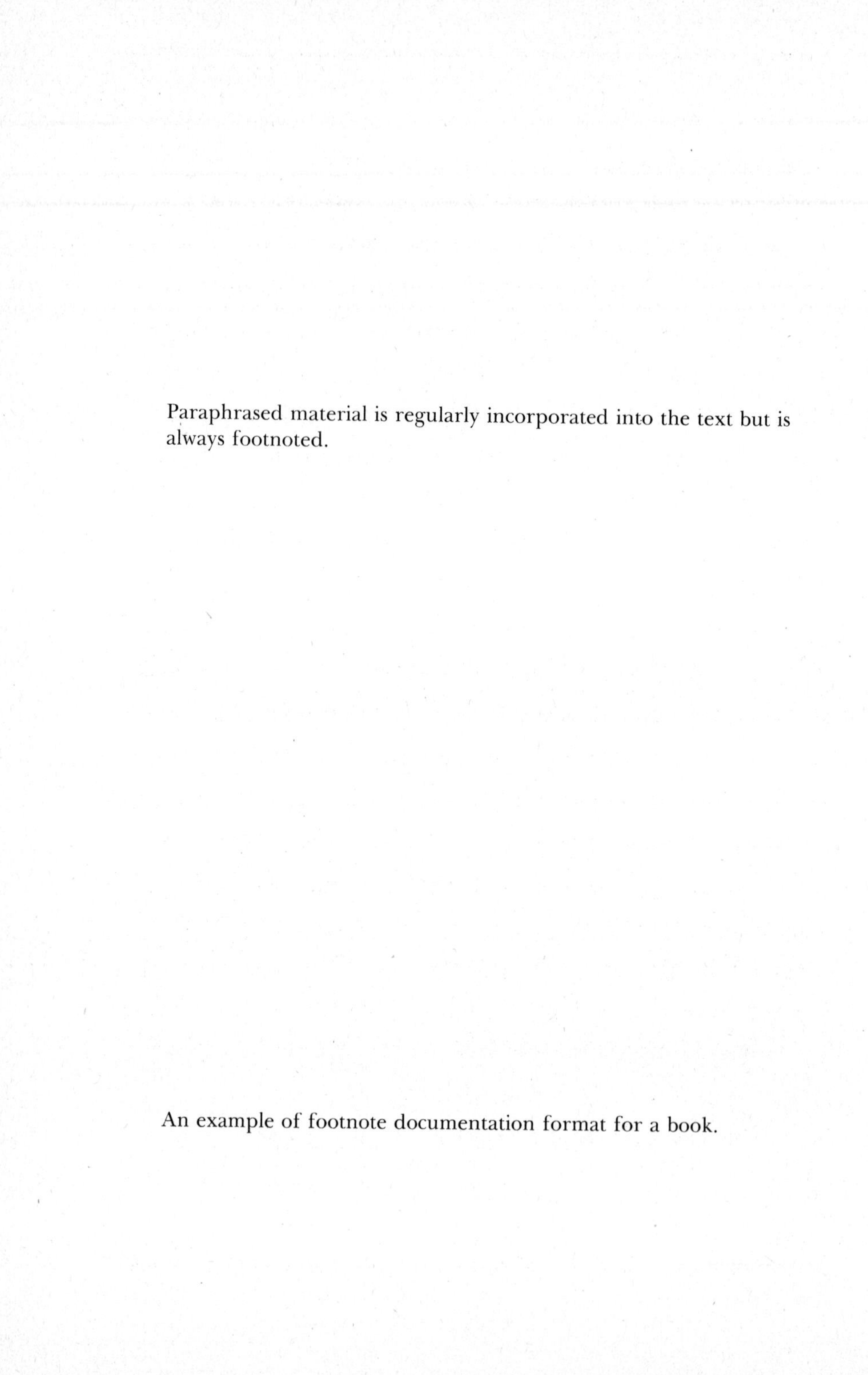

Paraphrased material is regularly incorporated into the text but is always footnoted.

An example of footnote documentation format for a book.

site upon which the house is to be built. In the past, builders of houses have avoided using hilly sites. These sites required too much landscaping, were hard to reach, and were generally not desired by the purchasing public. Architects now say that the ideal site for a house is on a hillside with a south-facing exposure.[4] Such "undesirable" lots may also be less expensive. The plans for the house should have the living area on the south side. This south-side wall should be made of glass which will capture and transmit the warm rays of the sun. The north underground wall should be well insulated; it should also be treated to eliminate dampness, effect good drainage, and keep out insects.[5] The advantage of the north underground wall is that the earth constantly remains at a temperature of 55°F. The inside temperature of the house can then be better controlled. If a hillside site is not desirable or available, the north wall of the house should be constructed solidly and have no openings. Also the

[4]National Solar Heating and Cooling Information Center, Passive Design Ideas for the Energy Conscious Consumer (Rockville, Maryland: National Solar Heating and Cooling Information Center, n.d.), p. 5.

[5]Alex Wade and Neal Ewenstein, 30 Energy-Efficient Houses You Can Build (Emmaus. Pennsylvania: Rodale Publishers, 1977), p. 174.

After a source has been named once in a footnote, subsequent references to it can be made through a shortened form. Use only the author's last name and the appropriate page number. (See page 273 for more explanation.)

north side should be lined with evergreen trees to keep out the cold and wind in the winter and to absorb the summer heat.

Another method that takes advantage of the earth's constant temperature is "berming." A berm is a narrow ledge or shelf. Berming is nothing more than surrounding the entire perimeter of a house with earth up to the window sills and then sloping the berm to the level of the lot. This method could actually pack the earth almost to the roof of the house. In this way it could be combined with solar collectors, rock storage bins, and air ducts within the berm to incorporate active solar systems into the structure. Berming by itself, however, can be a simple addition to energy efficiency in a structure.[6]

In addition to the site and the possibility of berming, the shape, the height, and the general layout of the house can also affect its energy efficiency. For instance, some architects feel that a circular house, although rather unconventional, is the best design. The perimeter of a circular house is the smallest; therefore, it gives the minimum exterior surface and

[6]National Solar Heating and Cooling Information Center, pp. 14, 15, 21.

resultant high savings.[7] A one-story house is the second-best design because it is easier to insulate than a two-story house.[8] Building a wooden house with double walls and double insulation in both walls and ceilings reduces energy consumption by astounding margins. Such a house built in the Giles Knoll subdivision in Fairfax, Virginia, by former Smithsonian designer Harry Hart used about 175 gallons of fuel oil throughout an entire winter as opposed to the average 1200 gallons used in the Washington, D.C., area. The heating bill of this family is a little less than $100 a year instead of the more normal $685 per year for this area.[9]

Other factors contributing to energy conservation by capitalizing on the sun relate to the placement of windows and doors and additions of porches. There should be no windows on the east and west sides of the house, for instance.[10] Skylights can also be useful to take advantage of the sun during the day. Doors should once again open into the old-fashioned vestibule which

[7]Henry T. Spies, et al., 350 Ways to Save Energy (and Money) (New York: Crown Publishers, Inc., 1974), p. 17.

[8]National Solar Heating and Cooling Information Center, p. 10.

[9]Grubisich, p. C-17.

[10]Grubisich.

is now called an "air-lock." This air lock traps the cold air, or hot air, thus eliminating the escape of the air which is in the house.[11] Greenhouses attached to the sides of houses can also act as a vestibule or air lock and can thus become energy savers. Finally, the front and back porches of many old houses are now becoming fashionable again since they act as awnings to shield the house from the cold and snow of winter and the heat of the sun of summer.

Some materials are better than others insofar as their ability to retain heat is concerned. Wood is perhaps one of the best materials to use. In _30 Energy-Efficient Houses You Can Build,_ Wade and Ewenstein say that wood soaked in creosote for posts and beams is probably one of the best materials to be used for the foundation of a home. This was a method used by the Pilgrims in 1620. A wooden frame for a house can be made more sturdy and add support if the siding is placed on the diagonal.[12] Cypress and redwood are good woods to use for neither requires much care and both are weather-

[11]Ronald Derven and Carol Nichols, _How to Cut Your Energy Bills_ (Farmington, Michigan: Structures Publishing Company, 1976), p. 12

[12]Wade and Ewenstein, p. 212.

resistant.[13] Brick, cement, stone, concrete, and glass are other materials which, if properly used, will either transmit heat or absorb and retain it.

Passive solar energy ideas can also design the interior of a house to take advantage of the sun and aid in energy conservation. Masonry fireplaces in the center of a house will radiate heat throughout the entire house. A two-story house will benefit from this central fireplace since heat rises to warm the second floor as well. Interior walls and ceiling can be made of wood, which radiates heat somewhat, instead of conventional plaster or plaster board, which do not. Wood can even be put to good use in a room such as the bathroom.[14]

Furnishings can aid in passive solar energy layout as well. Placing large pieces of furniture such as bookcases, china closets, couches, etc. along the outside walls of a house helps to insulate it. The use of venetian blinds or louvers can aid immensely in heating and cooling individual rooms in a house.[15] _30 Energy-Efficient Houses_ illustrates a concrete _banco_

[13]G. Kimball Hart, _et al_., _How to Cut Your Energy Costs_ (Washington, D.C.: U.S. News & World Report, Inc., 1978), p. 29.

[14]Wade and Ewenstein, pp. 54, 225.

[15]Hart, pp. 54-55.

(bench) placed directly beneath a window and adjacent to a fireplace. The banco camouflaged a fifty-five gallon drum of water. This water helped to retain the heat from the sun and from the fireplace, an ingenious way to use all of the elements.[16]

Many businesses and private individuals have begun to make use of solar energy. Some of these projects have been in existence for many years, although most of them use active solar design. Newspapers and magazines are filled with articles and advice about solar energy, and their concern has begun to include a vigorous pursuit of passive solar energy as the cheaper, more easily reachable goal of the consumer who wants neither to build a new house nor install a costly active solar system. Many people are already taking advantage of the tax credits and insulating their homes. On Maryland's Eastern Shore a home has been built incorporating brick under glass for the retention of heat. Builders are experimenting with additional energy packages for their customers. Overall, there is a strong surge to try to overcome the viselike grip which fossil fuels have on our economy and our lives.

In an early 1978 speech, President Carter compared the conservation of energy to "the moral equivalent of

[16]Wade and Ewenstein, p. 175.

The conclusion of the research paper is very much the same as the conclusion of an essay. This one sums up the paper's content with a projection for future use of passive solar energy. It then caps the entire discussion with a relevant quotation.

war." Perhaps this statement was too emphatic, but we need to be urged along to get things done. To this end, Congress has passed two laws which directly affect solar energy. Public Law 93-473, 93rd Congress, S.3234 established the Solar Energy Research Institute to research, develop, and demonstrate the use of solar energy. The second law, the Energy Tax Act of 1978, H.R. 5263, signed November 9, 1978, gives tax credits to those who wish to help in energy conservation. In his article "Spending to Conserve Energy Can Mean Tax Credits," E. Edward Stephens writes that the Energy Tax Act of 1978 will permit large credits to those who "buy solar, wind, or geothermal equipment to help heat or cool" their home.[17]

While not every United States citizen will benefit from this new legislation, many can tap solar energy in its passive if not its active mode. Those who will build new houses would do well to explore passive designs and tax breaks before planning the home. Others who have no plans for building new houses can still employ passive designs in existing houses. The day will come when technology will make it possible for us to use the rays of the sun to our best advantage.

[17]E. Edward Stephens, "Spending to Conserve Energy Can Mean Tax Breaks," The Washington Star, November 1978, Sec. B, p. 37, col. 1.

The Bibliography alphabetically lists all of the sources used in the research, not just those mentioned in the footnotes. Note that bibliography format differs slightly from footnote format. Check pages 257–60 for specific differences.

Bibliographic entry for a newspaper article.

Bibliographic entry for a book.

When a source has three or more authors, you can either use this format of author's name plus *et al.,* Latin for *et alia* (and others) or you may use the first author's name plus "and others."

When no author is given for a source, start the entry at the margin with the title. Use the first letter of the title (other than *A* or *The*) to place it in the bibliography in alphabetical order.

BIBLIOGRAPHY

"Building and Realty Revue." The Washington Star, November 10, 1978, Sec. E, p. 2, col. 3.

Cahill, Regina. "Poolseville Uses Wits to Save Kilowatts." The Washington Star, November 19, 1978, Sec. B, p. 10, col. 5.

Derven, Ronald, and Carol Nichols. How To Cut Your Energy Bills. Farmington, Michigan: Structures Publishing Company, 1976.

Grubisich, Thomas. "Fuel Costs Cut Sharply in Six New Virginia Homes." The Washington Post, December 9, 1978, Sec. E, p. 1, 17, col. 1.

Hart, G. Kimball, et al. How To Cut Your Energy Costs. Washington, D.C.: U.S. News & World Report, Inc., 1978.

National Solar Heating and Cooling Information Center. Passive Design Ideas for the Energy Conscious Consumer. Rockville, Maryland: National Solar Heating and Cooling Information Center, n.d.

"Solar Energy." The Sierra Club Bulletin, 4 May 1974, p. 16.

When several items by the same author are listed, write out the author's name only once. Thereafter, use ten hyphens to substitute for the name.

Spies, Henry T., _et al_. _350 Ways to Save Energy (and Money)_. New York: Crown Publishers, Inc., 1974.

Stephens, E. Edward. "Spending to Conserve Energy Can Mean Tax Breaks." _The Washington Star_, November, 1978, Sec. B, p. 37, col. 1.

U.S. Department of Energy. _Put the Sun to Work Today_. Washington, D.C.: U.S. Government Printing Office, 1978.

----------. _Solar Energy_. Washington, D.C.: U.S. Government Printing Office, 1978.

U.S. Department of Housing and Urban Development. _Solar Energy and Your Home_. Rockville, Maryland: National Solar and Heating Information Center, 1977.

Wade, Alex, and Neal Ewenstein. _30 Energy-Efficient Houses You Can Build_. Emmaus, Pennsylvania: Rodale Press, 1977.

about one of the crusades of Nader's Raiders against dangerous toys, perhaps, or unsanitary conditions in meat packing plants. A nursing student might explore the nature of a drug like Laetril, thought by some to be a miracle cure for cancer. A data-processing trainee might do some research on the mini-computer and its role in small business. A good way to find a topic which might interest you is to browse through a magazine, newspaper, or encyclopedia to see if you can find something you would like to know more about.

Once you have selected a general area for development, try to narrow down your study as efficiently as possible. When Delia Gerace began to work on the research paper you just read, she was generally interested in energy matters and thought she would like to write about the energy crisis. Although the broad subject of energy matters was too big for a ten-page paper, Delia was struck by some articles she had read about solar energy. As she began her research, reading widely in books and articles relating to the subject, she realized that her topic was still too broad. There was enough material for a book rather than a ten- to fifteen-page paper. However, she also discovered that a way of narrowing the subject would be to deal with only one of the two types of solar energy—active, that which relies upon solar collectors, and passive, the design adjustments that can be incorporated into building any structure. Once she limited the discussion to passive solar energy design, she had a topic suited to the approximate size of the paper assigned. When she began this research project, Delia knew next to nothing about solar energy. By the time she finished, she had gained a thorough understanding of the problems and systems as well as valuable experience in researching and integrating information.

Exercises

1. Pass judgment on the possible effectiveness of the following topics for a ten- to fifteen-page research paper.
   a. The Development of British Common Law from the Magna Carta to the Present
   b. Charlie Chaplin
   c. Margaret Thatcher: Britain's Iron Lady
   d. Crimes Against the Aged
   e. Hitler's Rise to Power
   f. The Invention of the Parking Meter
   g. Water Pollution

h. Canada's Bilingual Problem
i. Legalization of Prostitution in America
j. O. Henry's Short Stories

2. As the first phase of producing a research paper, define a workable topic suitable for a ten- to fifteen-page research paper. Try to find a subject in which you are interested as well as one which can be handled comfortably within the allotted scope. Two large topic areas from which you might choose a workable topic would be:
   a. A person, either a contemporary or someone from the recent past. Discuss his or her contribution to the cultural milieu. This should not be a biography, but an attempt to analyze someone's involvement in the problems of his or her time: e.g., Jimmy Carter, Paul Simon, Phyllis Schaffly, Saul Bellow; in short, a person integrally involved in some contemporary phenomenon—a musician, artist, sculptor, union leader, politician, etc.
   b. A valid contemporary problem: e.g., a problem in the prisons, a problem in higher education, an alternative energy source, violence in children's television, etc.

Preparing the Bibliography

Once you have narrowed the topic, you can begin the first stage of your research by accumulating a *bibliography*. The bibliography is the list of sources (books, magazines, newspapers, pamphlets, filmstrips, personal interviews, and so on) which you will use in the preparation of the paper. If your assignment is brief enough, you can just make a brief list of sources on a sheet of scratch paper. The more usual way of collecting bibliographic sources, however, is to put each entry on a separate 3 × 5 index card or a small slip of paper.

Finding the sources

You can begin assembling your bibliography in several ways. Sometimes the topic will dictate or restrict the sources you will want to use. If your topic is very contemporary, you may not find any book-length studies of it. If it is historical or political, you may find that most of your sources are lengthy volumes. If it relates to popular culture, your sources will be largely popular periodicals, such as *People, Time,* or *New York,* or interviews with people directly involved, maybe a street peddler or a social worker. If your subject is specialized, your sources will be specialized: medical journals, for instance, or volumes of literary criticism. To get well-balanced information, you might go through the various research tools in the following order, looking first for books, then magazine articles, then newspaper articles, and finally miscellaneous sources such as personal interviews or filmstrips.

To find books

Card catalog. This is a list of all the books in a particular library. The material in the card catalog is indexed in three ways: by author, by title, and by subject. Initially, the *subject headings* will be most helpful, although using them at times requires some ingenuity. For example, if you need information on "Educating the Mentally Retarded Child" and you find no such heading in the catalog, try the listing for a related subject such as "Special Education." Or possibly some of the books about mental retardation in general may have chapters on the education of the mentally retarded. Here is a sample of a card catalog entry under a subject heading Delia Gerace might well have used in her search for material on solar energy.

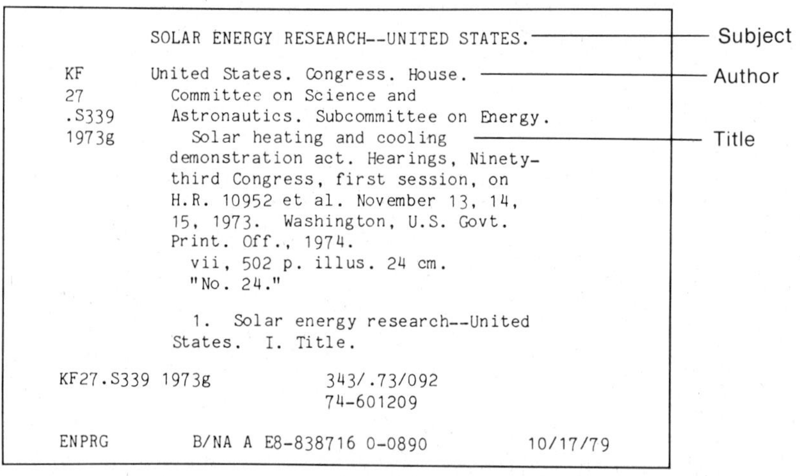

```
            SOLAR ENERGY RESEARCH--UNITED STATES.                Subject

KF          United States. Congress. House.                      Author
27            Committee on Science and
.S339         Astronautics. Subcommittee on Energy.
1973g           Solar heating and cooling                        Title
              demonstration act. Hearings, Ninety-
              third Congress, first session, on
              H.R. 10952 et al. November 13, 14,
              15, 1973.  Washington, U.S. Govt.
              Print. Off., 1974.
                vii, 502 p. illus. 24 cm.
                "No. 24."

                1.  Solar energy research--United
              States.  I. Title.

KF27.S339 1973g            343/.73/092
                           74-601209

ENPRG          B/NA A E8-838716 0-0890          10/17/79
```

You can also look for material under the name of an author you know has written a book about your subject. If Delia Gerace was aware that the Subcommittee on Energy of the House Committee on Science and Astronautics had done a report on solar energy, she could look under that committee's name as author if she did not know the actual title of their publication.

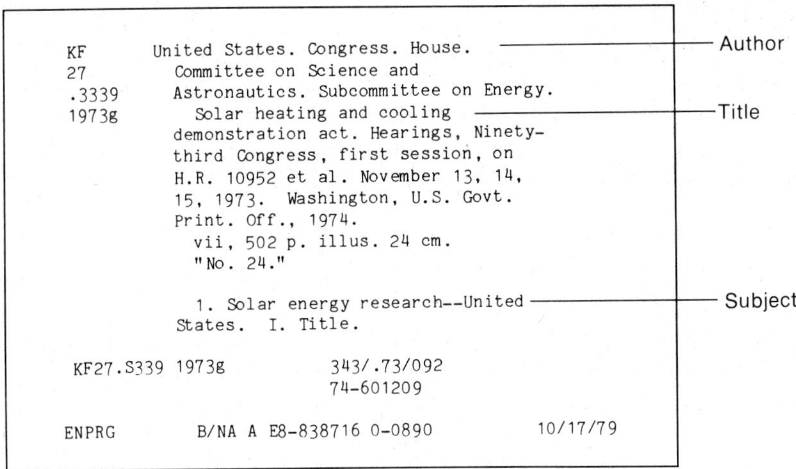

KF 27 .3339 1973g United States. Congress. House. Committee on Science and Astronautics. Subcommittee on Energy.
Solar heating and cooling demonstration act. Hearings, Ninety-third Congress, first session, on H.R. 10952 et al. November 13, 14, 15, 1973. Washington, U.S. Govt. Print. Off., 1974.
vii, 502 p. illus. 24 cm.
"No. 24."

1. Solar energy research--United States. I. Title.

KF27.S339 1973g 343/.73/092
74-601209

ENPRG B/NA A E8-838716 0-0890 10/17/79

If Delia did not know the title of the report she could simply search for a title of a book she knew was related to the subject of solar energy.

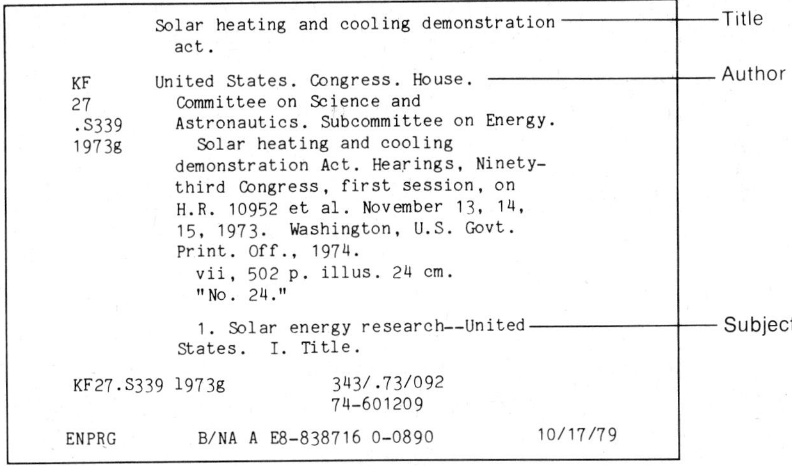

Solar heating and cooling demonstration act.

KF 27 .S339 1973g United States. Congress. House. Committee on Science and Astronautics. Subcommittee on Energy.
Solar heating and cooling demonstration Act. Hearings, Ninety-third Congress, first session, on H.R. 10952 et al. November 13, 14, 15, 1973. Washington, U.S. Govt. Print. Off., 1974.
vii, 502 p. illus. 24 cm.
"No. 24."

1. Solar energy research--United States. I. Title.

KF27.S339 1973g 343/.73/092
74-601209

ENPRG B/NA A E8-838716 0-0890 10/17/79

Union Catalog. This is a list of all the books available in the Library of Congress. These are indexed just as they would be in a card catalog—by author, title, and subject. You can use this catalog to learn what related books are to be found outside of your own library. Although the Union Catalog can be useful, not all libraries have it.

To find magazine articles

Reader's Guide to Periodical Literature. These big green volumes, published yearly, list magazine articles in alphabetical order by author and subject. They are an invaluable aid in tracking down articles, reviews, editorials, and the like relating to your subject. Specialized journals are not indexed in this publication; it is confined to the more popular magazines such as *Reader's Digest, Atlantic Monthly,* and *Harper's.* To make the best use of the *Reader's Guide* you must often look through many issues under a variety of headings. The *Reader's Guide* does not use standard bibliographic format; it uses its own abbreviations in its entries since it compiles such large amounts of information annually. Here is a sample entry, one which Delia no doubt scanned to settle on her solar energy bibliography.

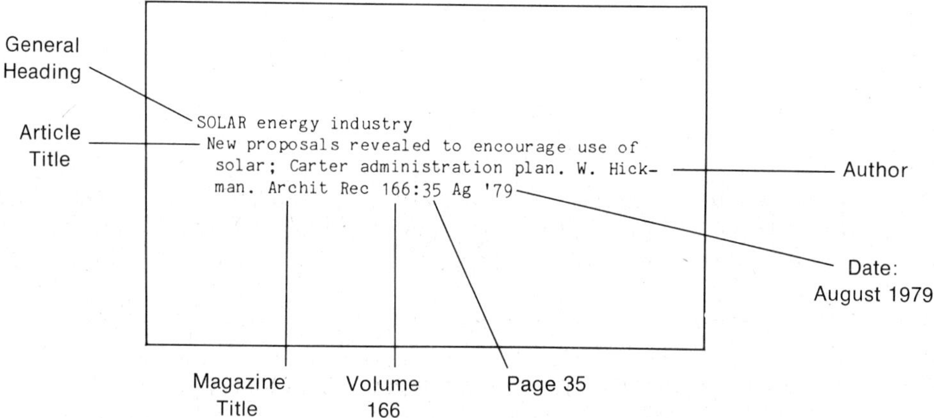

Special indexes. While you are in the reference section, you should also check any special indexes which might include material related to your topic. For example, if you are working on a paper about Jim Croce, check the *Music Index;* for a paper on computer time-sharing, consult the *Business Periodicals Index;* for a paper on malnutrition in America, try the medical index, the *Cumulated Index Medicus.* These indexes direct you to articles in the specialized and professional journals. The list below shows some of the special indexes which might be helpful and readily available according to common subjects:

Art	*Art Index*
Business	*Business Periodicals Index*
	Industrial Arts Index
Education	*Education Index*

Engineering	*Engineering Index*
Literature	*Book Review Digest*
	Dramatic Index
	Essay and General Literature Index
	Social Sciences and Humanities Index
Medicine	*Cumulated Index Medicus*
	Nursing Studies Index
Music	*Music Index*
Science and Technology	*Applied Science and Technology Index*
	Biological and Agricultural Index
Social Sciences	*Psychological Abstracts*
	Social Sciences and Humanities Index

Playboy Magazine Index. Along with its better-known items, *Playboy* frequently publishes excellent interviews, as well as general articles and reviews. It has its own index, however, since it is not included in the other indexes.

To find newspaper articles

The New York Times Index. This index is the most renowned for finding newspaper information. It provides a key to that giant newspaper's contents for the past several decades. Since the date when a news item appeared in the *Times* is likely to be the date when accounts of the same event were published in other newspapers as well, this index can help you research newspapers which have no indexes.

Other indexes of major newspapers. Some other newspapers—especially big city newspapers—have indexes of their own. Often if a newspaper has no printed index, it will have a telephone index which you can call. Some special interest newspapers, such as *Christian Science Monitor* and the *Wall Street Journal,* also have published indexes.

To find other kinds of material

Vertical file. This is an alphabetized collection of pamphlets, newspaper clippings, and such, available in some form in most libraries.

Audio-visual catalogs. These list a library's holdings in records, filmstrips, film loops, short films, and tapes.

Personal interviews. Interviews with people who have some specific knowledge of the subject with which you are dealing can be helpful.

Encyclopedias. You should use no more than one encyclopedia in your bibliography and it should be a good one—the *Encyclopaedia Britannica* or the *Encyclopedia Americana.* Both of these encyclopedias have a collection of carefully researched articles and may provide excellent background material on your subject.

Biography indexes. Indexes documenting information about the lives or achievements of individuals may be useful. Among them are the *Biography Index, Who's Who in America,* the *Dictionary of American Biography,* and the *Dictionary of National Biography.*

Bibliographic form

The research paper is quite formalized, with consistent patterns of documentation. These patterns form a universal method of recording information. The format offered here follows the standard Modern Language Association (MLA) Style Sheet, but there are other forms used in different disciplines. If your instructor wishes you to use another form, do so; the important thing is to be consistent. The format for the MLA-style bibliography entries can be imitated from the models on the following pages. You will need this information later for documenting the material you use in footnotes as well as for a final bibliography.

> Author (last name first; if no author is named, start with the title).
>
> Title (underline a book title; use quotation marks for an essay or article).
>
> Editor or translator, if any.
>
> Publication facts (generally includes place, publisher, and date of publication; the exact information to be specified for items of various types is indicated in the models that follow).
>
> Any information useful for finding the item (call number, particular library, and so on).
>
> Any information of special significance about the item ("written by a questionable authority," "one good chapter on . . . ," and the like).

Each bibliography card, then, will look something like this:

> KF
> 59
> .D446
>
> Derven, Ronald, and Carol Nichols. How To Cut Your Energy Bills. Farmington, Michigan: Structures Publishing Co., 1976
>
> Quick list of practical suggestions.
>
> Univ. of Penna.

On the following pages are the models for various bibliographic entries. When you prepare your bibliography cards, follow these models carefully, since in some respects different information is required for items of different kinds. It is true that you can collect bibliography items in a more random fashion on a sheet of notebook paper, but be sure you get enough information so that you can assemble a complete bibliography when you finally need to.

Books. This item shows what goes into a book entry as well as how to punctuate it:

AUTHOR. [last name first] TITLE. [underlined] EDITOR or TRANSLATOR. ["ed." or "trans." followed by name] EDITION. [except when it's the first] SERIES. [if applicable] NUMBER OF VOLUMES. [in Arabic numerals] PLACE OF PUBLICATION: PUBLISHER, DATE OF PUBLICATION.

You will not need all of this information for all books. Arrange and punctuate what you need as shown. For books of various types, the bibliographic entries are as follows:

One author

Crichton, Michael. The Andromeda Strain. New York: Dell Publishing Co., Inc., 1970.

Two authors

Postman, Neil, and Charles Weingartner. Teaching as a Subversive Activity. New York: Dell Publishing Company , Inc., 1969.

Notice that only the first author's name is given in reverse order.

Three or more authors

Boak, A. E. R., et al. The Growth of Western Civilization. 4th ed. New York: Appleton-Century-Crofts, Inc., 1951.

Either the Latin abbreviation *et al.* or the English "and others" can be used to indicate several authors.

An edited collection or anthology

Levtow, Harry, and Maurice Valency, eds. The Palace of Pleasure: An Anthology of the Novella. New York: Capricorn Books, 1960.

Notice that in the entry for a work of this sort, with selections by many authors, the editors' names are listed first, in the position usually reserved for the author.

An edited version of a particular work

Shakespeare, William. Love's Labour's Lost. ed. Richard David. London: Methuen and Company, Ltd., 1958.

A translation

Mishima, Yukio. The Sailor Who Fell from Grace with the Sea. trans. John Nathan. New York: Alfred A. Knopf, Inc., 1965.

An edition other than the first

Weiss, Leonard. Case Studies in American History. ed. Kenyon A. Knopf. 2nd ed. New York: John Wiley & Sons, Inc., 1971.

More than one volume

McMichael, George, et al., eds. Anthology of American Literature. 2 vols. New York: Macmillan Publishing Co., Inc., 1974.

Magazine Articles

AUTHOR. [last name first] "TITLE OF ARTICLE." [in quotation marks] TITLE OF MAGAZINE, [underlined] VOLUME NUMBER, [in Arabic numerals] (DATE) [in parentheses with no comma following if just year is given; without parentheses but with comma following if the journal is weekly or monthly] PAGE NUMBERS. [use "p." or "pp." if magazine is weekly or monthly; use no "p." for any other]

With an author

Rosenstein, Harriet. "An Historic Booby Prize--Seduction and Betrayal: Women in Literature." Ms., July 1974, pp. 35-37, 85-87.

Without an author:

"Festival Days in New York." Time, 22 October, 1973, p. 61.

Newspaper articles

AUTHOR. [last name first] "TITLE OF ARTICLE." [in quotation marks] TITLE OF NEWSPAPER. [underlined] DATE, [day, month, year] PAGE NUMBERS. [Section, page, column]

With an author

Shales, Tom. "Up, Up but Not Away." The Washington Post, 7 January 1975, Sec. D, p. 17, col. 3.

From a newspaper magazine section

Allen, Henry. "The Poet's Poet." Potomac: The Washington Post, 5 January 1975, pp. 10, 18-20.

Without an author

"Many Buyers Ignore U.S. Gold Sales." The New York Times, 7 January 1978, Sec. 3, p. 26, col. 2.

Pamphlets

AUTHOR [last name first] OR AGENCY. TITLE. [underlined] PLACE OF PUBLICATION: PUBLISHER, DATE OF PUBLICATION.

With an author

Alexandrov, I. The Preaching and Practice of the Chinese Leaders. Moscow: Novosti Press Agency Publishing House, 1971.

Produced by an agency or company, with no author named

U.S. Civil Service Commission. Working for the USA. Washington, D.C.: U.S. Government Printing Office, 1972.

PEPCO. Electricity: How to Get the Most for the Least. Washington, D.C.: PEPCO, n.d.

Without an author or producing agency and with scant publication data

Cal 3-30. Pamphlet advertising the Cal 3-30 boat (n.d.).

Special items

Essay in an edited collection

Kazin, Alfred. "Sons, Lovers, and Mothers." D. H. Lawrence: A Collection of Criticism. ed. Leo Hamalian. New York: McGraw-Hill Book Company, 1973.

Encyclopedia article with an author

Breen, Walter Henry. "Numismatics." Encyclopaedia Britannica, 15th ed., (1967).

Breen, Walter Henry. "Numismatics." Encyclopaedia Britannica, 1967 ed.

Either of these forms—specifying edition and date or just date—is acceptable. No other publication information need be given. However, in any particular research paper the same form should be used throughout. Many encyclopedia articles are signed with initials instead of a full name; you may be able to identify the author by checking the list of contributors in the last volume of the set. If the work is alphabetically arranged, volume and page number may also be omitted, unless the reference will cover only one page of a several page entry.

Encyclopedia article without an author

"Drillpress." Do It Yourself Encyclopedia, 1955.

Personal interview

Grant, Helen. Principal of Dana Street Elementary School, Wilkes-Barre, Pennsylvania. Personal interview. 7 January 1979.

Recording

Croce, Jim. Photographs and Memories. ABC Records, Inc. ABCD-835.

Filmstrip

Scenes from King Lear. Warren Schloat Productions, 1973.

Television or radio program

The Ascent of Man. PBS Telecast. Narrator, Dr. Jacob Bronowski. 24 January 1975.

Public document

U.S. Constitution. Art. 5, sec. 3.

Exercises

1. Using the bibliographic format indicated here for books, magazines, etc., organize and punctuate the following items in their appropriate format.
   a. A book by Eugene D. Genovese entitled Roll, Jordan, Roll, copyrighted in 1974, and published by Random House in New York.
   b. The second volume of an anthology entitled America in Literature, edited by Alan Trachtenberg and Benjamin DeMott, copyrighted in 1978 and published by John Wiley & Sons, Inc. in New York.
   c. A translation of Fyodor Dostoyevsky's The Brothers Karamazov by Constance Garnett published by the New American Library in New York in 1957.
   d. An article entitled Scarlet O'Hara's Millions by Fletcher Knebel in the December 3, 1963 issue of Look magazine. The article is on pages 39–42 in volume 27.

e. An unsigned article entitled Collective Marriage in the April 28, 1972, edition of Life magazine. The article covers pages 72–74 and is found in volume 72.
f. An article in the Washington Star newspaper on January 21, 1977. The article's title is The Inaugural Diary. It is found on pages A–1 and A–4 and was written by Michael Satchell and Rebecca Leet.
g. A personal interview with your local mayor.

2. Collect about ten sources of various types (books, magazines, pamphlets, etc.) to formulate a working bibliography for your own paper. Record the information on 3 × 5 cards as shown on page 230.

Collecting Information

Once you have collected the bibliography cards, you are ready to find the sources themselves, to examine them to see if they will be of use, and to take notes from them if they contain material relevant to your topic.

Locating materials

Books. Books are usually found on the library's open shelves arranged according to the call numbers on their spines. If the library has closed book stacks, you must request the books from a central desk.

Magazines. Magazines are either in bound volumes on the library's open shelves (in the periodical section) or on microfilm. Most libraries have a listing of their periodical holdings either on a cardex or in a booklet. This listing tells which titles the library has, their dates, and whether they are on microfilm or on the open shelf. If your library does not have the specific volume you need, you may be able to find it elsewhere. Most libraries have listings that show which magazines are available at various libraries in that area.

Newspapers. Newspapers take up a lot of space so libraries that keep the actual newspapers usually stockpile them for no more than five years. You will generally have to ask the librarian to unearth the issue you need. Microfilm copies, on the other hand, will go back decades. Most libraries have *The New York Times* on microfilm; some have other newspapers as well.

As you begin your research, you may find that lugging mountains of books home is a chore and that some books—encyclopedias, volumes of magazines—cannot be removed from the library. You should not hesitate to make photocopies of useful articles or chapters. You should also become familiar with the microfilm reader. Don't give up on a source simply because you must read it on microfilm. Microfilm readers are easy to operate, and many of the machines have copiers built right into them.

Note taking

As you begin to read your material intensively, take notes to record the numerous facts, statements, opinions, and quotations that will become the basis of the research for your paper. Often, if you are writing just a short paper based on a few magazine articles, you might Xerox the articles, underline important material, and assemble the paper in criss-cross fashion, drawing on the information you highlighted on the copies. For a longer paper, however, a paper for which you are using more than just one or two sources, you need a more elaborate procedure to record information accurately. If you take notes neatly and carefully, you will save yourself the agony of realizing at 2:00 A.M. on the essay's due date that you lack certain vital information, but the library is closed. You can speed the painstaking process of recording information for the paper by following these steps:

1. Alphabetize your bibliography cards and give each one an identifying number.
2. Do not take notes haphazardly on sheets of notebook paper or on the backs of envelopes. Instead, record them on 4 × 6 cards (or 4 × 6) pieces of paper). The cards are much more flexible than large sheets of paper, since they can easily be arranged and rearranged as you experiment with various ways of organizing your material.
3. In taking notes, employ whatever method is quickest for you. If you know shorthand or notehand or have your own private kind of speed writing, by all means use it. Unless you are a really fast typist, do not attempt to type note cards. These cards need to be legible only to you, since you are the one who must work from them.
4. Do not write on the backs of cards except perhaps to finish a thought. If you write on only one side, you will be able to lay out everything in front of you when you are ready to organize the paper, with all of your material immediately visible.
5. To be of value, a note card should include four important pieces of information: (a) source number, (b) heading or title, (c) page number, (d) the note itself.

In doing her research on passive solar energy systems, Delia Gerace collected about forty note cards from her fourteen sources. They all looked, more or less, like this one for the material on berming she used in her paper. As she read that information, whether or not she knew that she would use it, she jotted it down on a 4 × 6 card.

Berming ⑦

Berm - a narrow ledge or shelf

Surround house with earth up to window sills.

Take advantage of constant earth temp. - 55°F

pp 14-15

⑨

Used on Edward Davis' house - Duluth

p. 60

Each item in the note has a function.

Source number. Because you may wish to include in your paper a footnote giving the source of the information, record that source on the card. There is no need to write down author, title, and publication information in full. Instead, give each bibliography card an identifying number or letter and use that to identify the source of information on the card.

Heading or title. To a surprising extent, you can organize the notes while you take them. As you work through a source, you will think of general headings or titles that apply to the material. Then, on any one card you put notes relating *only* to the heading on that card. Later, when you are organizing the paper, you will not have to read through all of your cards to find the material on one aspect of your subject. For example, if you decide to include in a paper on Martin Luther King, Jr., a section on his early life, you will find on the cards headed "Boyhood" all the material pertinent to that part of the paper. Eventually, you may have fifteen or twenty such headings. Since you are organizing by subject, not by source, you can put information from more than one source on the same card. Thus, in the sample card on berming most of the information is from source 7 but the reference to the actual example of the Edward Davis house in Duluth is from source 9. If you take notes in this fashion, by the time you finish your research, your subject headings will in themselves virtually constitute a rough outline.

Page numbers. Include the exact page or pages on which the information is found. You will need these page references if you use the material in your paper and need to document it in a footnote.

The note itself. The note itself consists of the information you deem worthy of jotting down for possible inclusion in your paper. It can take one of four forms: quotation, paraphrase, summary, or personal comment.

Quotation. Another individual's exact words will frequently provide excellent support for a major point of your thesis; however, use quotes carefully. Quote directly, and exactly, only those passages that are so strikingly phrased, so particularly cogent, or so important to your subject that presentation of the exact words is of value. Overquoting weakens your paper since the sources may end up saying more than you do. It could also turn the paper into a string of short quotations loosely connected by a few words from you.

Paraphrases. Passages from your sources which you express in your own words are paraphrases. Most of the material you collect on note cards should be paraphrased.

Summaries. A summary is a paraphrase in a sense. However, when you summarize you take a large chunk of material—several paragraphs, several pages, even a whole book or article—and compress it into perhaps just a paragraph.

Personal comments. With the knowledge you are rapidly accumulating on your subject, you will find yourself reacting to the material you unearth: you may oppose or support a critic; you may question the findings of a researcher; you may think of solutions to problems related to your subject. In the final paper, your reactions will probably find expression in introductions, conclusions, bridges, transitions, topic sentences, and such. They need not be documented. As you take notes, you may find it helpful to jot down these reactions, clearly identified as your thoughts, not your source's, whenever they come to mind.

Exercise

Begin reading and taking notes on what you read. Using the form just discussed, take notes as you go along.

Writing the Paper

When you have finished collecting notes from your several sources, you are ready to write the paper. If you have taken notes with care, you should be armed with all you need to write the paper and should not have to scramble back to the library to collect more information or to refine the information you already have. Your next task is to organize a plan for the paper. While the research paper may be longer than the essays you have written, it will be constructed very much like them—with an introduction culminating in a thesis statement, a body, and a conclusion.

Organizing the plan

Form a thesis statement. You already have a general idea of what the paper's focus will be: The focus has of course guided the research you did. But it may flex and change as the research progresses. Sometimes, in this fashion, the focus can be reexamined and refined. Now you should embody that general focus in a thesis statement, which will determine the direction of the whole paper. In the solar energy paper, the focus was that passive solar energy systems could save us money. Put into a formal thesis statement, the focus became:

> While we can choose either active or passive solar design systems, applying simple, passive designs to our houses would allow us to employ solar energy without costly outlay or extensive equipment.

Organize a rough sketch. If you are to build onto that thesis statement systematically, you will need a plan for developing it. Group your note cards according to their headings and make a list of those headings. Then you can arrange them in a logical sequence, creating a rough sketch for the paper with almost no effort. Delia Gerace made a list of all the major headings on her cards and put them into a practical order. The rough sketch for her paper looked like this:

Passive solar energy can save money on energy consumpton.

- Active solar energy is . . .
- Passive solar energy is . . .
- Site
  - Hillside
  - South/north exposure
  - Berming
- Shape/layout of house
  - Circular/one-story
  - Double walls/double insulation
  - Windows
  - Doors
  - Porches
- Good materials
- Interior of house
  - Furnishings
- Popularity

She made this list by organizing the headings of the cards she wanted to use for the paper. The cards with headings that did not seem to fit in (either because of useless detail or irrelevant subject matter), she set aside. She was left with this sketch, copied from the cards that remained, most of which she followed to write the paper.

Preparing the rough draft. Using your outline and your note cards, you should be able to write the paper without directly referring back to any of your sources. As you reach each topic on the outline, you can simply lay out in front of you the cards bearing that heading . . . and write. In a sense, each segment of the outline is the basis for a little essay, and all of the material you need for that essay is to be found in one of those packs of cards. So your job is immensely easier than it might have been had you just scrawled all your notes on pieces of paper, with no organization, as you went along.

As you write the rough draft, indicate also any necessary documentation. For example, you might write in the margin "6 p. 2," meaning that the material in this paragraph came from source 6, page 2. When you are fully satisfied with the rough draft, you can go back through it and transform these rough notations into formal footnotes at the bottom of each page. To illustrate, a page of the rough draft Delia wrote as she created paper from sketch follows. You can see how the footnote indicators are simply numbers coded to her own set of cards and meaningful only to her. Later, as she is satisfied that she will not be adding any more information, she will change these into actual footnotes. You can see also that this is a very rough draft, written really only for her eyes. She uses all manner of shortcuts and abbreviations as a kind of note hand to speed her on her way.

Integrate quoted and paraphrased material carefully. Some of the material you quoted on your note cards will find its way into the paper as a quotation; some of it will be paraphrased. In both instances, you will need footnote documentation. In addition, you should also apply the following principles:

> Quote verbatim anything you borrow, whether it be two words or thirty-two.
>
> Enclose a quote of four lines or less in quotation marks and include it within the regular text:
>
>> As Eldridge Cleaver has so bluntly said in *Soul on Ice,* "We shall have it or the earth will be leveled by our attempts to gain it." At the time, his threat was real and his power to carry it out growing.
>
> When typing a quotation longer than four lines, separate it from the preceding typewritten line with a triple space, indent ten spaces, omit quotation marks, and type with double space:
>
>> James Baldwin wrote in his novel *The Fire Next Time:*
>>
>>> White people cannot, in the generality, be taken as models of how to live. Rather, the white man is himself in sore need of new standards, which will release him from his confusion and place him once again in fruitful communion with the depths of his own being.
>
> In a short passage, when you have a quotation within a quotation, use double and single quotation marks as shown:

~~Solar~~ Solar energy can be harnessed through either an active solar system or a passive sys. ~~thru 2 different ways~~, an active solar system combines technology & engineering to produce an ~~actual~~ functioning system of solar collectors & reators to both heat & cool a structure. such systems R not just dreams of the fut. As early as 1913, the Shuman-Boys solar pow. plant in Mead:, Egypt, was successfully pow. by solar steam of along the banks of Nile (18 p.21) But fossil fuels were plentiful & inexpensive so no incentive pushed solar energy. An elementary school in Fairfax, Virginia, a lib. in S Spring, Md, an indiv. house in Forestville, Md are some of the few bldgs which have been erected in the past decade attempting to grasp energy from the sun. But ~~such~~ active solar energy systems are xpnsive & cumbersome. A solar sys. that would sv 100 gal of fuel per htg seas might cost $5,000/$6,000 to build. It wud also require costly mntnc thruout the life of the sys. (10 p3)

insert Thomason house?

A passive solar energy sys. is a very diff. concept. Rthr than existing as a ~~functional~~ mach. with components, pass solar energy exists as a concept with many manifestations. These R more architechural & ldscp. designs many of which can B employed in an existing structure with almost no expense. The way a hs is built, the manner in which it is sited, the ~~form~~ way in which it is furnished can all help a consumer curtail heating costs.

think about inserting some actual building examples

> Of special interest is this byplay from Kurt Vonnegut's *Cat's Cradle:* "From the pitying way Minton and his wife looked at each other, I gathered that I had said a fat-headed thing. But they humored me. 'Yes,' winced Minton, 'I'm very pleased.' "

When you wish to omit a portion of a quoted passage, use an ellipsis—three dots (or four dots if you need a period to end the sentence after the ellipsis) with space between them:

> The event is described in Xaviera Hollander's *Happy Hooker:* "Business was booming, and I was making a fortune, but Carmen's Guest House was becoming an inconvenient place to stay . . . . So I started thinking about moving out of there."

Quote carefully, following exactly the wording, punctuation, capitalization, and so on of the original. If you find an error in a passage to be quoted (a grammatical error, perhaps, or a misspelling), indicate that the error is in the original by inserting *sic,* a Latin word meaning "thus":

> ". . . the elefant [*sic*] slowly lumbered down the path."

Anything inserted within a quote, to explain or to clarify it, for instance, should be enclosed in brackets, including *sic* discussed above:

> ". . . he [Martin Luther King] was born in Atlanta."

Paraphrases. Paraphrasing means more than rearranging the words of the original, changing a *but* to an *and* or a *we* to a *they.* Restate the main points of what you have read in your own way. If you paraphrase successfully, your paper will be dominated by a single style—your own—instead of being a blend of the mixed styles of the many sources from which you are drawing information. Here is a quoted passage from Robert Massie's *Nicholas and Alexandra* integrated into a student paper:

> The Tsar had fallen. It was an event of gigantic significance, and yet, neither in Russia nor abroad was this significance more than dimly understood. On the Sunday following the abdication, Paleologue visited three Petrograd churches: "The same scene met me everywhere; a grave and silent congregation exchanging grave and melancholy glances. Some of the *moujiks* looked bewildered and horrified and several had tears in their eyes. Yet even among those who seemed the most moved I could not find one who did not sport a red cockade or armband."

The paraphrase of this passage would be much shorter, with less description. It might look something like this:

> According to Paleologue, the day after the Tsar's abdication was a strange one. The people, tense, silent, seemingly wrapped in awesome melancholy, still all had red armbands on their sleeves or red cockades on their hats.

A paraphrase can include some short quoted phrases to keep the text flowing smoothly, but you must be scrupulous in crediting what is the author's. If you do not enclose these phrases in quotation marks on your note cards, you may have trouble with unwitting plagiarism when you finally write the paper—forgetting that those striking passages are not actually yours but belong to someone else, someone who should receive credit for them. In any event, do remember that the paraphrase also needs a footnote reference.

Summaries. When you summarize, your aim is to communicate the information you need without getting lost in the details or verbal complexities of the original selection, as you might in quoting from it or in trying to paraphrase the whole. You attempt to capture the essence of the material to be summarized while retaining the flavor of the original if possible:

> The first chapter of Pär Lagerkvist's novel *The Sibyl* simply and subtly introduces the main characters who will play such a powerful role in the story to follow: an old woman living on the mountain slopes above Delphi with her middle-aged, half-wit son. Their mysterious, isolated existence looked down over the temple, where each morning a young woman was ushered into the presence of the god to be filled with his powerful presence. This the old woman and her idiot son watched over with great knowledge, the wisdom of those who are strangely above such mysteries.

Exercises

1. Prepare a thesis statement for your own research topic.
2. Organize a rough sketch of your paper to support the thesis statement focus.
3. Prepare the rough draft for your paper from the sketch and notes which you have prepared.

Documentation

Any material you borrow from other sources must be documented. That means that the original sources must be given credit, in footnotes or endnotes, for their help in supporting your thesis. By acknowledging this help, you achieve two goals: You eliminate any suspicion of *plagiarism* (using someone else's material as if it were your own), and you provide references for the reader who may wish to learn more about your subject.

Footnotes are indicated in the text by a raised number placed at the end of the material to which they refer. You can put the actual notes either at the bottom of the appropriate page (footnotes) or on a separate sheet at the end (endnotes). Whether endnotes or footnotes are used, their format is the same.

There is no law governing how many footnotes you should have per page or per paper. There are, however, several circumstances in which footnoting is required:

1. To document a quotation.
2. To document a paraphrase.
3. To document summarized material.
4. To document maps, charts, diagrams, statistics, and so forth, if you have borrowed them from another source.

In general, whenever you borrow anything—word for word or paraphrased—you must acknowledge that borrowing in a footnote. If you are doubtful about whether to footnote something, you should probably do so to protect yourself against the accusation of plagiarism, intended or otherwise.

The one exception to this principle is for material considered *common knowledge*. Common knowledge is material which is so much a part of your subject that you find the same information repeated in a number of sources, making it difficult to tell what the actual original source was. After Delia Gerace had found several definitions of active and passive solar energy, she realized that those concepts were common knowledge in the realm of solar energy, so she did not footnote her definitions of them in her paper. The same is true for any subject. If after doing some research on George Meany or Vladimir Horowitz or cloning, you find certain information, such as a birth date or a formula or a definition, repeated regularly, you can be safe in regarding it as common knowledge. Such material does not need footnoting unless, for some reason, you quote someone's exact words in presenting it.

Basic footnote form

Like bibliographic entries and note cards, footnotes should be arranged in accordance with certain forms. Again, the form here is based on the MLA Style Sheet; while some disciplines may use other forms, the important point is to be consistent throughout your own paper. (Your instructor will tell you if you should use another documentation style.) While the footnote is *similar* to the bibliographic entry, it is *not identical.* Here, for example, are the differences in the bibliographic and footnote entries for the two most common sources, books and magazines:

For a magazine

Bibliographic entry

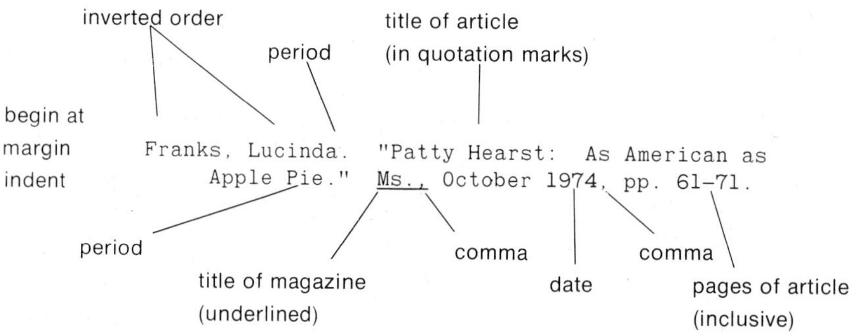

Footnote entry

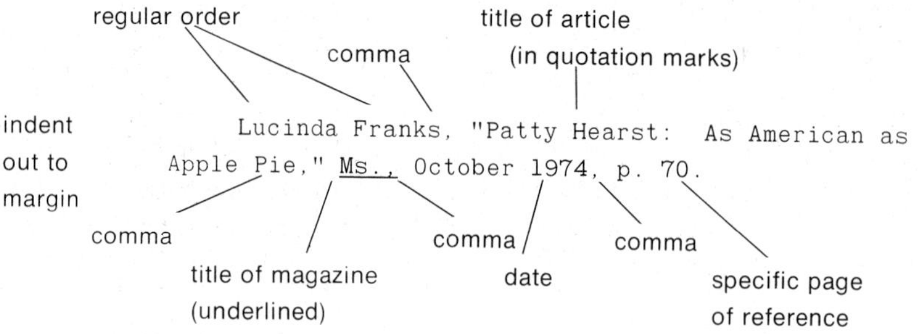

For a book
Bibliographic entry

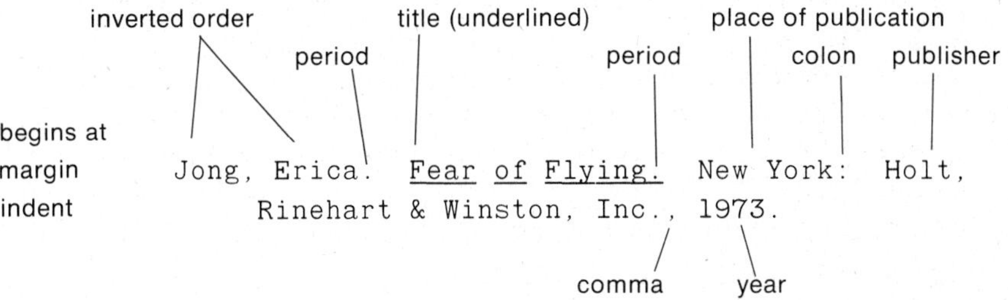

Footnote entry

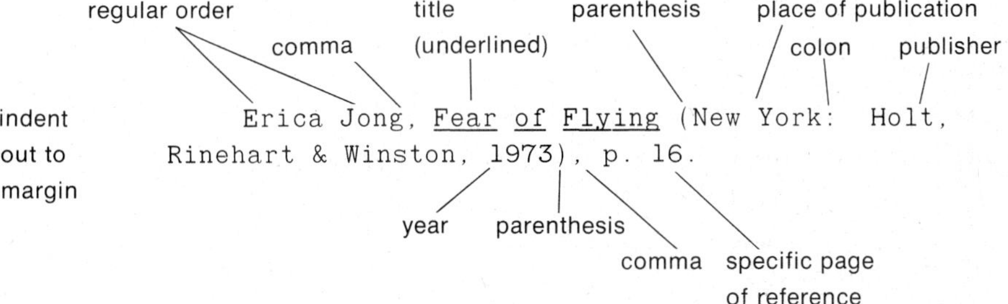

Subsequent references

The first time you write a footnote for any particular source, you write the entry out completely, according to the models on the next pages. But once you have cited a source, you can use a shortened form for any other references to that same source: Use the author's last name and the page number; if no author is given, use all of the title if it is short or part of the title if it is too long to repeat completely. Therefore, a second reference to Erica Jong's *Fear of Flying* would be a simple matter of author and page:

[7]Jong, p. 46.

If one author has more than one source listed in the bibliography, specify which title you intend in subsequent references to either source. For example, if you were using both *Fear of Flying* and an Erica Jong short story, "The 8:29 to Frankfurt," in the same paper, you would make later references to them in this manner:

[9]Jong, Fear of Flying, p. 25.

[10]Jong, "The 8:29 to Frankfurt," p. 7.

Another fine point of subsequent referencing occurs when you have two authors in your bibliography with the same last name. In that case, you must include the authors' first names as well to avoid confusion:

[7]Henry Miller, p. 25.

[8]Richard Miller, p. 102.

Explanatory footnotes

While most of your footnotes will provide documentation, sometimes you may want to explain something in a footnote—define a term, add interesting data, explain a minor point—almost anything which is relevant but which would interrupt the flow of thought if included in the main text. These footnotes are included in the same way as regular footnotes and are numbered right in sequence with them:

[4]Johnson, p. 78.

[5]Kafka has been accused at times of endowing his heroes with narcissism and self-indulgence, and there may be some basis for the charge.

[6]Swenson, p. 214.

Models of footnote formats

Books

[5]AUTHOR, [in normal order] TITLE [underlined] (PLACE OF PUBLICATION: PUBLISHER, DATE), [in parentheses] PAGE NUMBER. [preceded by "p." for one page or "pp." for several pages]

[5]Michael Crichton, The Andromeda Strain (New York: Dell Publishing Co., Inc., 1970), p. 29.

Magazine articles

[6]AUTHOR, [in normal order] "TITLE OF ARTICLE," [in quotation marks] TITLE OF MAGAZINE, [underlined] DATE, [day, month, year] PAGE. [preceeded by "p." for one page or "pp." for more than one]

With an author

[6]Harriet Rosenstein, "An Historic Booby Prize—Seduction and Betrayal: Women in Literature," Ms., July 1974, p. 35.

Without an author

[6]"Festival Days in New York," Time, 22 October 1973, p. 61.

Newspaper articles

[7]AUTHOR, [in normal order] "TITLE OF ARTICLE," [in quotation marks] TITLE OF NEWSPAPER, [underlined] DATE, [day, month, year] PAGE. [section (Sec.), page (p.), column (col.)]

[7]Tom Shales, "Up, Up but Not Away," The Washington Post, 7 January 1975, Sec. D, p. 17, col. 3.

Pamphlets

[8]AUTHOR OR AGENCY, [in normal order] TITLE [underlined] (PLACE OF PUBLICATION: PUBLISHER, DATE), [in parentheses] PAGE NUMBER. [with "p." or "pp.," as appropriate]

With an author

[8]I. Alexandrov, The Preaching and Practice of the Chinese Leaders (Moscow: Novosti Press Agency Publishing House, 1971), p. 6.

Produced by an agency or company, with no specific author named

[8]U.S. Civil Service Commission, Working for the USA (Washington, D.C.: U.S. Government Printing Office, 1972), p. 3.

[8]PEPCO, Electricity: How to Get the Most for the Least (Washington, D.C.: PEPCO, n.d.), p. 2.

Without an author and with scant publication data

[8]Cal 3–30, pamphlet advertising the Cal 3–30 boat (n.d.).

Special items

Essay in an edited collection

[9]Alfred Kazin, "Sons, Lovers, and Mothers," D. H. Lawrence: A Collection of Criticism, ed. Leo Hamalian (New York: McGraw-Hill Book Company, 1973), p. 24.

Encyclopedia article with an author

(Publication information beyond volume and date is unnecessary but volume and page number are necessary when the reference covers only one page of a multi-page article.)

[10]Walter Henry Breen, "Numismatics," Encyclopaedia Britannica, 15th ed. (1967), 16, p. 761.

[10]Walter Henry Breen, "Numismatics," Encyclopaedia Britannica, 1967, 16, p. 761.

Encyclopedia article without an author

[10]"Drillpress," Do It Yourself Encyclopedia, 1955, 3, p. 92.

Personal interview

[11]Helen Grant, Principal of Dana Street Elementary School, Wilkes-Barre, Pennsylvania, personal interview, January 7, 1979.

Recording

[12]Jim Croce, Photographs and Memories, ABC Records, Inc., ABCD-835.

Filmstrip

[13]Scenes from King Lear, Warren Schloat Productions, 1973.

Television or radio program:

[14]The Ascent of Man, PBS Telecast, Narrator, Dr. Jacob Bronowski, January 24, 1975.

Public document

[15]U.S. Constitution, Art. 5, sec. 3.

Exercises

1. Refer back to pp. 234–35. Create footnote documentation for the seven bibliographic items you devised there. Note the sometimes subtle differences in format.

2. Examine the intended documentation of your own paper. Carefully create footnotes for your materials needing documentation. Follow the format lists on pages 248–50 very carefully.

Preparing the Final Copy

When you are ready to type the final draft of your paper, check this list of mechanical details:

1. The paper should be typed (or handwritten if your instructor permits) so that it looks like the sample research paper included earlier. Fasten the finished paper together with paper clip, staple, or folder. A folder with interior side pockets for note cards or rough draft is a good one to use.

2. Use regular bond typing paper of standard size—8-½ by 11 inches. Make corrections with correction tape or some type of white-out, if possible. Some errors, such as misspellings, can be corrected neatly above the error. You would be wise to keep a carbon or a photocopy of the paper for yourself.

3. Set standard margins—1-½ inches on the left; 1 inch on the top, right, and bottom.

4. Arrange the title page as shown in the sample student paper or use some variation as explained by your instructor. Necessary information to be included is usually the title of the paper, your name, the title of the course, the section number, the instructor's name, and the submission date.

5. Include a formal outline if your instructor requests one.

6. Page numbers, in Arabic numerals, go in the upper right-hand corner of each page except for the first page and any other page which has a heading, such as Endnotes or Bibliography. These pages are included in the numbering sequence even though their actual numbers are omitted. The title page is not counted in the numbering.

7. Double-space throughout, except for footnotes and bibliography entries (see below).

8. Use the appropriate form for quotations. Quoted matter of four lines or less is enclosed in quotation marks and incorporated into the text in normal sentence fashion. Quotations of longer than four lines have a triple space above, are indented ten spaces from the left margin, and are double-spaced, without quotation marks.

9. Check the form of the footnotes carefully, remembering the following details:

In the text of the paper, footnote numbers, raised one half space, go at the end of the material being documented.

Footnotes can appear at the bottom of each appropriate page or they can appear as endnotes on a single sheet before the bibliography at the end of the paper.

Single-space within footnote entries; double-space between them. Use a quadruple space between text and notes if notes are at the bottom of each page.

Raise the footnote number one half space. Begin each entry with a five-space indentation; all other lines extend out to the margin.

Only the first reference to a source requires a full-length footnote. Subsequent references need only the author's last name and the specific page number. (See also pp. 273–74.)

10. Check the form of the final bibliography carefully, remembering the following details:

The bibliography begins on a separate page, headed Bibliography, at the end of the paper.

It should include all of the sources you have consulted substantially, even those not mentioned in the footnotes.

The items are *not* numbered; they are presented in alphabetical order according to the first word of the entry—author's name or title.

If there are several titles by one author, these should, in addition to being alphabetically placed in the Bibliography by author's last name, be arranged alphabetically by title within their own grouping. (In some disciplines, the entries will be arranged by publication date; check with your instructor.) The author's name is written out only for the first title; in the subsequent entries, type ten hyphens instead.

Single-space within each of the entries; double-space between them.

Begin each entry at the margin; indent all other lines five spaces.

Chapter Exercise

Using the ten items listed in "Preparing the Final Copy," go through your rough draft to adjust page numbers, footnote and bibliography format, and quotation punctuation. As you prepare your final copy, pay special attention to the finished form of the paper, proofreading and ensuring neatness as well as good order in margins, spacing, and outline and title page format.

Chapter Checklist

1. A research paper combines an examination of the available oral, visual, and written materials relating to your subject with an integration and interpretation of them to produce a new presentation of the topic.
2. Use the same principles for selecting a research paper topic as for an essay topic—one that fits the size of the assignment and one in which you have some interest.
3. Investigate all possibilities for sources: books, magazines, pamphlets, newspapers, etc., as well as any oral or audio-visual materials.
4. Record bibliography items on 3 × 5 cards according to the format on pages 231–34.
5. Take notes in whatever shorthand fashion you wish while you are reading your sources. Do so by subject heading rather than by source summary. Use the format suggested on pages 236–38.
6. Create a thesis statement and rough sketch before actually writing the draft of the paper to make sure that all of the parts seem to work well together.
7. Footnote all borrowed material whether it is quoted, paraphrased, or summarized. Carefully follow the format offered on pages 246–50.

Checking the Details: A Brief Handbook

Almost anyone over ten chuckles when an earnest seven-year-old scrawls on a cardboard sign: "LEMINADE 10¢." The quaint spelling and the backward cent sign are cute. As the seven-year-old gets older, however, the friendly chuckles change to snickers and sneers if the grammatical mistakes and the spelling errors continue. Standard rules of grammar and punctuation protect us from such attention and keep us from seeming foolish in the eyes of educated people.

Knowledge of sound mechanical elements underlies the survival kit notion upon which this book is built. Some of these elements are basic and come naturally; some serve as refinements for the editing phase of writing a paper. Writers suffer different lapses: one strings out run-on sentences; another regularly creates fragments; a third mixes subject and verb agreement; and a fourth misplaces modifiers. While some students need intensive review to correct their problems, others just need a mop and broom to clean up a paper once the ideas are etched into a draft. Either way, uncorrected, poor mechanics make a negative comment about the writer.

This handbook offers a brief guide to quick, clear mechanical information. It defines terms and illustrates rules, fixing the grammatical odds and ends sprinkled throughout the book into one place for ready access. It is not meant to be a complete guide; it merely highlights the basics. To make easy use of the handbook as a companion to a dictionary as you write a paper, put a marker at the beginning page of this section. For the most part, standard rules make good sense. This chapter will help you apply them to your own essays and papers.

Parts of Speech

Nouns	**Adverbs**
Pronouns	**Prepositions**
Verbs	**Conjunctions**
Adjectives	**Interjections**

An understanding of the parts of speech will help you to use them correctly and to follow the discussions of grammatical errors. See Chapters 2, 3, and 4 for the effective use of nouns, verbs, and modifiers.

Nouns

A **noun** is the name of:

a person: President Roosevelt, Mary Jane, Harold Robbins, swimmer
a place: Baton Rouge, William and Mary College, living room, closet
an object: carrot, camera, pencil, needle, Oldsmobile 88
a quality: kindness, flexibility, ignorance
an action: skating, laughing, tiptoeing

A *proper noun* names a particular person, place, object, etc.

President Roosevelt
Baton Rouge
Oldsmobile 88

A *common noun* names a general person, place, object, etc.

swimmer
closet
carrot

A noun functions as:

a subject: the doer of an action
an object: the receiver of an action
a complement: a noun following a linking verb and identifying the subject
an appositive: a noun placed next to another noun to help explain it

subject — appositive — object of preposition — indirect object — direct object
V Was for Victory, a book about World War II, shows its readers America

object of preposition
on the home front.

Pronouns

A **pronoun** is a substitute for a noun. It does not designate a specific person, place, object, etc.; instead it refers back to a previously mentioned noun, which is called an **antecedent.**

antecedent
The shark lurched toward the overturned boat.

pronoun
Greedily, it waited for the right moment.

A pronoun agrees in number with its antecedent. A personal pronoun with a singular antecedent should be singular; one with a plural antecedent should be plural:

He took the chewing **gum** from his mouth and pressed **it** under the table. *(singular)*

She beat back the **tigers** as they tried to escape from the cage. Afraid of the whip, **they** cowered behind the door. *(plural)*

Pronouns come in several varieties. *Personal pronouns* refer to individual people or things. Their form may change to show ownership (possessive case) or use as direct or indirect object (objective case):

subjective	*possessive*	*objective*
I	my, mine	me
we	our, ours	us
you	your, yours	you
you	your, yours	you
he	his	him
she	her, hers	her
it	its	it
one	one's	one
they	their, theirs	them

I know Mickey. *(subjective)*
He is **my** friend. *(possessive)*
I can tell a story about **him.** *(objective)*

Relative pronouns link a dependent clause to a noun:

who	which	whomever
whom	that	whatever
whose	whoever	what

The firemen ***who*** *volunteered for the search party* found the child shivering and tearful in the ravine.

Interrogative pronouns ask questions:

who	whose	what
whom	which	

Who sat on the home ec teacher's package of cream cheese?

Demonstrative pronouns point out or refer to nouns:

this that those these

This is absolutely the last time I will let you borrow my mink jacket to impress your dates.

Indefinite pronouns refer to indefinite people and things:

all	some }	+	{ one
any	any }		{ thing
some	every }		{ body
each	no }		
either			

Someone reported seeing a bear heading toward the shopping center.

Reciprocal pronouns substitute as an object for a compound or plural noun:

each other one another

The students giggled at **each other** when their science teacher brewed some potato whiskey in a makeshift classroom still.

Reflexive pronouns add "-self" or "-selves" to personal pronouns to show that the object or subject complement refers back to the subject.

Count Dracula groomed **himself** with care as he prepared to dine out that evening.

Intensive pronouns use the "-self"/"-selves" addition to show a pronoun in apposition:

Babe Ruth **himself** could not have hit a better home run.

Verbs

A **verb** shows the action, condition, or process in a sentence. Most verbs show action:

The woman *coddled* her son.
The salesperson *switched* the car's odometer.
The American colonies *revolted* against their British overlords.

A *linking verb* indicates state of being:

be	seem	sound
become	smell	feel
remain	appear	taste
grow	look	

The flapper **looked** out of place in the 1950s issue of *Life* magazine.
I **was** Fu Manchu's prisoner.
A briar patch **grew** by the fence.

The **parts** of a verb are

infinitive: to type
present: types
past: typed
past participle: typed
present participle: typing

Verb tense shows change in time by changing verb form. *Regular* verbs add "ed" to form the past and past participle:

He types. *(present)*	He has typed. *(present perfect)*
He typed. *(past)*	He had typed. *(past perfect)*
He will type. *(future)*	He will have typed. *(future perfect)*

Irregular verbs may change spelling to change tense:

He swims.	He has swum.
He swam.	He had swum.
He will swim.	He will have swum.

Transitive verbs require a direct object to complete their thought:

The fish ***bit*** *me.*
The furniture movers ***hefted*** *the piano.*
I ***bought*** *some gas* for my lawn mower.

Intransitive verbs are complete without an object:

A shot **echoed** through the school yard.
The chimney **narrowed** at the top.
The bathysphere **descended** too quickly.

A verb uses **voices** to show whether the subject of the sentence acts or receives the action. *Active voice* allows the subject to do the acting:

One unethical real estate *agent* **bought** all of the condemned houses.

Passive voice allows the subject to receive the action:

All of the condemned *houses* ***were bought*** by one unethical real estate agent.

Verbals are the parts of a verb which can serve as modifiers or as nouns in sentences. The *infinitive* form of a verb (to kick, to reach, to laugh) can be a noun or a modifier:

infinitive as modifier
To reach the jar of peanut butter, the two-year-old dragged the stool to the cupboard.

infinitive as direct object
The young widower planned **to invest** his inheritance in blue chip stocks.

A *gerund,* the present participle of a verb (kicking, reaching, laughing) can function as a noun:

gerund as subject
Laughing is good therapy.

The present or past *participles* of a verb (kicking/kicked; reaching/reached; laughing/laughed) can serve as modifiers:

present participle as modifier
Angrily **kicking** the can of worms, the boy tossed his rod and reel aside.

past participle as modifier
Having kicked the can of worms, the boy tossed his rod and reel aside.

Adjectives

An **adjective** modifies (describes or clarifies) a noun or pronoun:

muslin sheets **gold lamé** shoes **ragged** jeans

A phrase or a clause may also function as an adjective when it tells more about a noun or pronoun:

The prisoner **who escaped** is dangerous.

Adverbs

An adverb modifies a verb, an adjective, or another adverb to show:

degree	place
manner	time

An adverb answers the questions:

how: sniffed **cautiously**
how much: **really** sorry
when: came **then**
where: over **there**

A phrase or clause may also act as an adverb when it shows degree, manner, place, or time for a verb, adverb, or adjective:

> He has been depressed **since he lost his money in that gold mine scheme.**

Prepositions

A **preposition** connects a noun or pronoun to other words in the sentence to show specific relationship:

around	below	above
over	under	on
in	into	behind
before	to	toward

A preposition may join a noun to form a *prepositional phrase:*

> He found the skeleton ***in*** *the cave.*
> The brandy spilled ***on*** *the Oriental rug.*
> The cat hid ***behind*** *the sofa.*

Conjunctions

A **conjunction** links words, phrases, and clauses. A *coordinating conjunction* suggests equality between words or word groups:

and	yet	nor
but	or	for

two nouns
The pen **and** the sword offer two contrasting alternatives.

two clauses
Never had I seen such a marvelous jewel, **but** alas never would I see it again.

two phrases
Either put the fish in the pan **or** in the refrigerator.

A *subordinating conjunction* adds extra detail to the basic subject/verb of the independent clauses:

since	because	after
when	whenever	although
as	as if	as though
if	before	how
in order	that	once
provided	so that	that
till	unless	until
whether	while	why

Whenever *I eat too fast,* I get sick.
He hit a home run ***after*** *he smacked the bat against the fence.*
Because *of my allergy,* I need weekly shots.

Interjections

An **interjection** accents feelings or emotions with short exclamations:

Oh darn!	Help!	Eek!
Wow!	Oh!	

Sentence Grammar

Sentence parts

subject	**direct object**	**complement**
predicate	**indirect object**	

A sentence is a group of words expressing a complete thought. A sentence always has a subject and a predicate; it may at times have a direct or indirect object or a complement. See Chapter 3 for more information about sentences.

A **subject** is a noun or noun substitute which either performs an action or is in a state of being. It usually comes before the verb:

I gave him the empty box of Cheerios.

A **predicate** indicates the action or state of being of the subject. It contains the verb plus its modifiers:

I **gave** him the empty box of Cheerios.

A **direct object** is a noun or noun substitute which answers the questions *what* or *whom* asked by the verb. The direct object usually comes after the verb:

I gave him the empty **box** of Cheerios.

An **indirect object** is a noun answering the question *to what* or *to whom* the action is directed.

I gave **him** the empty box of Cheerios.

A **complement** is a noun or adjective which follows a linking verb and tells something about the subject.

Jennifer is a **rock climber.** *(noun as complement)*
She is quite **agile.** *(adjective as complement)*

Sentence types

simple	**complex**
compound	**compound-complex**

A **sentence** is also an *independent,* or *main,* clause, a group of words with a subject and verb that can stand alone and make sense by themselves. A *dependent,* or *subordinate,* clause is a subject and verb that can not stand by themselves to make sense. The combinations of independent and dependent clauses form the four types of sentences: simple, compound, complex, and compound-complex.

A *simple sentence* has one independent clause and no dependent clauses:

The youngest swimmer won the race.

A *compound sentence* has two or more independent clauses and no dependent clauses:

The youngest swimmer won the race, but he was exhausted by the end.

A *complex sentence* has one independent clause and one or more dependent clauses:

After he had swum with all his might, the youngest swimmer was exhausted.

A *compound-complex* sentence has two or more main clauses with one or more dependent clauses:

The youngest swimmer won the race, but he was exhausted after he had swum with all his might.

Sentence Problems

Fragments	**Comma Splices**
Run-On Sentences	

Depending upon the way clauses are connected within a sentence, that sentence will be wholesome and healthy, or it will suffer from one of the above problems.

Fragments

A **fragment** is a dependent clause or phrase used incorrectly as a sentence. By itself it does not make sense. Because it is dependent for its meaning upon something which is not present in the sentence, it is incomplete.

> Because I have no children to worry me. *(subordinate clause)*
> Drinking iced tea. *(verbal phrase)*
> Out of a can. *(prepositional phrase)*

A fragment can be cured by connecting it to an independent clause:

> Because I have no children to worry me, I can spend twelve hours a day working on my PhD.

Or a fragment can be converted into an independent clause:

> Drinking iced tea is a constant summer habit of mine.

Run-on sentences

A **run-on sentence** links two or more independent clauses without punctuation to separate them:

> Freedom of speech is abused so is freedom of the press.

A run-on sentence can be cured through proper punctuation.

1. Insert a period to make two sentences:

> Freedom of speech is abused. So is freedom of the press.

2. Insert a semicolon to separate the main clauses:

> Freedom of speech is abused; so is freedom of the press.

3. Use a comma and a conjunction:

> Freedom of speech is abused, and so is freedom of the press.

4. Rewrite the clauses to make one dependent upon the other without changing the sense of either:

> If freedom of speech is abused, so is freedom of the press.

Comma splices

The **comma splice,** or *comma fault,* is a kind of run-on sentence that separates two independent clauses with only a comma:

> Organized crime grew rich from bootlegging alcoholic beverages during Prohibition, by midcentury it had successfully switched to selling narcotics.

The comma splice is repaired in the same fashion as the run-on sentence.

1. Change the comma to a period to make two sentences:

> Organized crime grew rich from bootlegging alcoholic beverages during Prohibition. By midcentury it had successfully switched to selling narcotics.

2. Change the comma to a semicolon to separate the main clauses:

> Organized crime grew rich from bootlegging alcoholic beverages during Prohibition; by midcentury it had successfully switched to selling narcotics.

3. Add a conjunction to the comma:

> Organized crime grew rich from bootlegging alcoholic beverages during Prohibition, but by midcentury it had successfully switched to selling narcotics.

4. Rewrite the clauses to make one dependent upon the other without altering the sense of either:

> Although organized crime grew rich from bootlegging alcoholic beverages during Prohibition, by midcentury it had successfully switched to selling narcotics.

Agreement

Subject/Verb Agreement
Pronoun/Antecedent Agreement

Subject/verb agreement

Subject/verb agreement means that subjects and verbs match in number. A *singular* subject needs a *singular* verb:

singular subject — singular verb

The carpenter hammers nails.

A *plural* subject needs a *plural* verb:

plural subject — plural verb

The carpenters hammer nails.

Problems occur with subject/verb agreement from three directions:

subject identification **dialect interference**
subject number

Subject identification can be confusing in three ways.

1. Sometimes interrupting words, phrases, or clauses separate subject from verb:

Henry Ford, who berated his rivals both with his attitude that "change is not always progress" and with a successful series of unchanging Model T's, **would shudder** to see the new models of Cadillacs, Chevrolets, Buicks, and even Volkswagens that zoom onto today's marketplace yearly.

2. Sometimes the noun follows the verb:

Perched atop the telegraph pole **were** six **crows.**

3. Sometimes the constructions "There is" or "There are" create difficulty, since the noun then must follow the verb:

There **are** no good **reasons** for the secretary's dismissal.

Subject number is sometimes made difficult by compound subjects and collective nouns.

1. A *compound subject* is two or more words, phrases, or clauses linked by a conjunction:

Monica and Suzette bought lottery tickets.

The **pubs and alleys** of London were his home.

Depending on which conjunction is used, the subject may need a singular or plural verb.

And usually takes a plural verb:

Benjamin and Aaron are two names which have again become popular as names for newborn male infants.

Or, nor, either . . . or, neither . . . nor sometimes take singular and sometimes plural verbs.

a. If both subjects are singular, the verb is singular:

Neither **Pan Am** nor **TWA has** had a strike in several years.

b. If both subjects are plural, the verb is plural:

Neither **parties** nor **dinners** in fancy restaurants **help** him forget he has been jilted.

c. When one subject is singular and the other plural, the verb agrees with the nearer subject:

Either the **cameras** or the **projector has** to be left behind.

2. A *collective noun* is a noun which suggests a group of objects, places, or persons in a singular form:

team couple committee troop

If you consider the group as a unit, use a singular verb:

This **couple is** buying the Victorian mansion on Cedar Avenue.

If you consider the group as a collection of individuals, use a plural verb:

The **couple were** arguing regularly before their separation.

Dialect interference may also lead to agreement problems. Native speakers of black English or other dialects which differ from standard English may experience a problem with the rules of agreement of general English—especially with "-ed" and "-s." For some dialect speakers, it is not only habitual but quite logical to say:

Celestine walk down the street.
He pick up his date.
He be coming.

While the logic of a particular dialect may not require the "-ed" or the "-s," standard English does. In a first draft you may not pay too much attention to this standard subject/verb agreement, but try to do so when you polish a paper.

Pronoun/antecedent agreement

A pronoun must agree in person and number with its antecedent.

Personal pronouns have singular and plural forms. A singular noun needs a singular pronoun and must also be appropriately masculine, feminine, or neuter:

The china **doll** fell from **its** shelf.
Marta drove **her** tennis serve into the net.

A plural antecedent needs a plural pronoun:

The **bricklayers** walked off the job, neglecting even to get **their** pay.

A pronoun which refers to a compound joined by *and* is plural:

Michelangelo and Leonardo da Vinci have **their** names etched in the memories of every art student through **their** monumental achievements.

A singular pronoun is used to refer to nouns joined by *or* or *nor:*

Neither ***The Black Hole*** **nor** ***Battlestar Gallactica*** continued **its** hold on the popular imagination as *Star Trek* did.

A *relative pronoun* has the same number as the number of its antecedent:

Barbra Streisand is one **performer who does** best in comic roles. *(performer as singular)*
Barbra Streisand is one of those **performers who do** best in comic roles. *(performers as plural)*

An *indefinite pronoun* suggests an indefinite number, so determining whether it is singular or plural is sometimes difficult. Some indefinite pronouns are singular by rule:

everyone	someone	everybody	somebody
anyone	no one	anybody	nobody

Everyone was trying to get gasoline at the same time.

Spoken practice often represents these pronouns as plural:

Everyone spent **their** money far too quickly at the bazaar.

With the concern over the sexist overtones of *his,* the plural pronoun referring to *everyone,* etc., is becoming more acceptable. The more grammatically correct reference to eliminate sexist overtones would be to use *his or her, his/her,* or some other variation:

Everyone should put **his or her** name on the blackboard before leaving.

There are moments, however, when the singular version would not make as much logical sense as the plural:

Everyone was trying to get gasoline, and I couldn't blame **them.** I was, too.

Punctuation

End Punctuation
Internal Punctuation
Special Convention
Capitalization

Punctuation marks can plague any writer who does not know where to put them. Punctuation marks are important; they can change sense, shape it, or cloud it depending on the writer's real intent. A classic example of punctuation changing meaning occurs in this group of words:

> Woman without her man is nothing.

Altering the punctuation changes the thought completely:

> Woman! Without her, man is nothing.

Punctuation marks show pauses, ask questions, and show surprise. Although our ear tells us on occasion where to punctuate, the best guide is to be familiar with the rules.

End punctuation

period .
question mark ?
exclamation point !

Period. A *period* is the end punctuation for any sentence that states a command or makes a statement:

> By 1902 the free public high school had become an American institution.
>
> Take a bath.
>
> Switching cabs to confuse his pursuers, the CIA agent tried to escape from San Francisco.

Exclamation point! An *exclamation point* follows an emphatic statement:

> You saw Zulu warriors in Omaha!
>
> Ouch! The needle slipped.
>
> Disneyworld is fantastic!

More than one exclamation point is unnecessary. Also, exclamation points should be used sparingly in all writing.

Question mark? A *question mark* concludes a question:

> Why do you waste your life pining over that lazy bum?

Do you want some coffee?

Are you ready to quit?

Internal punctuation

comma ,	**dash –**
semicolon ;	**parentheses ( )**
colon :	

Comma, A *comma* is an internal mark of punctuation suggesting pauses between words, phrases, and clauses within a sentence.

1. Use a comma to connect two independent clauses joined with a coordinate conjunction:

I would give you this television to put in your dormitory, but it is the only one we have left at home.

2. Use a comma to separate an introductory subordinate clause or long introductory phrase from the main part of the sentence:

Whenever I feel the urge for peace and quiet, I go camping in the Smokies.

Looking long and hard for a summer job, I finally found one making doughnuts in a bakery.

3. Use a comma to separate items in a series:

In World War II the Allied nations were the United States, Russia, France, Britain, Canada, and many others.

The bar was sleazy, dark, and almost empty.

4. Use a comma to surround interrupting elements:

William Wordsworth, I believe, lived to be quite an old man.

There are only three tickets. You, therefore, must stay at home to watch the children.

5. Use a comma to set off certain modifiers that are not essential to the sense of the sentence:

Johnny Carson has hosted his television program, *The Tonight Show*, for many years.

In the event that the added material is actually essential to the meaning of the sentence, do not use commas:

Any group *(no comma)* that wishes to demonstrate in front of the White House *(no comma)* must apply for a permit.

Omitting the phrase "that wishes to demonstrate in front of the White House" would change the meaning of the sentence. Therefore, commas do not surround the added material since it is necessary.

6. Use a comma to accommodate certain conventions.

a. In dates and addresses:

The treaty ratifying the United States purchase of the Panama Canal Zone was signed on January 22, 1903.
My high-school friend now lives in Rome, New York.

b. In direct address:

Don't be stubborn, Marietta; your father wants you to come home.
Paul, bring your tapes to my house tonight.

c. In setting off some quoted material:

Ben announced proudly, "I got the job with IBM."

Do *not* use commas in these instances:

1. To separate two independent clauses:

NOT: He baked a blueberry pie, it was a little watery but we ate it just the same.

2. To separate two words or phrases joined by *and:*

NOT: Saccharin, and cyclamates have come under heavy fire recently.

3. To separate a subject from a verb:

NOT: The marble top table which sat in the corner of my mother's living room, will pass on to my sister who lives in a New York brownstone.

4. To separate a verb and its object:

NOT: In his solo flight across the Atlantic, Lindbergh earned a world record and a world-wide reputation.

Semicolon; A *semicolon* is the mark of punctuation that separates two independent clauses which are not joined by a coordinate conjunction, but which are closely enough related to remain as one sentence:

On August 6, 1945, an atomic bomb was dropped on Hiroshima; three days later a second bomb was dropped on Nagasaki.

A semicolon may also connect items in a series when one or all of the items already contain comma punctuation:

> Stephen Crane wrote several powerful short stories: "The Open Boat," which shows a universe indifferent to man; "The Blue Hotel," which captures some of Crane's western experiences; and "An Episode of War," which presents a brief picture of battle.

Colon: The *colon* is a punctuation mark which calls attention to the matter following it. It is used before a series that ends a sentence and in some way explains or defines a term just preceding:

> Each man must one day face at least one of the four horsemen of the Apocalypse: Pestilence, War, Famine, and Death.

A colon, rather than a comma, may be used to introduce a quotation you want to draw attention to:

> Although many fiction writers today have a tendency to disparage plot in favor of character, as one critic put it: "Those characters can not exist in a vacuum."

There are also mechanical conventions that call for the use of a colon.

1. Between title and subtitle:

   Two Sisters: A Memoir in the Form of a Novel

2. Between Biblical chapter and verse:

   Deuteronomy 3:2

3. In time references:

   4:30 p.m.

4. In a salutation:

   Dear Ms. Wilkinson:

Dash— A *dash* is a special mark of punctuation (typewritten as two hyphens) that creates a pause longer than that of a comma. It has several uses.

1. Stressing a word or phrase at the end of a sentence:

   The rifles, pistols, bayonets, and swords were all neatly lined up—on the floor.

2. Marking an interrupted or unfinished construction:

   He sputtered, unable to complete his sentence, "You—you—."

3. Setting off an interrupting word or phrase:

> I have finally achieved a childhood dream—to live on a houseboat—which will come to pass as soon as I withdraw twenty thousand dollars from the bank.

Note that interrupting material within a sentence is enclosed by dashes; that is, there is a dash before the interruption and also after it.

Parentheses ( ) *Parentheses* set off interruptions of lengthy or purely supplemental material:

> Traveler's checks (first copyrighted by American Express in 1891) are as vital to a modern traveler as is a suitcase.
>
> Theodore Dreiser (1871–1945) was a "naturalist" who did not receive appropriate recognition in his own time.
>
> The power behind the anti-gun–control lobby is the NRA (National Rifle Association).

Special conventions

quotation marks	" "	**italics**	_____
ellipses	. . .	**apostrophe**	'
brackets	[ ]	**hyphen**	-

Quotation marks " " *Quotation marks* have three functions: to set off direct quotations; to lend occasional emphasis to certain words; and to indicate titles of poems, short stories, chapter titles, songs, paintings, essays, and magazine articles.

1. Double quotation marks set off direct quotations, words which are quoted directly from a source:

> Walt Whitman's poems give expression to what he termed his "barbaric yawp."

Single space and indent quotations which are four or more lines long. Omit quotation marks:

> In his notes for his novel *The Last Tycoon*, F. Scott Fitzgerald described his ambitions:
>
> > I want to write scenes that are frightening and inimitable. I don't want to be as intelligible to my contemporaries as Ernest, who, as Gertrude Stein said, is bound for the Museums. I am far enough ahead to have some small immortality if I can keep well.

Use single quotation marks to set off a quotation within a quotation:

> Before the class ended, the English instructor announced, "For tomorrow you should read Twain's story 'The Notorious Jumping Frog of Calaveras County.' "

Depending on type, other punctuation marks go inside or outside of the quotation marks:

a. Periods and commas go inside of closing quotation marks:

> "Okay," he said, "you can start working at 6:00 tomorrow morning."

b. Question marks and exclamation points go inside of the closing quotation marks if the quoted material is a question or an exclamation:

> Her father asked, "Don't you ask anymore before you borrow the car?"

c. Place question marks and exclamation points outside of the quotation marks if the sentence is a question or exclamation but the quotation is not:

> Which of the folk groups from the sixties recorded the song "Puff, the Magic Dragon"?

d. Semicolons and colons go outside of the quotation marks:

> First read the Hemingway story "A Clean, Well-Lighted Place"; then read "The Girls in Their Summer Dresses."

2. Quotation marks are occasionally used to highlight a word or give it special emphasis:

> I didn't "want" to get that swine flu shot; my parents forced it on me.

3. Certain titles are indicated by quotation marks.

a. Short poems:

> Randall Jarrell's "The Death of the Ball Turret Gunner"

b. Short stories:

> Katharine Anne Porter's "The Downward Path to Wisdom"

c. Chapter titles:

> Chapter 1 of Ray Ginger's *Age of Success* is "Ways of Life at the End of Reconstruction."

d. Song titles:

> Simon and Garfunkel's "In My Little Town"

e. Paintings:

Edward Hicks's "Peaceable Kingdom"

f. Essay titles:

James Baldwin's "Stranger in the Village"

g. Magazine articles:

"A Psychiatrist's Casebook" in *McCalls*

Ellipses . . . *Ellipses* show that material has been omitted from a quotation. If an omission occurs at the end of a sentence, use four dots:

> J. K. Obatala's article "The Unlikely Story of Blacks Who Were Loyal to Dixie" points out:
>
> > Incredible though it seems, many slaves made financial and material contributions to the Confederacy. . . . It became a custom for slaves to hold balls and concerts and give the money . . . to aid soldiers' families and to other patriotic causes.

***Brackets* [ ]** *Brackets* enclose supplemental comments (either editorial or informational) within quotations:

> An article in *American Quarterly* stated: "The G-man [in the movies] was different from the other detective heroes because he spent less time with his girl and more time in the classroom, in the laboratory, and on the phone to Washington."

Always quote the words of the original exactly. Whenever any errors occur in the original, insert *sic* (Latin for "thus") within brackets:

> "The combination of hydrogen and oxygen produced H_3O [*sic*]."

***Italics (Underlining)* ____** *Italics* (indicated by underlining in handwritten or typed manuscripts) have three functions: to indicate titles of books, newspapers, periodicals, plays, motion pictures, television series, long poems, album titles, and long musical compositions; to emphasize an occasional word; and to indicate some foreign or scientific words.

1. Italics are used to indicate several types of titles.

a. Books:

Daniel Defoe's *Robinson Crusoe*

b. Newspapers:

Christian Science Monitor

c. Periodicals:

People magazine

d. Plays:

Christopher Marlowe's *Dr. Faustus*

e. Motion pictures:

Birth of a Nation

f. Television series:

The Avengers

g. Long poems:

Milton's *Paradise Lost*

h. Albums:

Handel's *Seven Sonatas for Flute and Harpsichord*

i. Long musical compositions:

Rimski-Korsakov's *Scheherazade*

2. Occasionally, italics give a word, phrase, number, or letter a special emphasis:

> I have spent six *days* waiting for you to telephone.
> The 1980 U.S. Olympic hockey team didn't win the bronze medal; they won the *gold!*

Words used as words and letters used as letters also receive emphasis:

> My daughter always gets *A*'s on her report card.

Foreign or scientific words that have not yet become common in standard English are italicized:

> Having spent several years in the Orient, the Herndons had indeed become *gens du monde.*

Apostrophe **'** An *apostrophe* serves three functions: It forms contractions, plurals, and possessives.

1. An apostrophe indicates omitted letters in a contraction or in parts of dates or other numerals:

can't	shouldn't	'76	rock 'n' roll

2. An apostrophe forms the plural of letters, symbols, words, and abbreviations followed by periods:

> The typewriter keys seem to botch the *A*'s, and the #'s.
> When you write a paper, use *and*'s instead of &'s for the conjunction.

3. An apostrophe uses various combinations to form possessives.

a. Add apostrophe plus *-s* to form the possessive of most singular nouns and some indefinite pronouns:

> Martha**'s** friend volunteered to collect everyone**'s** contributions to the cancer fund.

b. Add either apostrophe and *-s* or only the apostrophe to form the possessive of singular nouns ending in *-s:*

> Cass'**s** (Cass') legs shivered as she stood in her short costume on the outdoor stage.

c. Add apostrophe plus *-s* to plurals which do not end in *-s:*

> The women**'s** movement is mellowing, some say.

d. Add only the apostrophe to plurals ending in *-s:*

> The sailors' ship must stay in dry dock two weeks longer than planned.

e. Add apostrophe plus *-s* to the last word of a compound or word group:

> My sister-in-law**'s** sailboat can beat almost anything out on the bay when the wind is up.

f. Add apostrophe plus *-s* to show individual ownership; add apostrophe and *-s* only to the last name to indicate joint ownership:

> Dana**'s** and Rose**'s** coats were confused since they were both dark red.
> Diana and Bob**'s** car just sped past.

Hyphen - A *hyphen* has three functions: to connect two words as one adjective, to link root words to prefixes or suffixes, and to indicate a fraction or compound number.

1. Use a hyphen to connect two words as an adjective:

> Although he is a computer analyst, his knowledge is really not up**-**to**-**date.

2. Generally, use a hyphen to link roots to prefixes or suffixes:

> Her ex**-**husband decided to try to collect alimony from her since her $50,000 a year salary was much higher than his.

This practice was once far more common than it is today. When in doubt, check a dictionary.

3. Use a hyphen to indicate a fraction or a compound number:

> The drinking age in many states is once again being raised to twenty-one.

Capitalization

The conventions of capitalization are needed in each of the following instances.

1. The first word of a sentence:

> **We** understood John Barth's novel *The Sot Weed Factor* better after reading Voltaire's *Candide.*

2. The pronoun ***I***
3. Proper names of persons, places, things:

> **N**ick flew to **P**aris on **P**an **A**merican's "**C**lipper **C**ruise" to attend the **B**rewmasters **C**onvention held near the **S**eine during the second week in **J**une.

4. Names of organizations, groups, holidays, historical events, days, months, etc.

> The **G**irl **S**couts of **A**merica scheduled their jamboree for **J**uly 2–4 (**T**uesday to **T**hursday) as fitting tribute to **I**ndependence **D**ay celebrations held nationwide.

5. Titles preceding a name:

> **V**ice-**P**resident Jim Stewart
> **P**rofessor Henrietta Klinger

6. Common nouns if they are part of a proper noun:

> Sylvester **S**treet
> **A**unt Peggy

7. North, south, east, and west only when they refer to specific regions:

> The **M**idwest proved attractive to many Scandinavian farmers.

8. The first word and all important words in a title of a book, article, etc.:

> ***T**he **K**andy-**K**olored **T**angerine-**F**lake **S**treamline **B**aby*
> ***M**asterworks of **W**orld **L**iterature*
> "**C**hapter **T**hree: **B**oyhood in **B**erlin"

Index